"Policy is the lever that controls healthcare markets. In *The Customer Revolution in Healthcare*, Dave Johnson calls on us to move that lever in a new direction to encourage market-based reforms that will better serve the needs of patients."

—David Durenberger,
former US senator from Minnesota

"Dave recognizes that healthcare is about empowering people to achieve their best health. His clarity of vision, supported by his deep understanding of the future that is already here, comes together in his book, a must-read for students of healthcare strategy."

—Nancy Kane, PhD,
professor of management in the Department of Health Policy
and Management at Harvard School of Public Health

"We cannot improve the health of the population unless they are engaged fully in the effort with us. Dave Johnson has given everyone a road map for this engagement with all the signposts, directions, and barriers clearly visible. Do we have the courage to go down this road together—providers, payers, and patients? I, for one, am ready for the journey, and kudos to Johnson for his ability to lead us there."

—David B. Nash, MD,
founding dean emeritus at Jefferson College of Population Health

"*The Customer Revolution in Healthcare* aligns with AdventHealth's promise to consumers that we will help them 'feel whole'—providing care to the whole person in mind, body, and spirit. Dave Johnson's manifesto points out the need for much stronger consumer advocacy, better provider coordination, and new financial solutions to better meet their needs."

—Terry Shaw,
president and CEO of AdventHealth

"In this book, Johnson calls out how different sectors of the healthcare market contribute to our broken system. But he also outlines ways we can transform the industry to deliver better care at a lower cost that consumers want."

—Craig Sammit, MD,
president and CEO of Blue Cross and Blue Shield of Minnesota

"Johnson calls us out on the false choice of restricted care access or unconstrained cost growth. The questions he raises seem revolutionary, but shouldn't be. In his vision of a transformed healthcare delivery system, data is free from clinical, operational, and financial silos. It flows to frontline clinicians, powered by AI capabilities, so caregivers can focus on patients. That flow will fuel the customer revolution."

—Mudit Garg,
founder and CEO of Qventus

"As a health system CEO and cancer survivor, I have a unique perspective and see the business through the customer's eyes. In this book, Dave Johnson shines a light on all those dark corners we don't like to look at. He points us to the uncomfortable conversion we all must make for the healthcare system to respond to this evolving reinvention of an industry. For those of us who have a passion for transforming healthcare, Dave Johnson's book provides a candid overview of the challenges we've long admired and a pragmatic road map to a much-needed evolution of our industry."

—Peter Fine,
president and CEO of Banner Health

"I've seen the lack of true consumer involvement in the healthcare system as one of its major flaws. In this book, Johnson lays out how an industry that has historically struggled to identify its true customer could revolutionize itself with new attitudes, structures, and regulations. It calls out many longstanding practices that need to change. It's a must-read for policy makers and industry insiders alike."

—Joseph J. Fifer, CPA,
president and CEO of HFMA

"The market is moving toward consumerism and value. Every single person working in healthcare, either directly providing care or in the back office, has an opportunity and an obligation to do it better. Dave understands that consumerism and value are not just the latest trends; they are the driving force for meaningful change."

—Marc Harrison, MD,
president and CEO of Intermountain Healthcare

"Some problems are so enormous and multidimensional that they are hard to grasp, and competing interests, money, and politics make solutions seem unattainable. Johnson provides clarity around the fundamental flaws within the US healthcare system, and the revolutionary forces that have been unleashed that might just fix it. His book shows the negative historical forces that brought us here, but it is also full of hope. This optimism is based on the moral imperative for each of us to participate in the customer revolution happening in healthcare today."

—Lyric Hughes Hale,
editor in chief of EconVue

"Health systems' potential for innovation is limitless. Dave Johnson's new book, *The Customer Revolution in Healthcare* delivers a must-read road map for those interested in driving and participating in this innovation."

—Eric Langshur,
cofounder of Abundant Venture Partners

"David Johnson's *The Customer Revolution in Healthcare* provides a sharp diagnosis of the causes of healthcare's high costs and fragmentation, along with a strong prescription for a new system that is structured and financed based on changing consumer needs."

—Kenneth Kauffman,
chair of Kauffman Hall

"US healthcare is a system in name only. Dave Johnson not only frames the entrenched interests frustrating consumers with costly administrative friction, he compellingly articulates a customer-centered solution. His latest book should be required reading for understanding a when, not if, revolution that will transform US health and care."

—Don Trigg,
EVP of strategic growth at Cerner Corporation

"These aren't preachy or puritanical prognostications of where healthcare should go, but a leading thinker giving a deep analysis of the forces at work that will drive and shape the healthcare of the future."

—Paul Kusserow,
president and CEO of Amedisys

"Our traditional healthcare system serves no one well. The future will be clinician-led and patient-centered. The power of Johnson's new book is the clarity he brings to why and how this shift will happen: suddenly and sooner than many believe."

—Ronald A. Paulus, MD,
president and CEO of Mission Health

"Johnson discusses how we need to broaden our thinking about where care is delivered to better serve customers at different points in their health and wellness journey. In *The Customer Revolution in Healthcare*, Johnson outlines ways to think differently about the physical assets in our healthcare system and calls for breaking down barriers that separate industry stakeholders. Johnson challenges us to think and act smarter in order to improve health outcomes and drive down costs. We need to take his advice."

—Thomas J. Derosa,
CEO and director of Welltower

"*The Customer Revolution in Healthcare* builds upon Dave Johnson's deep industry insights to highlight the transformative power of consumerism on the health system, sharing strategic insights for market innovation and regulatory advancement, to deliver better results for all."

—Amir Dan Rubin,
president and CEO of One Medical

THE
CUSTOMER
REVOLUTION
IN HEALTHCARE

Delivering Kinder, Smarter,
Affordable Care for All

DAVID W. JOHNSON

New York   Chicago   San Francisco   Athens   London   Madrid
Mexico City   Milan   New Delhi   Singapore   Sydney   Toronto

1 2 3 4 5 6 7 8 9   LCR   24 23 22 21 20 19

ISBN: 978-1-260-45557-1
MHID: 1-260-45557-2

e-ISBN: 978-1-260-45558-8
e-MHID: 1-260-45558-0

This publication is designed to provide accurate and authoritative information in regard to the subject matter covered. It is sold with the understanding that neither the author nor the publisher is engaged in rendering legal, accounting, securities trading, or other professional services. If legal advice or other expert assistance is required, the services of a competent professional person should be sought.
—From a Declaration of Principles Jointly Adopted by a Committee of the American Bar Association and a Committee of Publishers and Associations

Library of Congress Cataloging-in-Publication Data

Names: Johnson, David W., author.
Title: The customer revolution in healthcare : delivering kinder, smarter, affordable care for all / by David W. Johnson.
Description: New York : McGraw-Hill, [2020]
Identifiers: LCCN 2019010770 (print) | LCCN 2019018247 (ebook) | ISBN 9781260455588 () | ISBN 1260455580 () | ISBN 9781260455571 (hardback) | ISBN 1260455572 ()
Subjects: LCSH: Consumer-driven health care. | Medical care. | Medical economics. | Patient satisfaction.
Classification: LCC RA416.3 (ebook) | LCC RA416.3 .J64 2020 (print) | DDC 338.4/73621--dc23
LC record available at https://lccn.loc.gov/2019010770

To frontline doctors, nurses, technicians, and caregivers,
may we serve you better

In memory of Barbara Johnson,
Mary Brady, and Gordon McLeod

CONTENTS

FOREWORD

David Johnson and I share a passion for fixing the broken US health-care system. We want US healthcare to be dramatically better for all—which means making it do more for less. After reading these words, regardless of your politics, you will agree that this is both necessary and possible.

In a world where pundits routinely offer something-for-nothing solutions for improving US healthcare, what is different about Dave Johnson's approach? Let me start by telling you how Dave has influenced my thinking and how this remarkable book offers you a chance to learn everything that Dave has taught me.

My passion for improving US health care led me to create the Health-care Policy Leadership Council in 2016 at Harvard's Kennedy School. The council convenes leaders from the industry's diverse sectors for frank, off-the-record, deep-dive investigations of the system's fault lines and failings. Everyone is in the room: government, commercial payers, hospitals, pharmaceutical companies and device makers, venture capitalists, physicians, and academics. We disagree. We listen. We learn.

Our gatherings are awesome to behold because it's one venue where data and evidence reign supreme. Academics present research that shines an unflattering light on vested interests in healthcare and on the anemic performance of so many well-intentioned policies. Pharma execs spar with Medicaid administrators on drug prices. Payers and providers expose their limitations in delivering value-based care. Each council meeting is a PhD-level seminar on the real-world operations of America's biggest industry. It's also shock therapy for leaders who want to break mindsets, and who want to stop the cycle of saying things like "there is waste everywhere in healthcare . . . except in my organization."

Dave is an HKS graduate, a founding member of the council, and among its most active voices. With his unique background, his expansive knowledge, and his contagious energy and engaging manner, Dave finds connections everywhere and offers insights that other analysts miss. This is the tour guide and friend that you want.

As I turn the pages, I feel something very special—here is an individual whose views about the industry have been shaped by learning and listening, not shouting and self-interest. Dave is aspirational while remaining resolutely pragmatic. This is so rare in healthcare today.

You have in your hands a very different healthcare book with a message that you won't come across every day. From the beginning, the story crackles with moral indignation as Dave indicts an American Healthcare Industrial Complex that serves its own needs at the expense of the American people.

Dave's methodical analysis of the System's perverse financial incentives explains the incredible waste and unnecessary harm the System generates. He identifies formidable force multipliers with the power to usher in a new era of Revolutionary Healthcare. He explains how their collective market-driven capabilities will differentiate and reward companies that deliver the right care, at the right time, in the right place, at the right price.

The careful identification of these multipliers is key. It's not enough to just call for revolution in healthcare, for that is just a slogan; US healthcare policy conversations and campaigns are littered with such wretched slogans. We need to distinguish slogans from goals, and then propose policies that deliver on those goals, while relying on evidence to choose between competing strategies.

Evidence of this movement abounds in the enhanced primary care providers, focused factories, asset-light providers, and retail clinics changing the way healthcare is delivered and consumed. Together, such revolutionary upstarts are working to create a more human and efficient system that meets the needs, wants, and desires of all Americans. Enlightened incumbents are starting to follow.

Note the title's emphasis on "for all." Dave argues that it's time for a constructive debate on universal health insurance. The United States is a rich country and Americans deserve access to appropriate and affordable healthcare services. Dave identifies a path toward a pluralistic and universal health coverage that emphasizes equity, value, and choice

Dive into *The Customer Revolution in Healthcare*. I think you will feel the same call, and join us in America's battle for a healthcare system that will make us proud—and healthy.

Amitabh Chandra, PhD
Economist, Professor of Public Policy, and Director of Health Policy Research,
Harvard Kennedy School of Government; member, COB Panel of Health Advisers

AUTHOR'S NOTE

I've dedicated this book to the heroic frontline doctors, nurses, technicians, and caregivers who are the face of healthcare to the millions of Americans who require their services every day. They do this often at the expense of their own health, fighting a system at odds with providing the right care at the right time in the right place at the right price. We simply have to make their work lives easier, more enjoyable, and more productive. My hope is that *The Customer Revolution in Healthcare* helps in achieving this most important goal.

I also have dedicated this book to Barbara Johnson, Mary Brady, and Gordon McLeod, who died during its writing.

THE MOTHERS

My mother Barbara Johnson and my mother-in-law Mary Brady were born nine days apart in March 1932 and died three weeks apart in August 2017. They traveled life's road on an identical timeline that converged when I met and married Terri Brady, my life partner for 35 wonderful years.

Barbara and Mary were born during the Great Depression, grew up during World War II, came of age during the Korean War and the prosperous 1950s, married, gave birth to six children, divorced, suffered the death of children (for Barbara, my brother Danny and sister Carol, and for Mary, three infant children), rebuilt their careers, achieved professional success, retired, and lived to an old age. Other than my wife Terri, they have been the two most important women in my life.

My mother was born in Salt Lake City and moved with her family to Mahnomen, Minnesota, when she was six years old. Mahnomen is a small rural community in northwest Minnesota that lies entirely within the White Earth Indian Reservation. It was in Mahnomen that Barbara developed her passion for reading, love of learning, and attachment to disadvantaged children.

Before marriage and children, Barbara earned a bachelor's degree from Macalester College and taught elementary school. In 1967 Barbara moved with her family to Barrington, Rhode Island, where she embraced life by the seashore. She remained active in the League of Women Voters and helped found the Rhode Island Association for Children with Learning Disabilities. After her divorce, Barbara earned a master's degree in education and returned to the classroom, where she specialized in teaching students English as a second language (ESL). For almost 20 years, Barbara taught inner-city students from diverse backgrounds in Providence, Rhode Island. Her classrooms were alive with energetic learning, murals, experiments, and displays. In retirement, Barbara took up "a second residence" at the Barrington Public Library. My brother Doug used to joke that Mom was either at the library or thinking about going to the library.

On a Bill Clinton campaign swing through Rhode Island in 1996, Barbara shook hands with the president outside Barrington High School. Clinton complimented Mom on her sweatshirt, which read "So many books, so little time." She was giddy for weeks. Among the greatest gifts a parent can give a child is intellectual curiosity. I received that gift in abundance.

My mother-in-law was a lifelong Cascade, Iowa, resident. Cascade is a small rural community southwest of Dubuque. After graduating from Marycrest College, Mary taught school for several years before starting a family. In the 1970s she pursued professional education in insurance at the University of Iowa.

After her divorce, Mary became the owner of J. C. Herard Agency, an insurance business established by her father in the 1920s. She was a long-standing member of the Iowa Independent Insurance Agents and among the few Iowa women who owned and operated independent insurance agencies. She grew that business through the years by providing consistent, exceptional, and personalized service.

Mary was the type of engaged, multipurposed individual that makes small towns thrive. She supported the American Legion Auxiliary, the Shady Rest Auxiliary, the Cascade Chamber of Commerce, the Tri-County Historical Society, and the Cascade Library Board. She raised funds to build the new Aquin Elementary Catholic school and the Ellen Kennedy Fine Arts Center. She loved theater, politics, Iowa sports, home design, bridge, sewing and quilting, music, travel, and coffee at Grandma's Kitchen with "the ladies." She was a loyal supporter of Cascade High School's cross-country teams and drama productions. I enjoyed Mary's wry sense of humor, commitment to education, love of history, and incredibly close mother-daughter relationship with Terri. Mary was Terri's matron of honor at our wedding.

Not surprisingly, my mother and mother-in-law got along famously. All they needed was coffee and conversation to pass the hours away. We miss them both very much.

GORDON NEIL MCLEOD, MPP 1983

Friends are the family we choose. In the fall of 1981, 76 students enrolled in a ridiculously quantitative Masters of Public Policy program at Harvard's Kennedy School. Among that intrepid group were my future wife and six guys who would become lifelong friends. We met in math review, survived HKS, and set out to conquer the world.

A simple NCAA basketball pool has been sticky glue holding us together through the decades. For a group of quantitative ninjas, our pool is lame—teams drawn at random and assigned to eight participants. I've won only once in 38 years (with the University of Maryland in 2002), but who's counting! That's a black swan event if there ever was one. We've pursued diverse careers in diverse locations but have kept our strong connections intact. In August 2018, we somehow managed to spend most of a week together with our wives in France. The peaches have never tasted sweeter.

But now there are just six of us. As I finished writing this book in April 2019, we lost our great friend Gordon McLeod to a nine-year battle with cancer. Gordo was an accomplished and innovative media executive. He ran digital media at *Sports Illustrated* and the *Wall Street Journal*, debated Steve Jobs on technology (always risky) at a News Corp. management retreat, and was president of the Newsday Media Group. He was a food and wine connoisseur, athletic, compassionate, opinionated, and conversational. Gordo had a great sense of humor accompanied by an obnoxious laugh and an insatiable curiosity in what others were doing.

When I visited Manhattan, Gordo and I would go for long meandering runs through Central Park. His observations regarding the media, public opinion, politics, government, and business were fresh, unvarnished, and insightful. In fact, Gordo only approved of the title *The Customer Revolution in Healthcare* after throwing up on several previous title suggestions.

Always warm and gregarious, Gordon's humanity increased as he ferociously fought the cancer that stole his mobility and independence.

He accepted the surgeries, tried experimental treatments, doubled down on physical therapy, learned to walk with a cane, and rarely complained. His death was sudden because he never gave in to his cancer.

Two days before he died, Gordo e-mailed me about a healthcare tech conference. After a few exchanges, I wrote, "You're a tough sonofabitch." He responded, "Not by choice." I beg to differ. He was tough because he wanted to live as best as he could for as long as he could on his own terms. As we mourn his loss, I'm also in awe of how he lived his life. He leaves behind an amazing and accomplished wife, Melanie Grisanti; two remarkable daughters, Grace and Jane; and many friends, including six HKS geeks. We miss him terribly but carry his generous spirit with us.

FINAL THOUGHT

My enduring hope for *The Customer Revolution in Healthcare* is that it gives readers a deep understanding of the following:

Why the economics and spirit of American healthcare are fundamentally broken; and

What the marketplace, government, communities, and individuals can do to restore the system's integrity.

Revolutions reconfigure the world order. Healthcare needs to recapture its commitments to humanism, balance, and value to earn back the trust of the American people. As it does so, enlightened health companies will create a new birth of possibilities that lead Americans to better, healthier, more productive lives.

The Healthcare Industrial Complex

On January 17, 1961, three days before leaving office, Dwight D. Eisenhower spoke to the nation one last time as its president. Eisenhower's observations regarding war, peace, government, and the emerging "military industrial complex" are timeless, visionary, and compelling (Figure I.1). They reflect a deep understanding of human nature, democratic institutions, and moral leadership.

Almost 60 years later, Eisenhower's analysis of the threats posed by inappropriate institutional behaviors applies to US healthcare. America's Healthcare Industrial Complex™ (the System) is far more insidious and virulent than the military industrial complex against which Eisenhower warned. Understanding the System's nefarious operating dynamics and the dangers they pose to American society are necessary and constructive first steps toward its elimination and replacement with a new American healthcare that is kinder, smarter, and affordable. Before charting that course, let's return to President Eisenhower and his concerns for America's future.

Given Eisenhower's storied military and political career, most listeners expected an "old soldier's" valedictory. That did not happen. Instead, the president dissected the moral dimensions of global leadership:

> America is today the strongest, the most influential and most productive nation in the world. Understandably proud of this preeminence, we yet realize that America's leadership and prestige depend, not merely upon our unmatched material progress, riches and military strength, but on how we use our power in the interests of world peace and human betterment.[1]

Until the end of World War II, America had never had a permanent armaments industry. While necessary to keep the peace, Eisenhower

FIGURE I.1 Eisenhower warns of the military industrial complex in farewell speech.

warned Americans of the grave dangers to a free society posed by an emerging "military industrial complex":

> This conjunction of an immense military establishment and a large arms industry is new in the American experience. The total influence—economic, political, even spiritual—is felt in every city, every state house, every office of the Federal government. We recognize the imperative need for this development. Yet we must not fail to comprehend its grave implications. Our toil, resources and livelihood are all involved; so is the very structure of our society.
>
> In the councils of government, we must guard against the acquisition of unwarranted influence, whether sought or unsought, by the military industrial complex. The potential for the disastrous rise of misplaced power exists and will persist.
>
> We must never let the weight of this combination endanger our liberties or democratic processes. We should take nothing for granted. Only an alert and knowledgeable citizenry can compel

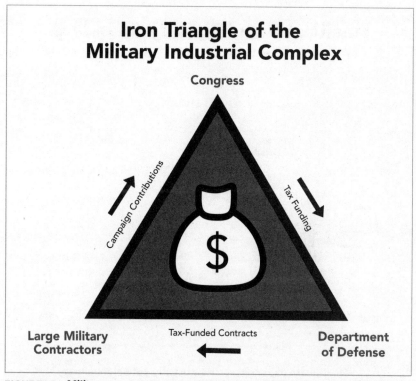

FIGURE I.2   Military contractors, the Department of Defense, and Congress fuel each other's growth and protect each other's funding.

the proper meshing of huge industrial and military machinery of defense with our peaceful methods and goals, so that security and liberty may prosper together.

Eisenhower coined the term "military industrial complex" to describe how an unholy trinity of the Defense Department, Congress, and military contractors work to promote their own interests at the expense of American society. Figure I.2 shows how money and influence flow between the three component parts of the military industrial complex.

Almost 60 years later, President Eisenhower's warnings remain more applicable to America's broken healthcare system than to the military establishment. In 1961, military spending and healthcare expenditures constituted 9 percent and 5 percent of the US economy respectively, as measured by gross domestic product (GDP). Today, healthcare consumes 18 percent of GDP, the military only 3 percent (see Figure I.3).

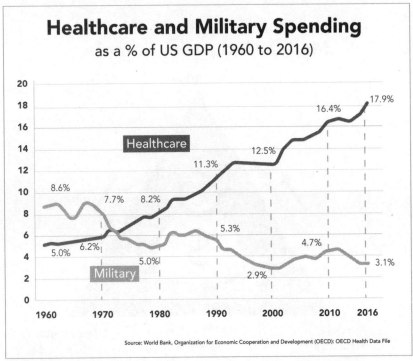

Healthcare and Military Spending
as a % of US GDP (1960 to 2016)

Source: World Bank, Organization for Economic Cooperation and Development (OECD): OECD Health Data File

FIGURE I.3 **Healthcare expenditures now greatly outweigh military expenditures.**

The United States spends far more on healthcare per capita than any other advanced economy yet experiences much lower health status. The developed country with the next highest percentage of healthcare expenditure is France at 12 percent of its GDP. Life expectancy in France is almost four years longer than in the United States. In fact, American life expectancy is now declining for the first time in the nation's history.

The average birth in the United States costs 21 percent more than a royal birth in Great Britain (Figure I.4). Prince William and Princess Kate welcomed eight-pound-seven-ounce Louis to this world on April 23, 2018, in the posh Lindo Wing at St. Mary's Hospital in London. The cost for a non-Cesarean birth at Lindo in 2015 was $8,900. An equivalent birth in the United States that year cost $10,808. Does that turn every American-born baby into a prince or princess?[2]

The Healthcare Industrial Complex is the military industrial complex on steroids. Congress, a massive healthcare bureaucracy, and an even

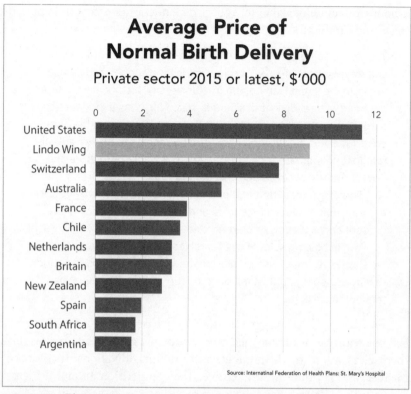

Average Price of Normal Birth Delivery

Private sector 2015 or latest, $'000

Source: International Federation of Health Plans; St. Mary's Hospital

FIGURE I.4 **Births cost more in the United States than in other developed countries.**

more massive healthcare industry conspire to drive US healthcare spending ever higher without delivering commensurate health benefits.

Healthcare's all-consuming appetite for resources steals from more productive sectors of the American economy. More important, the healthcare services the System delivers are not the services the American people need, want, and deserve. The Healthcare Industrial Complex is the root cause of America's healthcare crisis.

THE SCIENTIFIC-TECHNOLOGICAL ELITE

After explaining the dynamics of the military industrial complex, Eisenhower issued a second warning against an emerging "scientific-technological elite" that is dependent upon government contracts and funding:

> Today, the solitary inventor, tinkering in his shop, has been overshadowed by task forces of scientists in laboratories and testing fields. In the same fashion, the free university, historically the fountainhead of free ideas and scientific discovery, has experienced a revolution in the conduct of research. Partly because of the huge costs involved, a government contract becomes virtually a substitute for intellectual curiosity. For every old blackboard there are now hundreds of new electronic computers.
>
> The prospect of domination of the nation's scholars by Federal employment, project allocations, and the power of money is ever present and is gravely to be regarded.
>
> Yet, in holding scientific research and discovery in respect, as we should, we must also be alert to the equal and opposite danger that public policy could itself become the captive of a scientific-technological elite.

Fast-forward to the current day, and Eisenhower's prophecy has become reality in academic medicine. Academic medical enterprises rank themselves according the numbers and amounts of National Institutes of Health (NIH) funding they receive. The competition among principal investigators (PIs) retards collaboration and creates research silos.

The vast majority of NIH funding targets biomedical breakthrough research that supports the Healthcare Industrial Complex's ability to consume ever-greater percentages of societal resources. More disturbingly, medical research underinvestigates how social determinants of health (housing, transportation, poverty, food insecurity, etc.) influence the American people's health status. The System funds the research that pays, not the research that generates the greatest benefit for society.

MORTGAGING AMERICA'S FUTURE

Finally, Eisenhower warned against excessive public spending and public debt:

> As we peer into society's future, we—you and I, and our government—must avoid the impulse to live only for today, plundering, for our own ease and convenience, the precious resources of

tomorrow. We cannot mortgage the material assets of our grand-
children without risking the loss also of their political and spiritual
heritage. We want democracy to survive for all generations to
come, not to become the insolvent phantom of tomorrow.

Healthcare-related debt is the leading cause of personal bankruptcy.
Healthcare is the largest and fastest-growing budget item for federal and
state governments. It's the leading driver of deficit spending. If President
Eisenhower were to give his farewell address today, he would surely cite
the bloated and inefficient healthcare system as a fundamental threat to
the nation's prosperity and quality of life.

Other presidents have pushed for reform. President Franklin D. Roosevelt tried to include public funding for health insurance in his New
Deal legislation but dropped his proposal because of fierce opposition
from the American Medical Association. After World War II, President
Harry S. Truman called for universal coverage in his Fair Deal legislation. Instead, employer-sponsored health insurance emerged as the
principal health insurance funding mechanism.

As the civil rights movement unfolded, President Lyndon B. Johnson
gained passage for the landmark legislation that established Medicare and
Medicaid. Though ensuring care for the elderly and poor, these massive
new programs contained perverse economic incentives that have spawned
50+ years of fragmented care delivery and relentless expenditure growth.

In the early 1970s, President Richard M. Nixon proposed market-
based reforms that prefigured the Affordable Care Act (ACA) but failed
to win support from Democrats. In the 1990s, Republicans, with help
from the insurance industry, blocked President Bill Clinton's expansive
healthcare reform proposals.

President George W. Bush expanded Medicare's prescription drug
coverage and modernized the Medicare Advantage program. President
Barack Obama applied market-based reform principles pioneered under
Republican Mitt Romney in Massachusetts to enact the Affordable
Care Act with no Republican support. Fierce and unrelenting political opposition to the ACA has defined healthcare policy debate since its
passage.

Sadly, a century of reform initiatives has accomplished very little.

As the political balance swings toward Democrats after the 2018
midterm elections, there is renewed interest in a single-payer "Medicare
for All" health system. That approach runs the substantial risk of locking
in the System's current dysfunction even as it increases access. As Albert

Einstein famously observed, "The definition of insanity is doing the same thing over and over again but expecting different results."

We, the people, get nothing close to commensurate value for our healthcare expenditure. American healthcare fails to generate superior health outcomes, provide universal access to appropriate and affordable care services, or foster healthier communities.

The problems are not *in* the System. The problem *is* the System. It's time to fight the Healthcare Industrial Complex, blow it up and replace it. The coming revolution will not be top down but bottom up. In fact, it's already underway.

WE THE PEOPLE

In Philadelphia, on July 4, 1776, the representatives of the Second Continental Congress formally adopted the Declaration of Independence. This document announced that the 13 colonies would no longer suffer under the unjust rule of a distant power. As the signers stated,

> when a long train of abuses and usurpations, pursuing invariably the same Object evinces a design to reduce them under absolute Despotism, it is their right, it is their duty, to throw off such Government, and to provide new Guards for their future security.—Such has been the patient sufferance of these Colonies; and such is now the necessity which constrains them to alter their former Systems of Government.

Two and a half centuries later, American citizens retain the inalienable rights of life, liberty, and the pursuit of happiness but confront a different form of tyranny. The sprawling Healthcare Industrial Complex imposes itself unjustly on Americans at great human and economic cost. The System does not serve the American people's interests, meet their needs, provide for their welfare, minimize their financial burdens, or support their pursuit of better, healthier lives.

For complex conditions and "miracle" treatments, American healthcare is the best money can buy. From the inside, where it counts, the System generates subpar outcomes. It treats sickness but does not promote health. It ignores convenience, service preferences, affordability, and value. It rewards vested interests. It needlessly harms individuals and communities. It is a drag on national productivity, quality of life, and living standards.

The System is a dispiriting, frustrating, corrupting, burdensome, and lethal combination of bad medical practices, bad policy design, and bad market behaviors. Its villains are easy to identify: Big Medicine, Big Pharma, Big Insurance, and Big Government. The System consumes societal resources with vigor and exhibits an appalling indifference to societal needs. It's time to revolt. It's time for healthcare customers to use their purchasing power to demand health and healthcare services that meet their needs.

The unsung heroes of American healthcare are everywhere. They are:

- The doctors and nurses who deliver expert care with compassion despite the churn of 15-minute appointments and the mind-numbing demands of data entry.

- The patients, family members, and social workers who arrange care, coordinate information, and resolve problems by stitching together a broken system through their unpaid or under-paid labor.

- The administrators who overcome red tape and bureaucratic processes to meet real needs. They are technicians, technologists, and support staff who somehow keep the wheels turning.

- The executives and leaders who steer their organizations along a righteous path despite counterincentives that offer greater rewards for mediocrity, ruthlessness, and indifference.

- The entrepreneurs and visionaries striving to build better tools and services for a system that does its best to thwart or reject new approaches.

It shouldn't be so hard to do the right thing, but the System is unrelenting in pursuing its own interests. When push comes to shove, the System wins, and the people lose. The good news is that a new era is dawning. Revolutionary Healthcare is coming with payment models that reward service and value.

New delivery models are liberating healthcare professionals to provide personalized care with compassion, empathy, and shared medical decision making. They are giving patients and families the information, tools, and services they need to be powerfully engaged in their own health outcomes, decisions, and priorities. New technologies are making it easier to learn, communicate, and act. As a result, enlightened organizations are winning by delivering service excellence, not by exploiting regulatory loopholes or optimizing payment formularies.

In this new era, the market rewards integrity, kindness, innovation, service, performance, and quality. When that happens, the villains will no longer be the System. Instead, our common enemies will be injury, disease, suffering, anxiety, waste, and inefficiency.

There is no stopping this revolution because healthcare's customers and consumers are mad as hell. Their battle cry is a market-driven declaration for better value.

BALANCE AND SKEPTICISM

Lost in the political healthcare reform discussion is the necessity of achieving balance among competing interests: individual and societal needs; costs and benefits; government and private markets; influence and justice; reward and sacrifice; consumption and investment. Healthcare is dangerously out of balance and needs to regain it. Americans shouldn't have to live their lives in caves to afford great healthcare services.

Let's return to Eisenhower. His lifetime of leadership under the most demanding circumstances gave him a hardheaded appreciation for the role balance plays in governance while striving for the twin goals of "world peace and human betterment." Eisenhower fundamentally understood that human beings can be agents for good or evil. Productive societies accentuate human potential and limit human depravity. In this sense, Eisenhower's worldview exhibits a theological wisdom about human nature.

Reinhold Niebuhr was a contemporary of Eisenhower and the twentieth century's most influential theologian. Niebuhr's books and sermons addressed the need for moral action while acknowledging the flawed nature of human reasoning and judgment. As acclaimed historian Arthur Schlesinger Jr. observed, "Niebuhr's analysis of human nature and history came as a vast illumination. His argument had the double merit of accounting for Hitler and Stalin and for the necessity of standing up to them."

Niebuhr synthesized humanity's creative-destructive dynamism eloquently in his 1944 book *The Children of Light and the Children of Darkness*:

Man's capacity for justice makes democracy possible, but man's inclination toward injustice makes democracy necessary.

Eisenhower's leadership embodied "Niebuhrian" logic. Managing the affairs of nations requires a healthy dose of skepticism regarding human motivation. Applying Niebuhrian logic to healthcare reveals a harsh truth. The American healthcare industry operates the US healthcare system for its own benefit, not for the benefit of the American people.

Since Eisenhower's time in office, the conjunction of congressional, industrial, and bureaucratic interests has spread beyond the military and infected the entire US healthcare system. Healthcare is on its way to consuming 20 percent of the US economy and has demonstrated no ability to restrain its voracious appetite. The scale of healthcare's malfeasance threatens societal well-being at the national, state, community, and individual levels.

America has the ability to create and operate a healthcare system that meets the real health and healthcare needs of the American people with fairness, compassion, and effectiveness. To paraphrase Niebuhr, healthcare's capacity for innovation makes value possible. Healthcare's proclivity for waste makes value necessary. The future state of the nation depends on whether and how the American people take up this challenge.

THE CUSTOMER REVOLUTION IN HEALTHCARE

American healthcare operates within an artificial economic environment. Health companies exploit inefficient and perverse payment formularies to maximize revenues. An outdated regulatory structure and government capture encourage monopoly and monopsony business practices.

The result is a wasteful, fragmented, high-cost healthcare delivery system that neglects customer needs and delivers suboptimal care outcomes. The System is a tangled mess of bureaucratic bungling, profiteering, crony capitalism, and soul-destroying institutionalized care.

The Healthcare Revolution is coming. A confluence of better healthcare purchasing, technological advances, consumerism, and entrepreneurial innovation are turning healthcare inside out, upside down, and right-side up.

First, some definitions.

- **Customers** are the organizations and people paying for healthcare services. In the US healthcare system, customers are usually governments and corporations, not end users. The buyers of healthcare are the real drivers of change.

- **Consumers or patients** are the end users of health and healthcare services. The more that patients think and act like customers, the faster the Healthcare Revolution will advance.

- **Revolution** is the two-step process of decommissioning the System and replacing it with a new American healthcare system that rewards outcomes, customer service, and value.

- **Revolutionaries** are the individuals and organizations leading the bottom-up, market-driven transformation to a new American healthcare system.

The Customer Revolution in Healthcare has three parts: "Revolutionary Conditions," "Revolutionary Forces," and "Revolutionary Healthcare." Part I, "Revolutionary Conditions," details the reasons the American people must declare independence from the System. Part II, "Revolutionary Forces," describes the driving forces disrupting the System from the bottom up and empowering revolutionary health companies to victory. Part III, "Revolutionary Healthcare," describes how revolutionary upstarts and incumbents can deliver holistic health and healthcare services to all Americans.

Revolutionary Healthcare aligns payment with desired outcomes. It liberates caregivers, patients, and administrators and empowers consumers to make informed medical decisions. It requires governments to develop, apply, and enforce enlightened regulatory policies that support level-field competition. Supply and demand adjust to deliver the right care at the right time in the right place at the right price.

The System will not relent without a fight, but its days are numbered. Like the American war for independence, Revolutionary Healthcare empowers Americans to achieve greatness, advance humanity, and redefine the terms of engagement. It delivers the care people need, when and where they need it, at fair prices. It elevates and heals.

High-cost, inefficient, and impersonal healthcare is not our destiny. Enlightened health companies thrive under fair and transparent market conditions. They adapt to consumer needs and market demands by reconfiguring their business models to deliver healthcare that is appropriate, accessible, holistic, reliable, and affordable.

A modern-day customer revolution is remaking one-fifth of the US economy. This is a revolution that the American people want and need to win. Revolutionary Healthcare already has achieved critical mass in select markets, and it's spreading quickly. Revolutionary Healthcare will transform the well-being, productivity, and life quality of all Americans and all communities.

The road to revolution is never easy. Revolutionizing healthcare is not for the faint of heart. It inspires disruptive, bottom-up, market-driven, and customer-centric competitors who capture market share by conquering inefficient and entrenched business practices. Healthcare revolutionaries win by delivering customers the services they want with great service and transparent, competitive prices.

The revolution will turn many sacred cows into hamburger. Powerful incumbents will adapt or disappear. New companies will emerge, change lives, and thrive. When the dust settles, revolutionized American healthcare will serve the people, not the System.

In the last sentence of the Declaration of Independence, the signers mutually pledged to each other their "lives, fortunes and sacred honor." The current generation of Americans owes itself and future generations nothing less. It's time to take up arms and deliver Revolutionary Healthcare to the American people.

PART I

Revolutionary Conditions

DON'T TREAD ON ME

There were no TV shows to capture the zeitgeist in prerevolutionary America, but there were some great political cartoons. Benjamin Franklin drew one of the most provocative (Figure PI.1). To inspire unity among the colonies, Franklin fashioned a snake cut into pieces with the slogan "Join, or Die." Each piece of the snake represented a segment of the American colonies. Franklin believed a united effort could rebuff the British while a fragmented one spelled doom.

That message became a rallying cry for those seeking independence from British rule. Paul Revere applied this image to the masthead of the pro-Revolutionary newspaper *The Massachusetts Spy*. Slowly but surely, the colonies came together to fight and defeat their common enemy.

The American colonies smoldered under Britain's heavy-handed management of their affairs. Britain controlled all regional trade, including the taxation of imports and exports. The English Bill of Rights, passed in 1689, forbade the imposition of taxation without the consent of Parliament. However, the colonists had no members in Parliament to represent their views. Their rallying cry became "No taxation without representation!"

No matter. A succession of punitive taxation measures made colonial life intolerable. Protests erupted. In the famous Boston Tea Party, the Sons of Liberty dressed in Indian garb and dumped chests of British

FIGURE PI.1 Benjamin Franklin political cartoon

tea into Boston Harbor on December 16, 1773. In response, Parliament passed the Coercive Acts, which stripped Massachusetts of its right to self-governance and closed the port of Boston.

Britain's attempts to squelch dissent backfired. Colonists believed their fundamental political, economic, and "inalienable" rights as British citizens were under attack. The frustration inexorably led to the creation of the Continental Congress and the Declaration of Independence on July 4, 1776.

To this day, Americans resist ceding autonomy to others and distrust big government. History has proven this libertarian instinct to be well founded. Yet, in American healthcare, the Healthcare Industrial Complex (the System) exhibits the worst characteristics and habits of cruel colonial masters.

The System is deeply bureaucratic, inefficient, unresponsive, and wasteful. It fails to listen, is mistake prone, and institutionalizes care without regard to consumer needs and preferences. It causes unnecessary suffering and frustration, particularly when consumers are most vulnerable. Essentially, the System disrespects American consumers in the same way that Britain disrespected the American colonists.

The Spirit of '76 and the distaste for "Taxation Without Representation" live on. The American people lack power, agency, and status when engaging the System. "We the People" confront terrible choices regarding care delivery. The System controls the factors of production, hides their true costs, and forces the American people to pick up the tab.

Part I addresses the "Revolutionary Conditions" that necessitate a customer-led revolt by the American people against the System.

- **Chapter 1, "Fundamental Flaws,"** describes the origins and mechanics of the System's "revenue-first" operating model.

- **Chapter 2, "Waste More, Want More,"** chronicles the System's ravenous appetite for consuming ever more societal resources and its tactics for frustrating real payment reform.

- **Chapter 3, "Taxation Without Representation,"** details how the costs and depersonalization of the System's grotesque and artificial economic model terrify regular Americans and exert a substantial economic drag on the nation's overall economy.

- **Chapter 4, "America's Self-Created Opioid Tragedy,"** narrates how the System's nefarious components conspired to create and spread the opioid crisis that is killing Americans at an alarming rate and devastating local communities.

When tyrannical forces push the American people, they push back. The British discovered this in 1776. Those promoting the System's anti-consumer agenda also will experience the revolutionary wrath of the American people.

CHAPTER 1

Fundamental Flaws

In September 2017, I presented at Becker's 3rd Annual Health IT and Revenue Cycle Conference at the Hyatt Regency in Chicago. The conference, one of the industry's largest, attracted more than 2,000 registered attendees with a massive exhibit floor dominated by revenue cycle companies. About 200 people attended my session, which I started by asking a series of questions.

"How many of you work at revenue cycle companies?"

About half raised their hands.

"How many of you have booths on the exhibit floor?"

The same people raised their hands again.

"How many of you saw a cost accounting company on the exhibit floor?"

Not a single person raised a hand.

Revenue cycle management is the process by which healthcare providers document their billable interactions with patients. Revenue cycle management companies are sophisticated businesses with smart and able people who help healthcare providers claim and capture as much of that revenue as possible. They provide the gasoline that makes the US healthcare system run.

Cost accounting, on the other hand, attributes specific component costs for producing goods or services. Some of those costs are direct, like labor and raw materials, while others are indirect, like management, facility overhead, marketing, research, and so on. In almost all businesses, managing expenses is essential to profitability. Given the formulaic nature of treatment payments, however, that's not true in healthcare.

Back to my speech. I joked that I didn't need to continue discussing why US healthcare struggles to provide better, more cost-effective care. The audience's answers had already illustrated a major theme of my speech. Almost all hospitals have robust revenue cycle capabilities to optimize revenue collection. Almost no hospitals have robust cost accounting systems because managing expenses is not a priority. Revenue cycle's predominance and cost accounting's insignificance are Exhibits 1 and 2 in the case of the American people against the System.

IRRATIONAL PRICES

Knee replacement surgery is the third most common operating room procedure in the United States, with over 966,000 performed in 2017.[1] The operation is straightforward and relatively standard across most hospitals and surgical centers. Surgeons remove the old knee and replace it with a mechanical joint. Rehabilitation usually starts the same day.

Gundersen Health System is a highly regarded six-hospital system headquartered in La Crosse, Wisconsin. Gundersen undertakes 400 knee replacement surgeries a year, and they are highly profitable. Until 2016, Gundersen's list price exceeded $50,000 per procedure. That list price was high compared with the $33,307 average US price in 2015.[2]

Providers rarely receive the list price, but it has relevance for select commercial transactions. Government payers establish their own prices and providers negotiate directly with insurance companies to set prices for specific procedures. Still, this discrepancy prompted Gundersen's leadership to ask why their list price for knee replacement surgeries was so high.

It turned out there was no particular reason. They found that $50,000 was an estimated price that inflated over time with 3 percent annual increases. Many hospitals might have left the matter there. Why kill the golden goose? Gundersen dug deeper for answers.

The *Wall Street Journal* chronicled the story of how Gundersen determined its actual costs for knee replacement surgeries.[3] The effort started in 2013 and took 18 months to complete. Gundersen meticulously analyzed every aspect of knee replacement surgery, from supplies to labor to facilities, and added up all the numbers. The total cost turned out to be $10,550 per knee. In other words, the list price of $50,000 represented an almost 500 percent markup on its actual costs. As Harvard economist Leemore Dafny notes, "When price isn't tightly linked to cost, that is a sign that the market isn't competitive."

Gundersen also identified systematic inefficiencies in its knee replacement surgeries that increased costs and impaired quality. These included variations in physician practice patterns, device choices, discharge procedures, error and infection rates, and post-acute rehabilitation. Gundersen saved $1,000 per replacement by using technicians instead of the surgical team to prepare the patient. It slashed its costs by switching to generic bone cement. It saved $800 with better postoperative care by eliminating certain implants that increased infection rates and extended patient recovery time.

Gunderson used this information to standardize and improve its protocols for knee replacement surgery from intake through surgery to discharge and recovery. These program improvements lowered costs and helped patients recover more quickly with fewer complications. Knee surgery at Gundersen dropped by $1,850 to $8,700, a 21 percent decrease.

Was the effort worthwhile? Gundersen had no pressing financial incentive to do its analysis and reduce its prices. Commenting on the lessons learned, Gundersen Health System CEO Scott Rathgaber put it bluntly, "We were inefficient. We didn't know it." Gundersen is now better positioned to compete with national providers and win business from large employers who make more discerning healthcare purchasing decisions.

Gundersen is exceptional in choosing to investigate its costs and apply that knowledge to performance improvement. America is exceptional in the amount of money it devotes to healthcare and the relative mediocrity of the outcomes that spending generates. Americans do not use more healthcare than people in other developed nations—they generally use less, but they pay substantially more for procedures.

When Gundersen Health System calculated the cost of a knee replacement surgery, it was practicing in-depth cost accounting. This is a rarity in healthcare. The "art" in cost accounting involves allocating direct and indirect, fixed and variable costs in accurate and systematic ways.

As Gunderson discovered, precise cost accounting reveals paths to superior performance. It liberates and empowers managers to improve quality by reducing waste. It makes businesses run better. As a result, companies can offer their customers better products and services at competitive prices. Cost accounting is a fundamental aspect of business operations. In healthcare, it's an afterthought.

Other industries routinely improve quality and eliminate waste through constant process improvement. It seems obvious. To fix the American healthcare system, we need to improve care quality and reduce care costs. That starts with understanding why more providers haven't replicated Gundersen's efforts to know its costs and standardize its protocols.

HEALTHCARE PRICING MECHANICS

Like other businesses, hospitals produce goods and services for "customers." Unlike other businesses, hospitals "charge" patients for every service they deliver, regardless of efficacy. As a result, healthcare business models focus on the amount of services they provide, not the effectiveness of the services.

Activity-based fee-for-service (FFS) payments are the gasoline that powers American healthcare. In essence, the more treatments providers deliver, the more payment they receive. From a purely financial perspective, it is more important to document that a treatment is billable than whether it is effective.

Central planners within the Centers for Medicare and Medicaid Services (CMS) create complex pricing formularies to determine how much to pay healthcare providers for specific treatments. Commercial and other governmental payers piggyback on these pricing formularies in establishing their payment mechanics.

The late Princeton economist Ewe Reinhardt used Figure 1.1 to depict Medicare's complex analytic methodology for calculating treatment payments. Medicare's actual methodology is even more complex. The payment process begins by calculating an average inpatient case rate sufficient to cover operating and capital costs for efficient facilities. In 2018, the operating base rate was $5,574, and the capital base rate was $454.

Medicare adjusts this base rate for geographic variation in labor and nonlabor cost as well as treatment complexity based on the primary diagnosis, coexisting medical conditions, and complications. The adjusted payment rate incorporates these geographic and care intensity factors. Then, Medicare adds payments to compensate hospitals for medical education and indigent care costs. It also makes allowances for high-cost outlier cases.[4]

Medicare's payment algorithm incorporates multiple factors, homogenizes complex relationships, and requires massive data entry for processing. Notably absent from the algorithm is payment for superior outcomes or penalties for inferior outcomes.

To its credit, CMS now incorporates some value-based payments and penalties into its care payments. Some employers and commercial insurers also are creating incentives for better care management, but these value-based payments are a small fraction of overall provider payments. These

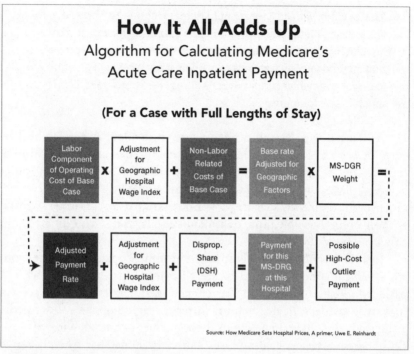

How It All Adds Up
Algorithm for Calculating Medicare's Acute Care Inpatient Payment

(For a Case with Full Lengths of Stay)

Source: How Medicare Sets Hospital Prices, A primer, Uwe E. Reinhardt

FIGURE 1.1 Medicare's complex payment formularies are easy to manipulate and not linked to quality outcomes.

incentives have not been large enough to meaningfully change inefficient or ineffective practice patterns.

Medicare pricing is a form of market socialism where central planners price, administer, and police market-level activities, such as medical treatment. They are replete with perverse incentives and unintended negative consequences. At best, Medicare's payment formularies invite manipulation. At worst, they inspire fraud and abuse.

WHY PRICES DON'T MATTER

In a March 2017 *New York Times* article, author Elizabeth Rosenthal chronicles America's dystopian system for coding and billing medical treatments.[5] Rosenthal concludes that the medical billing system itself is a primal cause of the nation's sky-high medical costs.

That system, with its lines of alphanumeric codes and arcane medical abbreviations, has given birth to a gigantic new industry of consultants, armies of back-room experts whom medical providers and insurance companies deploy against each other in an endless war over which medical procedures were undertaken and how much to pay for them.

Rosenthal's analysis illustrates a core truth about American healthcare: prices rarely matter. Healthcare companies strive to optimize revenue per treatment. Payments for healthcare services ping-pong between payers and providers as they manipulate complex payment formularies for their own advantage. While titans battle, consumers wrestle with incomprehensible bills, treatment denials, and uncoordinated care delivery.

In this revenue-first operating environment, prices separate from costs, value is ephemeral, waste is breathtaking ($1 trillion annually), and patients are an afterthought. Entrenched incumbents across all sectors (payers, providers, device manufacturers, drug companies, intermediaries, and consultants) engage in these payment contests with virtuoso skill and devastating success. The healthcare industry wins and society loses.

Differential payment for identical procedures is the defining feature of American healthcare. Complex billing codes are the currency through which commercial and governmental payers compensate hospitals and doctors for the treatments they provide.

Maximizing payment is Job 1 in almost all large health systems. They build robust revenue cycle capabilities to capture the most revenue possible. Sophisticated revenue cycle systems employ data mining, coding formularies, and predictive analytics to optimize claims collection.

Minor adjustments to treatment protocols can increase procedure payments substantially. Doctors change behaviors to incorporate these adjustments. They spend more time documenting treatments for billing purposes than providing care. This is a principal cause of physician burnout.

Commercial health insurance claims are substantially more lucrative for providers than public claims. Health systems and health insurers employ legions of highly trained coders to negotiate payment for specific claims. Health systems bill to maximize payment. Health insurers deny claims to minimize payment. Resolution often takes months.

These payment battles between large health insurers and health systems dominate US healthcare. They add enormous administrative complexity and cost without benefiting consumers. At US hospitals, administrative budgets are double those of Canadian hospitals.[6] American society pays for healthcare's profligacy through lower wages, lower productivity, and declining global competitiveness.

These perverse and counterproductive payment mechanics and the market distortion they create have their roots in World War II wage and price controls, tax policies, and the enabling legislation that created Medicare and Medicaid. The fault lies not in program intention, but in program design. By understanding the System's fundamental flaws, healthcare's revolutionaries can overcome and replace them with business models that meet customer needs.

HEALTHCARE'S FUNDAMENTAL FLAWS

Massachusetts General Hospital (MGH) is the third-oldest hospital in the United States. It has a venerable tradition of advanced teaching, fine clinical care, and scientific breakthroughs. In 2011, in the wake of its two hundredth anniversary, MGH published statistics on hospital mortality and costs from 1821 to 2010. We've combined the two trends in the Figure 1.2.[7] The numbers tell quite a story.

The up-and-down spikes in mortality data illustrate the haphazard nature of care through the mid-1900s. Hospitals were dangerous places. Medicine was rudimentary. In some years, as many as 14 percent of patients who entered Mass General died. People died for myriad and tragic reasons. Infection, childbirth, viruses, and other ordinary events could be death sentences.

With the advent of new medicines, enhanced diagnostics, and standardized medical practices, in-hospital mortality rates have plummeted. Since the 1990s, the death rate of Mass General patients has stabilized at just over 2 percent. The same cannot be said for costs.

Hospital costs have followed the opposite trajectory. They began to rise gradually during and after WWII as a result of the imposition of wage and price controls during WWII. Then they suddenly spiked upward in the mid-1960s after the legislative creation of Medicare and Medicaid. That steep upward climb continues today.

FIGURE 1.2 Opposite trajectories for mortality rates and discharge costs at Massachusetts General Hospital

Distortion #1: Price Controls

Prior to WWII, healthcare was a cottage industry, practiced primarily by charitable organizations with last-resort care offered in public "charity" hospitals. That is the reason most American hospitals are tax-exempt organizations. Today, healthcare is big business. It is the largest and fastest-growing sector of the American economy.

To curb spending and inflation during World War II, the government imposed wage and price controls on American businesses. In the tight postwar labor market, companies attracted and retained workers by offering healthcare benefits in lieu of wage increases. This was the origin of employer-sponsored healthcare coverage in America, and it has distorted healthcare's supply-and-demand dynamics. More health insurance leads to more healthcare services and higher prices.

Distortion #2: Tax Policy

Tax policy amplified the market distortion. In accordance with federal law, companies do not pay taxes on health insurance benefits. This tax policy increases the percentage of total compensation dedicated to health insurance benefits and reduces the percentage dedicated to wages. Companies get a "bigger bang for their buck" with each dollar increase in health benefits relative to wages. Health companies are the direct beneficiaries of these distorting economic and tax policies.

Corporate healthcare benefits is the US Treasury's single largest tax break. It costs the federal treasury $200 billion each year.[8] Unfortunately, generous health benefits lead to excessive healthcare consumption. This creates a form of what economists term "moral hazard" and increases unnecessary healthcare expenditure. Consumers interact with the health system more frequently than necessary and pursue treatments without regard to overall costs. The fee-for-service payment model exacerbates these tendencies.

> **Moral hazard.** A situation in which one party gets involved in a risky event knowing that it is protected against the risk and the other party will incur the cost. It arises when both the parties have incomplete information about each other.

Hospitals like Massachusetts General Hospital benefited from the increase in funds flowing into healthcare. On an inflation-adjusted basis, the cost per alive discharge at MGH was approximately $1,000 from its founding in 1821 until the beginning of WWII. Then, that cost tripled to $3,000 between the beginning of WWII and 1965.

Distortion #3: Medicare

A second and more catastrophic market distortion occurred with the creation of the Medicare and Medicaid programs that provide health insurance for older and lower-income Americans respectively. Medicare and Medicaid are landmarks of social policy. They increase care access for America's elderly, poor, and vulnerable.

In the mid-1960s, there was strong resistance to the Medicare and Medicaid enabling legislation, especially from physicians, provider organizations, and insurers. To pass the legislation, President Lyndon B. Johnson agreed to two provisions that underlie the stratospheric rise in Medicare's healthcare prices during the last 50+ years:

1. Fee-for-service payment for all treatments
2. No governmental interference in medical decision making

Together, these provisions guarantee payment to physicians and hospitals for all "reasonable" treatments administered to Medicare patients. Commercial plans followed Medicare's lead in designing and implementing payment formularies for medical services.

But there's more. To placate the American Hospital Association, the law also required Blue Cross Plans to *administer* the hospital benefit (Medicare Part A). This turned insurer organizations like Blue Cross Blue Shield into third-party administrators (TPAs). The provision rewarded health insurers in the same way that fee-for-service payment rewarded providers. As a result, health insurers take as much as 15 percent of the costs of Medicare claims to design and administer health benefit programs. In the open marketplace, these administrative functions are typically 2 to 3 percent of premium dollars.

In normal markets, demand for products and services drives supply. In healthcare, the supply of facilities and practitioners drives demand for their services. When there are more cardiac surgeons in a region, the System performs more cardiac procedures. This phenomenon is termed "Roemer's law" in reference to the work of Milton Roemer, a former professor at the UCLA School of Public Health. He concluded in the early 1960s that, "supply may induce its own demand in the presence of third-party payment."[9]

> **Roemer's law.** The theory of economist Milton Roemer that states "supply may induce its own demand where a third party practically guarantees reimbursement of usage." Roemer discovered this investigating how the number of hospital beds per capita affected hospitalization rates. He found that in regions with higher numbers of hospital beds per capita, the rates of hospitalization and length of stay were also higher.

Supply-driven demand, as Roemer termed it, explains high levels of unnecessary treatments delivered in the United States. This is a major component of wasteful healthcare spending, which many experts believe approximates $1 trillion.[10] Third-party payment causes economic dislocation in the following ways:

- It compensates "reimbursable care" whether or not it is appropriate.

- It discourages "appropriate care" when it is not reimbursable.

- It complicates the determination of what constitutes proper care, which in turn increases administrative costs.

- It separates the recipient of healthcare services from the payment for those services.

This blending of public and private activity without the constraints present in efficient markets has created a high-cost system with significant coverage gaps. Hospitals and payers maximize revenues within a closed payment system. Each sector is consolidating to improve its negotiating leverage. The result is that higher payments go to hospitals with the most negotiating leverage, not those that deliver the best healthcare services.

Payers use their leverage and enrollment systems to maximize revenue, shift coverage risk to others, and/or minimize payment for care services (the medical loss ratio). This pattern of payment and service provision generates confusion and uncertainty for consumers within the system. The lack of pricing transparency and the limited availability of outcomes data limit their ability to make informed decisions regarding healthcare purchases.

Accordingly, the System focuses on providing the costliest services in the costliest facilities. We have a massively overbuilt acute care delivery infrastructure—i.e., too many hospitals. America overtreats and overpays for costly acute care procedures. It undertreats and underpays for vital primary services, including chronic disease management, behavioral health services, and health promotion.

The cost per alive discharge at Massachusetts General Hospital illustrates the impact. It took off like a rocket ship in 1965. By 2010, MGH's discharge cost reached $30,000—a tenfold increase since Medicare's inception. It's much higher now.

As a result of policy decisions, including wage and price controls in World War II, not taxing health benefits, and the design of Medicare payment formularies, the United States has created and funded an artificial supply-driven economic model for healthcare service delivery. The

United States' massive level of nonproductive healthcare expenditures exerts a drag on the overall economy, reduces take-home pay, and terrifies individual Americans confronting major medical expenditures.

The System wins. The rest of us lose.

FOLLOW THE MONEY

After the Watergate break-in, *Washington Post* reporters Bob Woodward and Carl Bernstein worked tirelessly to determine who was ultimately responsible for the break-in and why. Whenever the trail went cold, Woodward sought the advice of a secret trusted source who became known in conspiratorial lore as "Deep Throat." To learn the truth, Deep Throat counseled Woodward to "follow the money."

If Deep Throat were a source in "Healthgate," he or she would say, "Follow the payment." Healthcare's payment complexity enables insurers, pharmacy benefit managers, health systems, drugmakers, and physicians to optimize revenues by gaming the current payment systems and regulatory regimes. Under fee-for-service medicine, process wins and outcomes lose.

Today, expenditures for healthcare services in America are, on average, twice that of other industrial countries around the world. The average price for a knee replacement, for example, is 40 percent higher than it is in Switzerland, the next most expensive country, and 53 percent higher than in Great Britain. Americans see doctors less often and have shorter hospital stays but lead the world in expensive procedures and costly services such as MRIs.[11]

A July 2018 *Wall Street Journal* article on why Americans spend so much on healthcare succinctly summarizes healthcare's gravity-defying economics.

> The U.S. spends more per capita on health care than any other developed nation. It will soon spend close to 20% of its GDP on health—significantly more than the percentage spent by major Organization for Economic Cooperation and Development nations.
>
> What is driving costs so high? . . . Americans aren't buying more health care overall than other countries. But what they are buying is increasingly expensive. Among the reasons is the troubling fact that few people in health care, from consumers to doctors to hospitals to insurers, know the true cost of what they are buying and selling.

Providers, manufacturers and middlemen operate in an opaque market that can mask their role and their cut of the revenue. Mergers give some players more heft to enlarge their piece of the pie.

Consumers, meanwhile, buoyed by insurance and tax breaks, have little idea how much they are really spending and little incentive to know underlying costs.

It's impossible to overstate the role money and profits play in the delivery of healthcare services: the use of hotel-like dining and entertainment amenities to attract high-paying commercially insured consumers; the location of facilities; the use of advertising; the choice of medical specialty by physicians; the determination of which diseases to cure; the mechanisms for setting prices; the documentation of services; the time spent with patients; the ways to influence referrals. The list goes on and on and on.

Healthcare analyst and futurist Joe Flower illustrates the System's operating mentality with his two core rules of healthcare economics:

- Rule 1: People do what you pay them to do.

- Rule 2: People do *exactly* what you pay them to do.

Flower's assessment is harsh, but directionally right. Following payment and profit almost always reveals the motivations of health companies.

There is nothing inherently wrong with for-profit enterprises, just as there is nothing inherently virtuous in being a nonprofit organization. Healthcare has many of each. What they share in common is a transactional payment system that does not align service provision with consumer needs. Connecting with customers and meeting their needs is the essence of great business practice. This is an alien concept in healthcare.

Examining the following components of the System's operating mechanics demonstrates how money and profits fundamentally shape the healthcare services the American people receive: physician compensation, Medicare fee splits, conflict of interest disclosure, and medical advertising.

Physician Compensation

In December 2018, the USC-Brookings Schaeffer Initiative for Health Policy issued a report examining how Medicare's policies influence the national mix of primary and specialty care physicians. They concluded the following:

> [T]he mix of physicians in the US has too few PCPs [primary care physicians] and too many specialists, the income gap between the two is a major determinant of the PCP/specialty mix, and Medicare physician payment policy is a major contributor to the income gap. Changes in GME [graduate medical education] payments to hospitals to favor training of PCPs have little potential to make a meaningful difference because other incentives affecting physicians in training and teaching hospitals are too powerful.[12]

Clearly, physician compensation influences practice selection. Figure 1.3 details physician compensation by specialty. Primary care specialties, including preventive, pediatric, family, and internal medicine, are the lowest compensated by a wide measure. Interestingly, in foreign medical schools the highest percentages of graduates are in the primary care specialties, with 30.3 percent in family medicine and 43.3 percent in internal medicine.

Only 32 percent of US physicians practice in primary care, and 68 percent are specialists. Other high-income countries have higher percentages of primary care physicians (PCPs) and lower compensation differentials between PCPs and specialists. Highly integrated US health companies also employ higher percentages of PCPs. For example, the percentage of PCPs employed by Kaiser Permanente is 45 percent.

Here's what's interesting. Robust primary care practices demonstrate both better outcomes and lower costs. Better preventive care and chronic disease management reduce acute admissions and the need for specialty care. This is the business logic driving the expansion of accountable care organizations, patient-centered medical homes, direct-contracting programs, and Medicare Advantage health plans. Ironically, market demand for PCPs is increasing as the supply of PCPs is decreasing. The Association of American Medical Colleges projects a PCP shortage of 14,800 to 49,300 by 2030.[13]

In normal markets, compensation for PCPs would increase to adjust their supply to market demand. That isn't happening in healthcare. The System's artificial economy overtreats and overpays for specialty care. This is a direct by-product of the complex payment formularies described earlier in this chapter. US medical students are making rational decisions to pursue specialty medicine. It's in their economic interests. The way the System pays for care distorts the physician mix needed to deliver optimal care. Money, money, money . . .

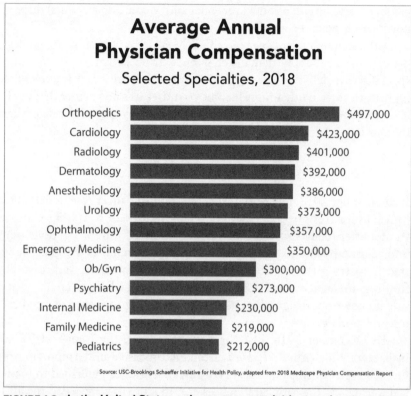

Average Annual Physician Compensation
Selected Specialties, 2018

Orthopedics	$497,000
Cardiology	$423,000
Radiology	$401,000
Dermatology	$392,000
Anesthesiology	$386,000
Urology	$373,000
Ophthalmology	$357,000
Emergency Medicine	$350,000
Ob/Gyn	$300,000
Psychiatry	$273,000
Internal Medicine	$230,000
Family Medicine	$219,000
Pediatrics	$212,000

Source: USC-Brookings Schaeffer Initiative for Health Policy, adapted from 2018 Medscape Physician Compensation Report

FIGURE 1.3 **In the United States, primary care specialties receive the lowest compensation.**

Medicare Payment Splits

The determination of how much Medicare pays for the different types of specialty care originates within the American Medical Association (AMA). Specialty associations dominate the process. Talk about the fox guarding the henhouse.

Each year, an AMA committee reviews Medicare billing codes and payment levels to recommend appropriate rates for primary and specialty procedures. Medicare typically accepts the AMA panel's recommendations. Medical specialty associations devote considerable resources to lobbying the committee. This process is political, not impartial and rational.

Strong specialty associations, such as the American Society of Cardiology, overwhelm primary care advocates. As a consequence, Medicare

payment (and by extension commercial and Medicaid payments) disproportionately benefit specialists.

Like so much in the System, this AMA-driven fee-splitting process
distorts market supply-demand dynamics. It pushes more revenue into
specialty care delivery. The result is excessive specialty care treatment at
higher prices than other high-income countries. It's no wonder that medical students disproportionately pursue careers in specialty care rather
than primary care. The System pays them to do this.

Conflicts. What Conflicts?

In September 2018, one of the world's foremost cancer researchers, Dr.
José Baselga, resigned as CMO of Memorial Sloan Kettering Cancer
Center after reports surfaced that he had received millions of dollars in
undisclosed payments from drug and device companies. Studies show
that industry gifts, speaker fees, travel costs, payments, and research
funding influence prescribing habits and even clinical trials. Outside money from drugmakers asserts a corrupting influence on medical
research and practice.[14]

In December 2018, just three months later, the *New York Times*
in partnership with *ProPublica* chronicled massive underreporting of
financial relationships by authors of research studies published in medical journals.[15] The article references a 2015 study that revealed the 100
highest-compensated doctors from device companies only revealed their
financial conflicts 37 percent of the time. Blame falls squarely on both
physician researchers for not reporting and the journals for not policing.
Despite multiple attempts to improve disclosure, many researchers still
fail to disclose with few repercussions.

Pay-to-play is alive and well in the System. It compromises the integrity of medical research. Moreover, it skews research activities toward
biomedical areas of interest favored by well-funded corporate sponsors.
Most important, it diminishes research's ability to advance medical
understanding and effectiveness.

Medical Advertising

With all their profits, health companies strive to unduly influence patients
and doctors as well as government officials. America and New Zealand
are the only countries in the world that permit direct-to-consumer advertising by drugmakers. The FDA outlawed the practice in the United

States until 1997. Today, drugmakers spend around $5 billion annually on televised ads.[16]

In 2011, the giant British drugmaker GlaxoSmithKline (GSK) sent $28.5 million to US institutions and researchers working on drug studies and spent $56.8 million on US doctors speaking about GSK products.[17] That year, the American drugmaker Pfizer spent $177 million total on similar promotion channels in the United States. In 2012, the British government levied a $3 billion fine against GSK for improperly promoting drugs. Chastened, it voluntarily ceased promotions. In 2018, it reversed that policy because of the competitive disadvantages the company had suffered.[18]

Health systems and insurance companies also advertise expansively. Insurers do this to push consumers toward their products and services. This is a customary practice within competitive markets as companies seek to connect with customers. What is unusual is that healthcare consumers rarely know the prices of advertised products and services, nor do they pay for the lion's share of their costs. This is another feature of the System's operating dynamics that distorts proper market function.

TRANSACTIONS WITHOUT CUSTOMERS

In healthcare, transactions occur without customers. Patients see doctors. Doctors tell patients what to do. After limited co-pays and deductibles, a third-party insurer pays for prescribed services. Healthcare transactions sever the direct buyer-seller interactions that establish supply-demand relationships in well-functioning markets.

In efficient markets, prices have the power of language. They signal information from sellers to buyers regarding the perceived value of offered products and services. There's a limit to how much companies can charge customers, particularly for routine services and commodity products. Transactions occur when buyers have the inclination and means to purchase desired products and services. In this way, buyers become customers. Transactions are value-based exchanges undertaken willingly by both parties.

In other markets, high-margin products and services attract competition. Over time, markets exert downward pressure on prices and revenues as new competitors enter the marketplace. For businesses to remain profitable, they must manage costs and improve operational efficiency while offering goods or services that customers value and want.

Without buyer-seller dynamics to guide pricing, the System relies upon complex payment formularies that lend themselves to manipulation and fraud. In their efforts to "win" disputes over treatment payments, both providers and payers have lost sight of the paramount role prices play within efficiently functioning markets.

This blind spot limits the ability of incumbent health companies to respond to market demands for greater value in healthcare delivery. They lack the internal capabilities to hear and react to market signals demanding better healthcare at lower prices. This deficiency creates opportunities for new business models to deliver superior healthcare services to value-driven customers who care about prices.

Hospitals, under the traditional fee-for-service payment system, have limited financial incentive to reduce costs. They seek to grow revenues by increasing volume. Incumbent managerial mindsets calcify attempts to bring value to healthcare delivery. They fail to see the link between better outcomes and lower prices. They frustrate attempts to disrupt unproductive business models that add costs without creating value.

Most important, incumbent mindsets prevent health companies from undertaking transformational change. Health companies make incremental improvements on flawed business models rather than embrace transformative business models with different capabilities and lower cost structures.

I use the term "indumbent" to describe this type of self-destructive, short-term thinking. Indumbent thinking prevented Kodak from recognizing the competitive threat posed by digital image technologies. Indumbent thinking prevents many health companies from appreciating existential threats to their high-cost and inefficient business practices.

With very few exceptions, US providers will quote cash prices for specific procedures, but they are unwilling to publish those rates. They worry about setting precedent with payers who could use transparent procedural prices to reduce payments for equivalent procedures.

This is indumbent thinking in action. Providers protect their near-term negotiating advantage with payers while leaving themselves vulnerable to the longer-term trend toward pricing convergence for routine procedures.

Healthcare companies may have the best intentions toward patients, but perverse economic incentives shape their operations. They do what the System pays them to do. That is the root cause of healthcare's dysfunction and the wasteful, costly, neglectful, and indifferent healthcare services that patients routinely receive.

Mark Twain famously observed, "It's not what you don't know that will kill you. It's what you know for sure that just ain't so." Indumbent mindsets believe current payment practices will continue for the foreseeable future. It just ain't so.

In the ongoing and seemingly never-ending debate over how our healthcare system got so broken, there is plenty of blame to go around. Depending on the issue at hand, we can point to health insurers or pharmaceutical companies or health systems or physicians or government or the food industry or unhealthy lifestyles and behaviors. Underlying all the finger-pointing, however, there is one principal force driving the System's dysfunction: unrestrained fee-for-service payment.

In the process, incumbent thinking often becomes indumbent thinking. New business models are emerging that deliver better healthcare for less money with transparency and great customer experience. Old-world managerial mindsets with payment-first instincts are ill-equipped to compete on price, outcomes, and customer service. Healthcare markets are changing. Health companies must adapt or die.

As Gundersen demonstrated when it researched its own cost for knee surgery, it's clearly possible for healthcare providers to know their costs and improve their performance through time-tested business strategies. That hospitals choose not to do so reflects the nature of FFS payment and how it rewards healthcare providers for treatment activity, not care outcomes.

In the land of the blind, the one-eyed woman is queen. Health systems that become more price transparent, align prices with costs, and sell value-oriented treatments will increase market share. Lagging health systems will lose relevance.

A CALL FOR REVOLUTION

When Americans complain about healthcare, they tend to focus on a specific incident or experience. A claim that goes unpaid because of a bureaucratic snafu. A bill that's shockingly high. A bad outcome from a procedure, a long wait time, a very expensive medication. At such moments, it's easy to get mad at the health plan, the hospital, the pharmacy, or the IT system.

All that anger, frustration, and despair is misplaced. Americans deserve to be angry, but their righteous anger should be directed at the System, not individual participants. America already spends more than enough money to provide superior healthcare to everyone in the country, but the System does not allocate healthcare dollars effectively. In this sense, fixing America's broken healthcare system is a distribution challenge, not a funding issue.

Social justice activist and theorist Angela Davis observes that reform fortifies the status quo. When it comes to healthcare, she's right. The System's problems are structural and massive. Incremental reforms are insufficient to overcome the System's inherent fragmentation and dysfunction. It's like putting a new coat of paint on a rusty old Camry and expecting it to run like a Tesla.

The System is rotten at its core. The benefits of America's excessive and ineffective healthcare spending flow to the System's incumbents who pursue their interests at the expense of the American people. If that isn't grounds for a revolution, I don't know what is.

CHAPTER 2

Waste More, Want More

The US healthcare industry has an insatiable appetite. The array of health systems, physician groups, insurers, device companies, drugmakers, pharmaceutical distributors, imaging centers, and ambulatory clinics consume societal resources with a relentless, unappeasable hunger.

Billing bears no clear relationship to services. The numbers can be astronomical, even after providers apply negotiated insurer discounts. Surprise bills have become routine: a NORC survey found that most Americans (57 percent) have received a bill for treatments they thought their health insurance would cover.[1] Surprise! Surprise! It's so common that Kaiser Health News and National Public Radio have partnered to feature an outrageous "bill of the month."[2] The stories are confounding. Here are a few.

- In New England, Sarah Witter broke two bones in her leg while skiing. To heal the bones, doctors inserted a metal plate, but that plate broke soon after the surgery, requiring a second surgery. Doctors assured Witter that she had done nothing wrong to cause the plate to break, but they billed for both surgeries anyway. Her insurer, Aetna, refused to pay some of the costs because the company believed they were too high. Then Witter learned she was on the hook for more than $18,000, including over $7,000 for the second surgery.[3] Breaks in her leg, break in the plate, no break in the bill.

- In California, Janet Winston sought testing for allergies at an in-network hospital with her Anthem Blue Cross insurance plan. The bill totaled over $48,000 before insurance discounts. Her portion of the final bill was over $3,000. The "usual, customary, and reasonable" charge for the allergy tests she took, however, was just $35.[4] That's a lot of scratch for those scratches.

- In Texas, Elizabeth Moreno had back surgery to address ongoing pain. The surgery was a success. At the end of a follow-up visit, an office staffer asked her for a urine sample. Long after payment for her back surgery and more than a year after the follow-up visit, Moreno receive a $17,000 bill for the urine sample.[5]

Each of these stories reflects price gouging, generated by providers and passed on by insurers to customers who have done everything right: they got insurance, they followed the rules, they stayed with preferred providers, they asked questions about their care. Still, they got slammed with unexpected, and unexpectedly high, bills for treatment.

These billing experiences reflect the fragmented and disconnected relationships between health companies and American consumers. Hospitals, doctors, device manufacturers, drugmakers, insurers, and multiple other service providers all interact to deliver and pay for care delivery with limited regard to outcomes and almost no regard to value. Consumers caught in the crossfire are casualties of an ever-larger Healthcare Industrial Complex™ (my term) that takes care of itself first and foremost.

The unchecked growth in US healthcare spending is a monstrosity of our own making. It must be stopped. The System's profligacy adds enormous unnecessary costs to care delivery without adequate investment in preventive care, behavioral health services, health promotion, chronic disease management, and old-fashioned primary care services. The System has become a significant drag on the overall economy as well as the leading cause of personal bankruptcies.

Without a revolution, US healthcare's systemic dysfunction will continue to wreak devastating and lasting havoc on individual Americans, their communities, and the nation's economic prosperity.

MONSTROUS APPETITE AND MONSTROUS WASTE

As a percentage of gross domestic product (GDP), US healthcare has been on a relentless upward climb for over 50 years, consuming societal resources at an alarming rate (Figure 2.1).[6] According to the Centers for Medicare and Medicaid Services (CMS), total health expenditures for 2026 are projected to be $5.7 trillion.[7]

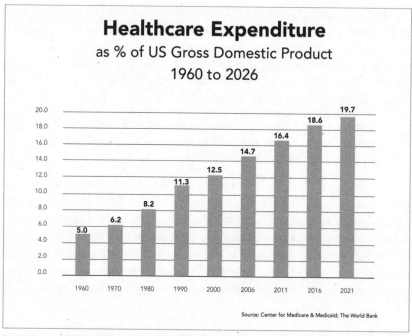

Healthcare Expenditure
as % of US Gross Domestic Product
1960 to 2026

Source: Center for Medicare & Medicaid; The World Bank

FIGURE 2.1 **US healthcare expenditure as a percent of GDP has almost quadrupled since 1960. More for healthcare means less for everything else.**

As a Peace Corps Volunteer in Liberia, West Africa, in the late 1970s and early 1980s, I learned to count in the local dialect, Grebo. Anything over the number 20 was simply "a lot." Grebo logic applies well to healthcare spending. A trillion is an unimaginably large number that's very difficult for the human brain to comprehend. Here's a way to think about it:

* A million seconds takes 11.5 days.

* A billion seconds takes 31.7 years.

* A trillion seconds takes 31,710 years.

At $1 trillion annually (a conservative estimate), healthcare wastes $2.7 billion each and every day. As a native Grebo speaker would put it, that's a lot. The size of the US healthcare system will soon surpass the GDP of Germany, the world's fourth largest economy. The US healthcare system's annual waste is equivalent to Mexico's GDP. The daily waste is 25 percent greater than Liberia's GDP.

In their April 2012 article "Eliminating Waste in US Health Care," published in the *Journal of the American Medical Association* (*JAMA*), authors Donald Berwick and Andrew Hackbarth declared that constructing an affordable healthcare system that addresses the vital care needs of Americans requires removing "non-value-added practices," or waste. As they put it, cutting waste

is a basic strategy for most industries today, i.e., to keep processes, products, and services that actually help customers and systematically removing the elements of work that do not.[8]

To that end, Berwick and Hackbarth estimated that US healthcare wasted between $558 billion and $1.263 trillion in 2011. They designated six categories of waste (failures of care delivery, failures of care coordination, overtreatment, administrative complexity, pricing failures, and fraud and abuse) with high and low estimates. Overall, Berwick and Hackbarth estimate "non-value-added practices" constitute between 21 percent and 47 percent of total national health expenditures. Figure 2.2 details their

Healthcare "Waste"
2011 vs. 2017
($ Billions)

Categories	2011 ($2.7 Trillion)		2017 ($3.5 Trillion)	
	Low	High	Low	High
Care Delivery Failures	102	154	132	200
Care Coordination Failures	25	45	32	58
Overtreatment	158	226	205	293
Administrative Compliance	107	389	139	505
Pricing Failures	84	178	109	231
Fraud and Abuse	82	272	106	353
Total	558	1263	723	1,638
% of Total Expenditure	21%	47%	21%	47%

Source: Berwick, Donald M. & Hackbarth, Andrew D. "Eliminating Waste in US Health Care." JAMA. 2012 307(14): 1513-1516

FIGURE 2.2 **$3.5 trillion was spent on healthcare in 2017. An estimated 21–47 percent is waste.**

findings with equivalent estimates for 2017 when total health expenditures equaled $3.5 trillion.

Little has changed in the practices of American healthcare organizations since that 2012 report, even as national health expenditures have increased from $2.7 trillion in 2011 to $3.5 trillion in 2017. Using Berwick's and Hackbarth's percentages, that translates into an additional $168 billion to $376 billion in new wasted healthcare expenditures. If anything, waste has probably increased in percentage terms. There is significant "pricing failure" embedded within drug manufacturing and distribution, particularly for new high-cost cancer drugs.

Most of what Berwick and Hackbarth label waste, American healthcare companies consider profit. Under fee-for-service medicine, every bureaucratic process, $400 bandage, $1,900 urine test, unexpected readmission, hospital-based infection, overextended stay, and unnecessary MRI goes straight to the bottom line. To the System's incumbents, healthcare's waste tastes so very good. Why ever give it up?

HEALTHCARE'S IRON TRIANGLE

The System's inability to improve is a source of singular frustration. Well-intentioned and well-resourced reforms to increase care value and eliminate medically unnecessary treatments have failed to produce material improvement.[9] There clearly is a deeper pathology at work. It was this line of thinking that led me to Eisenhower's 1961 farewell address and his warnings regarding the dangers posed to American society by the military industrial complex.

As detailed in this book's Introduction, Eisenhower coined the term "military industrial complex" to describe how an unholy trinity of the Defense Department, Congress, and military contractors work to promote their own interests at the expense of American society. Political scientists developed the phrase "the iron triangle" to describe the flow of money, people, and influence that promote excessive defense spending and sustain the military establishment.

The Healthcare Industrial Complex replicates the features of the military industrial complex on a much larger scale. First substitute the massive federal and state bureaucracies administering health policies for the Department of Defense. Then substitute the even more massive healthcare industry and its aligned interest groups for the defense industry. And voila, we have the three components necessary to misdirect healthcare resources.

- **Congress** with healthcare legislative responsibility and numerous oversight committees.

- **Federal and state healthcare agencies** with administrative and oversight responsibilities. Federal agencies include Health and Human Services (HHS), the Centers for Medicare and Medicaid Services (CMS), the Food and Drug Administration (FDA), the Centers for Disease Control (CDC), the National Institutes of Health (NIH), and aligned agencies. States typically have departments of health, insurance, and social services among others to administer and regulate state healthcare activities and policies.

- **Healthcare companies and advocacy groups** that deliver healthcare services, provide health insurance, manufacture medical drugs and devices, conduct medical research, provide medical education, and lobby for constituent interests including industry segments, specific patient populations, and health policies. Together, these activities constitute 18 percent of the US economy.

Healthcare's "iron triangle" in Figure 2.3 is far more powerful and destructive than the military's iron triangle has ever been.

Congress, the bureaucracies, and industry/interest groups work in the shadows to advance their parochial interests. The industry funds election campaigns for legislators who pass supportive legislation. Legislators provide funding and political support to healthcare-related agencies who administer lax regulations and grant special favors to industry.

At its extremes, this iron triangle of interests not only misdirects resources to overfund its multifarious activities, it actually kills people. Chapter 4 details the iron triangle origins of America's self-created opioid crisis.

MARKET-MEDICINE INTERACTIONS

Shortly after publishing my first book, *Market vs. Medicine: America's Epic Fight for Better, Affordable Healthcare*, I met with Jullia Quazi, a close friend and former investment banking colleague. Jullia told me a funny story about her precocious and freaky-smart six-year-old son, Kairan. Noticing the cover of my book, Kairan asked Jullia to ask me who won. When Jullia asked what he meant, Kairan responded, "Dave wrote 'Market vs. Medicine.' Who won, 'Market' or 'Medicine?'"

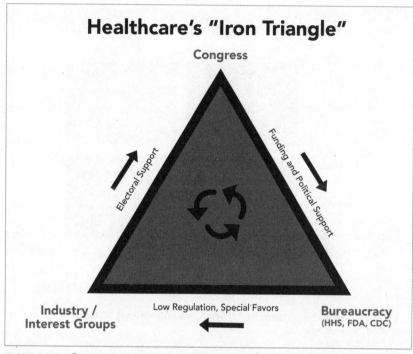

FIGURE 2.3 Congress, healthcare industry groups, and federal bureaucracy feed each other to maintain the Healthcare Industrial Complex, which affects more people and expenditures than the military industrial complex.

Out of the mouths of babes . . . If only, Kairan, there were a simple answer.

Good and bad medical practices abound in US healthcare, just as there are good and bad market behaviors at play. Clarifying the characteristics and implications of market-medicine interactions is essential for understanding US healthcare's structural flaws and how proper market function corrects them.

- **Good initiatives advance market-driven reform** by rewarding innovative organizations that deliver better outcomes, lower costs, and/or superior customer service. This is Revolutionary Healthcare.

- **Bad initiatives strengthen incumbents** through regulatory manipulation, market concentration, and/or lack of transparency to perpetuate the status quo system. This is Status Quo Healthcare.

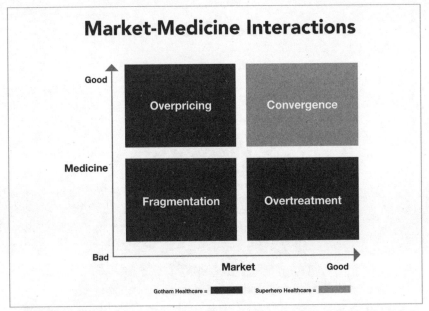

FIGURE 2.4 **Most healthcare in America is a suboptimal blend of bad market and medicine behaviors.**

The matrix in Figure 2.4 segments market-medicine interactions into four quadrants and identifies each quadrant's defining characteristic.

Bad medical practices and bad market behaviors are destructive and dangerous. They lead to fragmented, overpriced care delivery (lower-left quadrant) that is mistake-prone and ignores consumer needs. Hospitals that overcharge for services and neglect patients; outpatient clinics that have no connection to the larger care continuum; surgical units that work banker's hours despite urgent, 24/7 demand: these Status Quo practices riddle American healthcare and diminish quality and satisfaction while wasting societal resources.

Appropriately priced bad medicine (lower-right quadrant) constitutes overtreatment. An unnecessary MRI is wasteful even if it only costs $500. Moreover, unnecessary services or treatments may even be harmful. Mispriced appropriate care (upper-left quadrant) is also wasteful. An MRI may be necessary, but it's wildly overpriced at $5,000.

Fragmentation, overtreatment (too many units of care), and overpricing (too much cost per unit of care) are the three faces of Status Quo healthcare delivery. They thrive in opaque and unaccountable operating environments. Much of the healthcare waste detailed by Berwick and

Hackbarth originates here. The American people deserve better. They should expect great healthcare at fair prices.

The convergence of holistic care delivery within efficient markets with price transparency produces Revolutionary Healthcare (upper-right quadrant). There are pockets of Revolutionary Healthcare practiced in America, and I will describe them in detail in Part III, but they are the exception today, not the rule.

By definition, Revolutionary Healthcare is pro-market. It reinforces level-field competition, transparency, and accountability. In the process, it delivers value to consumers by meeting their needs for service, support, convenience, compassion, safety, affordability, and the best possible outcomes.

Pro-market health companies deliver the right care at the right time in the right place at the right price. They provide the care and services that patients need, want, and deserve. That's healthcare as it should be.

HEALTHCARE'S CHRONIC DISEASE

As discussed earlier in this chapter, authors Berwick and Hackbarth detailed the financial parameters of the System's staggering waste within six logical categories. They recommended systematically attacking each type of waste through regulation, education, and monitoring. Their goal is to reduce annual healthcare inflation so that it tracks the Consumer Price Index, which measures nominal inflation. This would put the System on a diet and a sustainable economic path. With guarded optimism, they believe that reducing waste incrementally is doable and offers the best hope for bringing healthcare costs under control over time.

Unfortunately, their analysis neglects the powerful economic motivations that drive wasteful healthcare spending. Those dynamics are more complex, interrelated, and pernicious than Berwick and Hackbarth present them to be. The Healthcare Industrial Complex resists incremental improvement because it has the intrinsic power to bend the government and marketplace to its desired ends.

The System limps along year to year. It's gaining weight, not exercising, not innovating, antisocial and narcissistic, irritable and abusive, lacks purpose, repeats mistakes, and is incapable of self-control. It's clear the System is suffering from a complex chronic disease that could be life-threatening to America if not treated.

Incremental reforms seeking to address the System's profligacy miss the mark. They treat the symptoms of the System's chronic disease, not its root causes. As with any chronic disease, successful treatment requires accurate diagnosis of pathologies, identification of root causes, and targeted treatments that address the totality of the disease.

US healthcare has three serious pathologies (revenue optimization, monopoly pricing, and monopsony pricing) caused by three pervasive root causes: payment complexity, unbalanced regulation, and government capture or influence-peddling (Figure 2.5). The System cannot heal and transform until reformers acknowledge and address the root causes of its chronic disease.

The System's pathologies rely on complexity, fragmentation, and "capture" of government officials to reward entrenched incumbents while adding unnecessary regulatory burden to sustain its bloated and ineffective bureaucracy. The System's chronic disease amplifies its pathologies through ineffectual regulatory structures with the following characteristics.

- **Complexity.** The Centers for Medicare and Medicaid Services (CMS) employs complex formularies to determine treatment payments. The marketplace is always smarter than central planners.

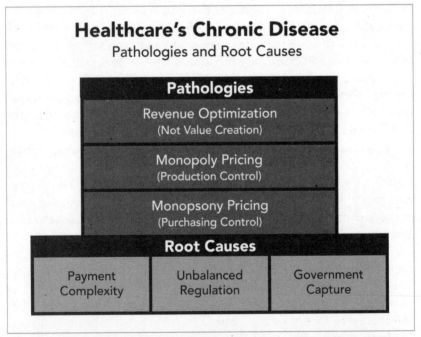

FIGURE 2.5 **Healthcare's destructive pathologies are a function of payment complexity, unbalanced regulation, and government capture.**

At best, the current payment formularies invite manipulation. At worst, they stimulate fraud and abuse. Moreover, regulatory and legislative attempts to change pricing mechanics (e.g., value-based pricing, MACRA, pilot programs) require detailed program submissions, complex reporting, and delayed performance assessment. It's no surprise that new healthcare payment initiatives rarely achieve the twin goals of reducing costs and improving outcomes.

- **Fragmentation.** The federal government regulates hospitals. State insurance commissions regulate health insurance companies. Payers and providers are actively pursuing vertical integration to respond to changing buyer preferences. Moreover, the FDA grants patents without regard to market pricing. As a result, device and pharma companies practice predatory pricing whenever they can. Like blind men describing different parts of an elephant, there is no regulatory body that sees the entire ecosystem. Lack of coherence weakens healthcare's regulatory framework.

- **Burden.** The System places an enormous regulatory and compliance burden on health companies through massive reporting requirements, internal auditing, and external enforcement, which increases administrative costs unnecessarily. The System's top-down, centralized approach to payment formularies, its patchwork approach to oversight, and its overweening and off-base monitoring result in a Byzantine set of regulatory policies that stifle innovation, reduce competition, add costs unnecessarily, and incentivize counterproductive care delivery practices.

- **Capture.** The capture of elected and nonelected government officials by the healthcare industry and its interest groups leads to pro-industry legislation and regulation. Industry experts insert their preferred language into legislation. That's how unhealthy frozen pizza became an allowable vegetable in public school lunches.[10] Revolving-door professionals circulate between industry and government positions. Conflict of interest is never far behind. They use insider access and relationships to advance industry interest. Lax enforcement of existing laws and regulations do little to prevent bad behavior. Fines paid by health companies for violations rarely alter corporate profitability.

In "Fundamental Flaws," Chapter 1 of this book, I detailed the System's insatiable pursuit of revenues over value. The root cause of this pathology is the complex payment formularies payers and providers rely upon to determine compensation for specific treatments. Health companies optimize to the payment formularies, not to the desired outcomes. The System's payment formularies tolerate manipulation and invite fraud.

The System's other two pathologies, monopoly and monopsony pricing control, result from excessive market concentration. Monopoly pricing occurs when companies capture sufficient production control to increase prices without fear of being undercut by competitors. Monopsony pricing occurs when companies exercise sufficient purchasing control that they can demand lower prices without fear that other buyers will pay more. Their root causes of monopoly and monopsony pricing are unbalanced regulation and government capture.

All healthcare is local, and so is the business of healthcare. The System's fragmentation has created hundreds of distorted local markets where payers and/or providers exercise unacceptable levels of pricing power. Market distortion also occurs when health companies capture sufficient production or distribution control for specific products (e.g., an "orphan" drug or a delivery device like the EpiPen) to generate excessive profits.

Let's shift our attention to Columbus, Ohio, and Chicago, Illinois, to examine cases of monopoly and monopsony pricing power. The System's fragmented regulatory framework undermines level-field competition and denies its benefits to consumers. The government either can't or won't implement pro-market regulatory reforms. After our spin through the Midwest, we'll dig into the other two root causes of the System's chronic disease: unbalanced regulation and government capture.

- **Monopoly.** A market structure characterized by a single seller, selling a unique product in the market. In a monopoly market, the seller faces no competition as the sole seller of goods with no close substitute and has the power of setting the price for products or services.
- **Monopsony.** A monopsony occurs when a single organization has market power as the sole purchaser for multiple sellers and can drive down the price of the seller's products or services according to the quantity that it demands.

Monopoly Pricing: Goodbye Columbus (Ohio)

With a metro-wide population of 2 million people and a growing diversified economy, Columbus is Ohio's capital city, home to Ohio State University and famous for its zoo, botanical gardens, and municipal parks system. People in Columbus must love hamburgers. Both Wendy's and White Castle have their corporate headquarters there.

Columbus also is a mecca for health systems. Sixty percent of the region's population carries high-paying commercial insurance, and no health insurance company has a dominant market position. UnitedHealth is the largest commercial insurer with 33 percent market share. By contrast, three well-funded, profitable, and highly integrated health systems dominate care delivery. Ohio Health (OH), Ohio State University Health System (OSUHS), and Mt. Carmel Health (MCH) had a combined market share of 83 percent in 2016. MCH is part of Trinity Health, among the nation's largest health systems. No health insurance company serving the Columbus area can afford to exclude any of these three providers from its networks, so OH, OSUHS, and MCH enjoy monopoly pricing power.

To the victors go the spoils. Since 2012, Columbus's health systems have already spent or are projected to spend $5 billion on new healthcare facilities, including a number of freestanding emergency department (ED) centers. That is a massive amount ($2,500 per person) of new facility investment for a region with 2 million people.[11] To generate adequate returns, hospitals in Columbus raised inpatient prices 20 percent and outpatient prices 30 percent between 2012 and 2016.[12] This compares to just a 5 percent increase in the Consumer Price Index (CPI) during the same period. Any way people in Columbus slice it, that's a lot of appendectomies and White Castle sliders.

Monopsony Pricing: Chicago Blues

In December 2015, the FTC challenged the proposed merger of Advocate Health Care with NorthShore University Hospital in federal court. Using a gerrymandered process that would make even the most partisan lawmakers blush, the FTC argued that the proposed combined company's concentration of hospitals in Chicago's North Shore would stifle competition, raise prices, and reduce service quality.

Examining metropolitan Chicago's competitive landscape, it is clear that Advocate-NorthShore's combined 22 percent market share in the six-county metropolitan region would not distort market pricing for healthcare services.

In fighting the Advocate-NorthShore merger, the FTC ignored the real 900-pound gorilla in the Chicago marketplace, Blue Cross Blue Shield of Illinois (BCBS). BCBS controls almost 75 percent of the region's commercial insurance market. Using monopsony purchasing power, it's the pricemaker in the Chicago marketplace.

BCBS was "officially" neutral regarding the Advocate-NorthShore merger. By contrast, the region's other health insurance companies supported the transaction.

The first trial began in the spring of 2016. It immediately became clear that BCBS virulently opposed the merger. The company had secretly spent months marshaling its arguments. Its opposition made no sense to me. I doubted it had any real concerns about excessive market concentration on the North Shore. Moreover, BCBS and Advocate had worked closely in structuring multiple insurance products. Why jeopardize the relationship?

To figure this out, I called an in-the-know health system executive. He speculated that BCBS feared the combined company might eventually offer a competing insurance product. That's when the light went on. BCBS had not challenged the merger to protect consumers against unfair hospital prices; it wanted to protect its dominant market position in the metro-Chicago commercial insurance market.

After three trials, two years, and millions in legal fees, Advocate and NorthShore terminated their merger discussions in March 2017. This was a pyrrhic and ironic victory for federal regulators. The FTC's win makes the Chicago marketplace less, not more competitive. Illinois consumers will pay higher rates for healthcare services because of BCBS's entrenched monopsony pricing power.

Unbalanced Regulation

The regulation of healthcare activities is split between federal and state agencies with overlapping jurisdictions, fragmented oversight, antiquated tools, and inconsistent leadership. The Federal Trade Commission (FTC) regulates hospitals, and state insurance commissions regulate commercial health insurers like BCBS.

Powerful market forces are reshaping healthcare delivery. New business models are emerging, and traditional lines between insurance provision and healthcare delivery are blurring. No regulatory body has the expertise and jurisdiction to establish a pro-market regulatory framework for integrated systems that combine insurance coverage with care delivery.

For example, the FTC relies on an outdated, inpatient-based index (the Herfindahl-Hirschman Index, or HHI) to determine market concentration, ignoring the substantial presence and accelerating growth of outpatient, commercial, home-based, and virtual care delivery. Mergers, like the Advocate-NorthShore combination, live or die on their HHI score. Digging deeper into the logic of the Advocate-NorthShore merger illustrates the ineptitude of the government's approach to evaluating its anticompetitive characteristics.

Advocate and NorthShore wanted to apply Advocate's sophisticated care management protocols region-wide to deliver better, lower-cost healthcare services. The companies were so confident their merger would create value that they committed to keep their prices in check and partner with a health insurer to offer a competitive health plan to the metropolitan Chicago marketplace. They guaranteed the new plan's price would be 10 percent below the region's lowest-priced HMO.

The FTC took none of this into consideration in challenging the merger. Instead, the FTC applied outdated or inappropriate measures to assess competition in hospital networks.

- The FTC used a gerrymandered North Shore service area to create a highly concentrated (greater than 50 percent) combined market share for Advocate-NorthShore. Its analysis excluded many competing hospitals, including St. Francis Presence and Northwestern Memorial, that would have reduced the merged entity's market share significantly.

- The FTC examined only inpatient admission and price data. Most healthcare treatments occur in outpatient settings and physician offices.

- The FTC did not consider Advocate's care management capabilities or the merged company's potential to deliver higher-quality, lower-cost care. Advocate has devoted enormous organizational energy to advancing care management. Advocate practices integrated delivery, evidenced-based medicine, and chronic disease management. Team-based caregivers engage patients, make fewer errors, and achieve superior outcomes. Indeed, Advocate was BCBS's partner of choice for accountable care programs.

- The FTC focused exclusively on per-unit hospital prices, not incremental costs associated with unnecessary treatments, medical errors, or readmissions, and even rejected Advocate-NorthShore's offer to cap post-merger hospital prices.

- The FTC did not consider nonhospital competitors offering equivalent services at lower prices.

- The FTC did not consider BCBS's market dominance and price-setting power in evaluating Advocate-NorthShore's potential pricing leverage.

Using this tortured methodology, the FTC concluded the proposed merger would "generate significant harm" to consumers on Chicago's North Shore. The FTC's methodology for challenging mergers epitomizes the System's fragmented, wrongheaded, and bureaucratic approach to regulating the healthcare industry at a time of dynamic and disruptive change. Similar structural deficiencies plague the FDA's approval processes for new drugs and medical devices and CMS's ability to police fraud and abuse.

Most important, ineffective regulatory oversight compromises the ability of enlightened and innovative health companies, like Advocate and NorthShore, to deliver more holistic healthcare services. Healthcare's entire regulatory structure needs overhauling.

Government capture (also called regulatory capture):
- Is a form of nonmarket failure.
- Occurs when a regulatory agency that was created in the public interest ends up advancing the political or commercial concerns of the very people, companies, or entities it is supposed to be regulating.
- Causes the interest of political groups or companies to become more important than those of the public.
- Leads to a net loss to society.
- Encourages rent-seeking behaviors.

Government Capture

Health companies often garner a higher investment return walking the halls of Congress and state legislatures than they do in the marketplace. Capturing favor with governmental officials is a natural go-to strategy for businesses reliant on government contracts and subject to governmental regulation and oversight. The question is not whether established companies will try to curry favor with government agencies. They always do. The question is whether and how government agencies can resist their solicitations.

It is no surprise that established health companies benefit from regulatory and policy manipulation. In 2017, the pharma industry spent almost $120 million more on lobbying than any other industry group. Hospitals, health insurers, nursing homes, specialty societies, healthcare professionals, medical device manufacturers, and other healthcare services companies are also big spenders in Congress. Let's look at the numbers (Figure 2.6).

In well-functioning healthcare markets, governmental regulatory policies ensure access, safety, quality, and privacy. Beyond protecting people, the government's most important responsibility is creating level-field competition through balanced regulation, targeted enforcement actions, and price/outcomes transparency. Unfortunately, healthcare markets do not function efficiently and are subject to manipulation by vested interests. A failed attempt by Massachusetts to lower its Medicaid drug cost through proven market-based strategies illustrates how government capture frustrates progressive reform.

In September 2017, the Massachusetts Office of Health and Human Services filed a Section 1115 Amendment Request to CMS seeking relief from skyrocketing drug prices in its Medicaid program (MassHealth). The waiver requested permission to incorporate provisions that would enable MassHealth to negotiate drug formularies like commercial insurers and pharmacy benefit managers (PBMs). Nine months later, in June 2018, after vigorous lobbying by Big Pharma, CMS denied the state's waiver request.

Medicaid is the largest and fastest-growing component of Massachusetts's state budget. It currently represents nearly 40 percent of total state expenditures. Increasing drug prices contribute disproportionately to spending growth. MassHealth's prescription drug costs more than doubled between 2010 ($917 million) and 2016 ($1.94 billion) with no relief in sight. This translates into a 13 percent compounded annual growth rate that threatens to crowd out other vital social and healthcare spending.

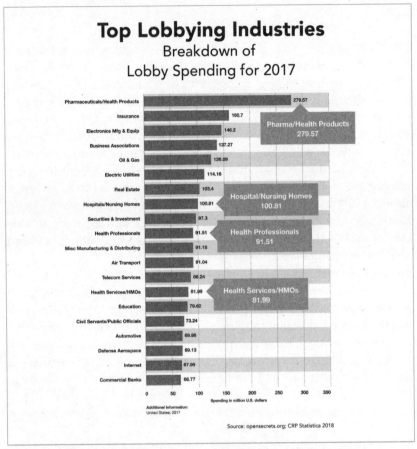

Top Lobbying Industries
Breakdown of
Lobby Spending for 2017

Source: opensecrets.org; CRP Statistica 2018

FIGURE 2.6   Government capture in action. Healthcare dominates congressional lobbying.

In essence, Republican Governor Charlie Baker's administration wanted CMS to grant MassHealth the ability to apply proven market-based practices (pioneered by commercial insurers and PBMs) to stabilize drug prices. Specifically, MassHealth wanted CMS to grant it the authority to implement the following new policies:[13]

- Adopt closed formularies with at least one drug available for each therapeutic class (i.e., disease).

- Exclude drugs "with limited or inadequate evidence of clinical efficacy" from formularies.

This discussion of these provisions may seem wonky, but they strike at the heart of Big Pharma's ability to force state Medicaid programs to pay sky-high prices for branded drugs. Revenue rules. Even with percentage discounts, drug manufacturers can raise prices to optimize revenue from sales to Medicaid programs. Figure 2.7 details the considerable revenue that pharma manufacturers generate by selling their blockbuster drugs to Medicaid programs.

Current practice requires Medicaid to offer beneficiaries all branded drugs for which pharma manufacturers provide discounts. Adopting closed formularies for a limited number of drugs would have allowed MassHealth to negotiate better discounts based on larger volumes for preferred drugs. The proposed waiver included provisions for patients to receive alternate drugs when medically necessary.

In contrast, commercial PBMs, as well as traditional Medicare and Medicare Advantage Rx plans, exclude higher-cost drugs from their formularies when there are effective lower-cost alternatives. In response, drug manufacturers offer substantial rebates to incentivize PBMs to include their drugs within specific disease formularies. With rising drug

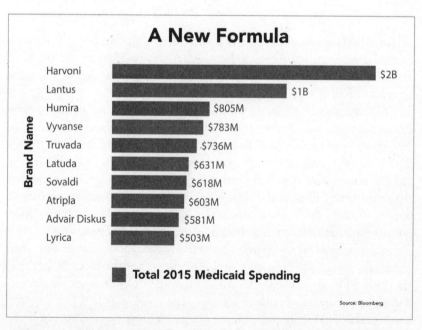

A New Formula

Brand Name	Total 2015 Medicaid Spending
Harvoni	$2B
Lantus	$1B
Humira	$805M
Vyvanse	$783M
Truvada	$736M
Latuda	$631M
Sovaldi	$618M
Atripla	$603M
Advair Diskus	$581M
Lyrica	$503M

Source: Bloomberg

FIGURE 2.7 **Big Pharma doesn't want to give up the big payments it gets for its branded drugs from Medicaid.**

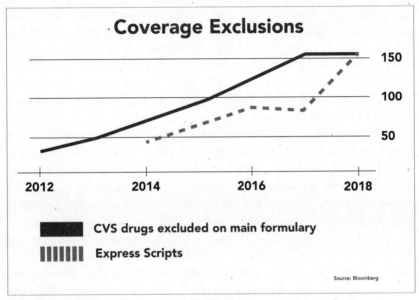

Source: Bloomberg

FIGURE 2.8 **Pharmacy benefits managers have grown increasingly aggressive about excluding certain medicines from coverage lists.**

prices, PBMs are more aggressively excluding high-cost drugs from their formularies. Figure 2.8 shows that the nation's two largest PBMs, CVS and Express Scripts, have more than doubled the number of excluded drugs since 2014.

MassHealth also wanted the ability to decide whether or not to cover drugs that had not demonstrated clinically effectiveness. Commercial insurers already enjoy this discretion. Enacted in December 2016, the 21st Century Cures Act grants expedited Food and Drug Administration (FDA) review and approval for drugs that "treat serious conditions and fill an unmet medical need." Thirty million Americans suffer from one of roughly 7,000 rare "orphan" diseases.[14] Expedited approvals mean drugs come to market without definitive evidence of their efficacy.

Pharmaceutical companies are actively developing drugs that treat these rare diseases because they're able to charge very high prices for drugs that gain FDA approval. Under current law, the FDA does not incorporate a drug's price into its approval process. As a consequence, FDA approval can translate into monopoly pricing power for drug manufacturers.

For example, Biogen and Sarepta Therapeutics received FDA approval in December 2017 for drugs that treat rare forms of muscular dystrophy. Clinical trials for these drugs have been promising, but not conclusive. Commercial insurers, such as Anthem and UnitedHealthcare, have resisted approving the drugs for widespread use because of their whopping price tags and their limited evidence of efficacy.

Biogen's Spinraza costs $750,000 the first year and $375,000 per year afterward. Patients must take the drug for life. Spinraza will not cure spinal muscular atrophy (SMA) but has demonstrated some efficacy in trials with very young children. The FDA has approved Spinraza for use with all SMA patients irrespective of age.[15]

Unlike commercial insurers and even Medicare, state Medicaid programs almost always pay for unproven and/or marginally effective high-cost drugs like Spinraza. If CMS had approved its waiver request, Massachusetts Medicaid would have had the administrative authority to decide when and when not to cover high-cost drugs for "orphan" diseases. Patients would have been able to appeal noncoverage decisions.

In denying the waiver, CMS made an offer (the ability to negotiate directly with manufacturers for all drugs) it knew Massachusetts would not accept. To do so would have required MassHealth to forgo rebates altogether. This would have been fiscal suicide. Rebates keep drug prices in check for 90 percent of drugs directed to Medicaid beneficiaries. Only 10 percent of drugs are budget-busters. MassHealth wanted to attack prices only on high-cost drugs. These are the same high-priced drugs that Big Pharma is lobbying to protect.

Had CMS approved the waiver, other states would have followed Massachusetts' lead and drug prices would have "come a-tumbling down." Big Pharma simply could not let that happen. Too much money was at stake. Inside baseball wins again. Denying Massachusetts' 1115 waiver request was a boon for Big Pharma and the System.

OVERBUILT AND UNDERUSED

The pantheon of waste that infects US healthcare includes overtreatment, predatory pricing, profiteering, shady dealing, and influence peddling. Add to that list a massively overbuilt infrastructure for delivering acute care services.

Take, for example, operating rooms. ORs, particularly inside hospitals, cost millions of dollars to build, yet the typical OR in America only runs one shift per day, four to four-and-a-half days per week. No other industry uses capital-intensive assets in such a limited way.

Providers underuse ORs for two principal reasons: (1) to placate surgeons who prefer "block" surgical time (predetermined time slots which they may or may not use); and (2) there's limited financial downside since the payment for a surgical procedure incorporates an agreed-upon facility fee. A 2017 article in the *Orthopaedic Journal of Sports Medicine* reported that facility charges for identical knee replacement surgeries were 350 percent higher in hospitals than in ambulatory centers ($13,200 versus $3,800).[16] Discrepancies in procedure prices don't matter when the facility fee is built into the payment rate.

Columbus, Ohio, isn't alone in building new facilities to provide more acute care services. FMI Corporation is a leading advisor on construction and infrastructure projects. It issues quarterly reports of actual and projected construction spending by industry sector. FMI's third quarter for 2018 projects steadily increasing growth in the healthcare sector (Figure 2.9).[17]

In July 2017, FMI reported that health systems "are moving [away] from large-scale new construction" projects. Instead health systems are investing primarily in outpatient care centers and to expand and renovate existing facilities.[18] While certainly true, dozens of health systems are currently undertaking massive campus "transformation" projects. Many will cost more than $1 billion, including announced projects for

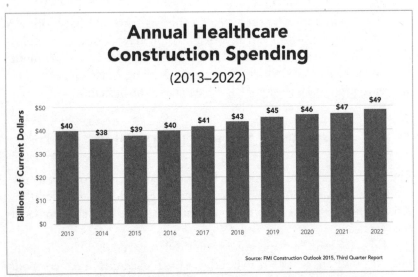

Annual Healthcare Construction Spending
(2013–2022)

Source: FMI Construction Outlook 2015, Third Quarter Report

FIGURE 2.9 An aging population and increase in chronic disease drive increases in healthcare construction.

Atlanta Children's, Atrium Health, Banner, BJC, Boston Children's, IU Health, Jackson Memorial, Mass General Hospital, NY Presbyterian, Ohio State, Stanford, Sutter, Texas Medical Center, UC San Francisco, University of Minnesota, University of Pennsylvania, and UPMC.[19]

This intense capital investment in centralized facilities is perplexing. Healthcare is a mature industry where the vast majority of treatment activity is routine, even commoditized. Typically, industries decentralize as they mature to be closer to customers with lower-cost and more convenient product and service offerings. This explains the rise of ambulatory clinics and retail clinics we are witnessing today, as well as the surge in in-home care and telemedicine services. Companies invest in these less expensive, alternative delivery channels to attract price-sensitive customers.

The decision by so many health companies to invest heavily in high-cost centralized campuses reflects confidence that current payment models will continue and generate sufficient revenues to repay the up-front capital investment. This is a huge strategic gamble.

With an already overbuilt acute care platform, it is probable that some providers will use their existing facilities more intensely to reduce per-unit costs. When prices matter, production and operating costs also matter. The decision to invest in capital-intensive facilities is becoming a "to be or not to be" question: invest today hoping for more high-return surgical procedures tomorrow; or don't invest in expectation of a future marketplace where cost, flexibility, and customer needs shape service demands.

To Invest or Not to Invest

Less than five miles separate Garfield Park from downtown Chicago. Despite the short distance separating them, they are entirely different worlds. The grim evidence is the 16-year difference in male life expectancy: 85 years in Chicago's Loop and 69 years in Garfield Park. This reduced life expectancy is due largely to lifestyle-related chronic illnesses and violence. Rush University Medical Center's CEO, Larry Goodman, describes visiting Garfield Park as "going back in time from a healthcare perspective."

One of the sobering realities of our healthcare system is that it has little impact on societal health. Up to 80 percent of the health of a population relates to lifestyle, social infrastructure, and genetics. To address the needs of the disadvantaged and chronically ill, healthcare organizations and other societal groups need to address the social determinants of health.

To that end, Rush University Medical Center, along with more than 50 healthcare, governmental, nonprofit, educational, and corporate partners, have created West Side United. Its goals are to "improve neighborhood health by addressing inequality in health care, education, economic vitality and the physical environment." Rush's advocacy and leadership within West Side United is essential, enlightened, and effective.

Here's the rub. Rush also must operate its high-cost health system. In April 2018, Rush announced construction of a new $500 million outpatient care center on its main campus.[20] The new facility will open in 2022.

Rush's proposed outpatient center illustrates how the System's needs divert resources away from broader societal needs. Chicago doesn't need more ambulatory surgery capacity. It has more than enough. Imagine, instead, the potential improvement in health status on the West Side that would result from investing $500 million to address social determinants of health.

It's difficult to blame Rush for its "business" decision. The System pays for surgeries, not for addressing negative social determinants of health. Heart and wallet separate. Under current funding formularies, the new outpatient care center will boost Rush's revenues and profits but do little for the impoverished communities just west of its main campus. Rush is feeding the System's chronic disease even as it works to strengthen Chicago's social fabric.

The economics of healthcare are perversely misaligned with market needs. Rush is doing what the System pays it to do. It is unrealistic to expect Rush or any health system to change the way it delivers care until their customers force them to do otherwise.

GOOD INTENTIONS AREN'T ENOUGH

Amid much fanfare in April 2012, the ABIM Foundation and *Consumer Reports* launched the "Choosing Wisely" campaign to promote more effective use of healthcare resources. The organization has partnered with over 80 medical societies (representing more than 1 million clinicians) to eliminate "low value" treatments that add cost without improving outcomes.

Choosing Wisely® Campaign

The goal of the campaign is to promote conversations between clinicians and patients by helping patients choose care that is:

- Supported by evidence
- Not duplicative of other tests or procedures already received
- Free from harm
- Truly necessary

It calls upon leading medical specialty societies and other organizations to identify tests or procedures commonly used in their field whose necessity should be questioned and discussed with patients.

Source: ABIM Foundation, sponsor of *Choosing Wisely*

Five-plus years later, medical specialty societies have identified and published 525 unnecessary treatments. *Choosing Wisely* has undertaken a massive education program to change physician behaviors and inform consumers. It has partnered with over 70 consumer and employer groups to spread the word. In its five-year report,[21] *Choosing Wisely* highlights the extensive outreach it's taken to advance the national dialogue on appropriate care. Accomplishments include the following:

- Selecting 45 specialty physician champions to advocate for better treatment protocols

- Funding 29 grantees to conduct research on appropriate utilization

- Being referenced in 1,330 medical journal articles during 2016

- Receiving almost 2 million visits to the *Choosing Wisely* website during 2016

Unfortunately, the activity has not translated into better health outcomes. An October 2017 *Health Affairs* article chronicles *Choosing Wisely*'s launch and progress to date.[22] The authors observe that "nationwide decreases in unnecessary care appear to be slow in coming." Several studies have found either minuscule decreases or increases in targeted low-value services.

The conclusion is inescapable. Despite its heroic effort, *Choosing Wisely* has belly flopped. It has not materially improved physician practices. Americans routinely receive unnecessary medical treatments that cost hundreds of millions of dollars annually. This result should surprise no one. Self-directed improvement programs cannot overcome American healthcare's gaping structural flaws by themselves. Major payment reform that rewards better outcomes and more efficient resource utilization must accompany industry-led transformation initiatives to achieve meaningful results.

In a *Modern Healthcare* interview, the report's lead author, Dr. Eve Kerr, explained the System's inability to eliminate wasteful medical treatments as follows:

> What we've learned is that it's just really hard to change practice [patterns]. Medical professionals have been practicing one way for a long time and patients expect that kind of practice. . . . That doesn't happen in five years. Culture is one of the hardest things to change and it takes the longest.[23]

Culture change is certainly hard and time-consuming. However, that alone cannot explain why the System fails to provide the right care at the right time in the right place at the right price; why it tolerates unacceptable levels of unnecessary, wasteful, and counterproductive care.

In other industries, payment follows value. Companies offer high-value products and services for which customers willingly pay, such as Apple's iPhone and Tesla cars. In healthcare, the System pays for treatment activities with minimal regard for treatment outcomes (i.e., value). Here's the hard truth. Physicians won't provide appropriate care consistently until we pay them to do exactly that.

While fee-for-service payment predominates, well-intentioned programs like *Choosing Wisely* will not eliminate inappropriate but profitable medical practices. They will have their successes, but the System's perverse operating and incentive structures will overwhelm voluntary reform efforts.

Muckraking journalist Upton Sinclair wrote, "It is difficult to get a man to understand something, when his salary depends on his not understanding it!"[24] Reform is pointless when uncoupled from economic incentives. Good intentions are not sufficient to induce health system transformation. Healthcare cannot improve incrementally. The System requires radical transformation to align industry and customer interests.

Until healthcare's buyers use their purchasing power to address the root causes of the System's endemic waste, corruption, and indifference to quality, Status Quo Healthcare will persist. Small numbers of advocates are not enough. It will take hundreds of companies and millions of American consumers to force the System to stop practicing the "old math" of fee-for-service payment and learn the "new math" required to deliver value to customers.

Real change will not happen until industry incumbents feel market pressure from competitors delivering high-quality healthcare services people really want at affordable prices. Demand-driven change fuels this revolution. Value-based care will emerge when customers pay for value.

CHAPTER 3

Taxation Without Representation

n 2018, NBC launched the medical drama *New Amsterdam* as part of its fall lineup. Its provocative tagline—"Break the Rules. Heal the System."—captures the anger and determination of passionate clinicians working against the Healthcare Industrial Complex (the System) to meet patients' needs.

The show originates from the book *Twelve Patients: Life and Death at Bellevue Hospital* by Eric Manheimer, who served as chief medical officer at the nation's oldest public hospital. When Manheimer started as Bellevue's CMO in 1997, he carried a notebook to record patient stories. Many of them, including his own battle with cancer, are remarkable, frustrating, inspiring, and depressing.

Manheimer's inquiries went beyond diagnosis and treatment because he believes the larger circumstances of a patient's life provided helpful context for what brings them to hospitals and the kinds of support they need. As Manheimer puts it,

> To understand patients and where they're coming from, you need a broader lens than just seeing them in a clinical office. You need to know more about where they're from and what's going on [in their lives].[1]

In the made-for-TV version, the hospital's new medical director is aptly named Dr. Max Goodwin. Dr. Goodwin invests time with his patients, particularly those on life's margins, and engages them in their care. His constant question is, "What can I do to help?" The hospital through which he maneuvers, however, obstructs him at every turn.

In true Hollywood fashion, Goodwin refuses to moderate his approach. He fights the good fight and wins more often than he loses. He eliminates waiting rooms, serves healthy food, creates a peace garden, and invests in mental health services. He implores physicians to "Be doctors again" and includes custodians in weekly staff meetings for their insights. Goodwin believes everyone who touches patients can make a difference.

At his first all-staff meeting, Goodwin fires everyone in the very profitable cardiac surgery department for (we find out later) overtreatment, poor quality scores, shifting excessive work to interns, and prioritizing billing over patient care. The cardiologist he appoints to rebuild the unit ("the right way") warns Max that "the whole system is rigged, so you can't just expect to come in here and help people."

New Amsterdam is great television, but it also provides a window into the American mindset. Its storylines reflect the widely shared public belief, born of actual experiences, that US healthcare is badly broken. While the System offers medical hope, it also delivers frustration, fragmentation, and financial harm. *New Amsterdam* is a cannon shot announcing a customer revolution against the System.

Network TV is often guilty of presenting glib versions of real life. Sometimes, though, it gets the cultural zeitgeist just right. This chapter explores how the System interacts with consumers at the market level; how it thwarts the needs and desires of patients, caregivers, families, employers, and communities. It will catalog the economic havoc the System causes the nation as it devours ever more of the American dream. The System taxes American resources, spirit, and sense of fair play.

As doctors Manheimer and Goodwin exemplify, it takes courage, commitment, collective effort, and a customer-first mentality to deliver great healthcare to consumers consistently. Who cares who shot JR? The stakes are far higher in this real-life revolution.

Woven into the fabric of American identity is opposition to tyranny and insistence on individual liberties. Resentment is growing as the System plunders the people's wealth, controls their care, and weakens their communities.

MARKET SIGNALS GONE HAYWIRE

For Americans, making independent purchasing decisions based on value comes as easily as breathing. Buyers and sellers execute transactions with clear prices and clear rules of exchange. Markets work best with informed customers. Consumers select from competing options while instinctively asking themselves value-specific questions: What's the price? How good is the service or product? Who else is selling it? How much do I need it? How soon do I want it?

Countless transactions occur every second of every day. Some regulatory rules and oversight (just enough) keep the guardrails in place to ensure those transactions are fair, transparent, and fulfilled.

The beauty of markets is that they accommodate a continuous and virtuous information flow that guides and improves the terms of exchange. Through their buying decisions, consumers "signal" what they value and how much they're willing to pay. Producers adjust to these signals and provide their goods and/or services as efficiently as possible so they can offer competitive prices and value to customers. They innovate to produce better products with features customers want. Over time, costs and prices tend to fall while quality and variety increase.

For example, my father purchased his first Hewlett-Packard calculator in 1973. It had four functions (addition, subtraction, multiplication, and division), one memory, and a $400 price tag ($2,320 in 2019 dollars). Today a solar-powered calculator has immensely more functionality at a fraction of the original $400 price.

Healthcare is different, many argue, from other businesses. Life, after all, is priceless, and healthcare consumers cannot always make optimal buying decisions. No one refuses expensive emergency care in a life-threatening situation. This argument, however, exaggerates healthcare's uniqueness and fails to recognize that most healthcare services (even emergency care) are routine with predictable outcomes. The result is that healthcare offers commodity services at premium prices.

The business of healthcare is not immune to the universal laws governing economics and human behavior. Overemphasizing healthcare's unique attributes leads providers to charge prices based on their production costs and negotiating leverage, not independent and transparent assessments of market value. This translates into differentiated prices for identical services. Lower-back MRIs can cost $300 or $3,000. Without market signals to guide producer behaviors, prices go haywire and consumers get burned.

PRICING DYNAMICS

In normal competitive markets, prices contain the basic information that buyers and sellers need to guide and optimize their economic decisions. Nobel Prize–winning economist Friedrich Hayek used the price of tin to illustrate the dynamic. Hayek maintained that markets and competition were the best mechanisms for calculating and coordinating economic choice. He believed that prices contain sufficient information to guide and adjust economic decisions. He stressed that decentralized planning by individuals and companies is the most effective system for allocating resources and generating wealth. To illustrate, Hayek contrasted how free-market enterprise and market socialism respond to increasing tin prices in Figure 3.1.

Under free-market capitalism with decentralized planning, primary and marginal users of tin "read " the pricing information and adjust consumption accordingly. In response, manufacturers substitute materials, improve production mechanics, and/or adjust prices. The cycle repeats until the market stabilizes.

In contrast, market socialism with centralized planning requires complex protocols to determine why the price of tin increased, establishes

Free-Market Capitalism vs. Market Socialism

The Prices Increase

Categorical Change

- Price contains meaninful information
- Marginal users find substitutes
- Essential users adjust
- Correlated product prices increase
- Market stabilizes and functions efficiently

Market Socialism

- Central planners study factors driving price increases
- Determine priorities for tin usage
- Assign and enforce prices
- Very complex
- Never have complete information
- Prone to mistakes
- Retards economic growth
- Stimulates black market trade

FIGURE 3.1 Centralized price setting leads to too many tin cups and not enough tin pans.

priorities for its use, assigns prices, and enforces market acceptance. Before long, complexity overwhelms managerial capabilities and it's easy to make mistakes, such as producing too many tin cups and not enough tin pans. Managed economies create imbalances in supply and demand, impede economic growth, and stimulate black-market trading of goods and services.

American healthcare is a mix of centralized (top-down) and decentralized (bottom-up) payment mechanics. As discussed in Chapter 2, centralized fee-for-service payment dominates. However, there also is a bottom-up payment component supplied by consumers through co-pays and deductibles.

While only a small (but increasing) percentage of total health expenditure, consumer payment obligations disproportionately influence healthcare utilization. Once plan subscribers fulfill their deductible obligation, for example, they have little incentive to restrain their consumption and often pursue unnecessary care with the active support of financially incentivized providers.

Alternatively, many consumers with high-deductible health plans (HDHPs) forgo necessary care because they cannot afford to make the up-front deductible payments. Deductible limits in HDHPs usually exceed $5,000. Forgoing necessary care accelerates disease progression and often leads to preventable and very expensive acute treatments.

Could there be a less effective way to guide consumers to the appropriate care at the right time? It gets worse. The System's payment dysfunction leads to absurd pricing for healthcare products and services.

ABSURD PRICES

Two customers buying identical vacuum cleaners at Best Buy and Target will pay the same approximate prices. However, two people lined up at the same pharmacy or visiting the same surgical center often pay very different amounts for the identical drug, treatment, procedure, or test depending on their health insurance and where they're receiving or picking up the prescribed treatment.

There are a million stories of unexpectedly high healthcare prices. Most confound reason. Vox Media spent a year collecting true accounts of emergency department bills that bore no relation to reality.[2]

Let's revisit and dig deeper into Janet Winston's "Allergy Test Is a Lot of Scratch" story from the introduction to Chapter 2. In 2018, Janet

Winston, a 56-year old professor living in northern California, sought treatment for a rash. She assumed her symptoms were allergy related, so she tried to make an appointment with her local dermatologist. The earliest availability, however, was months away. So Winston turned to Stanford Healthcare instead. Though a six-hour drive away, Stanford was in-network for Janet's insurer. Even so, Janet's bill for her allergy testing and doctor consultation was a mind-blowing $48,329. She owed 20 percent of that cost, almost $10,000.

What could Winston have done differently to avoid this unexpected bill? Very little, other than forgoing care. She knew the testing would be "expensive" but was unaware of its actual cost and had no reason to anticipate such an astronomical amount. A single skin-patch test typically costs as little as $35. In Winston's itemized bill from Stanford, each test cost $399. Her consult, in which a doctor explained her test results, cost a whopping $848. While appreciating the quality of her care and clarity of her diagnosis, Winston found the exorbitant treatment costs prohibitive and unjustifiable. She couldn't believe the System had squeezed her so ruthlessly.

Recall that Stanford was in-network for Winston. Her reasonable expectation was that this special relationship would protect her from extravagant billing. It did not. Winston's insurer, Anthem Blue Cross, likely included Stanford in network because of its market presence and strong brand. Indeed, studies have shown that Stanford, like most well-positioned health systems, negotiates higher payment rates than competing institutions. This is monopoly pricing power in action. It drives up health insurance premiums and hits consumers in their pocketbooks.

That $48,329 charged to Winston's insurer was not the end of the story. Anthem Blue Cross pushed back and negotiated a lower payment with Stanford for Winston's treatment. Stanford agreed to a substantially lower payment of $11,376.47. Although this was a relief to Winston, it still put her on the hook for $3,103.73. After even more negotiations, Winston agreed to pay Stanford $1,561.86 for her portion of the bill.[3]

Though frustrating and bewildering, Winston's billing experience inside the System is common. "Buyer beware" is the operating mentality when revenue optimization is the end goal. Hospitals catalog their list prices for all services, procedures, drugs, and diagnostic tests—which often have no correlation to underlying costs—on a centralized "chargemaster." Winston undoubtedly received Stanford's full charge-master rates for her treatments. Clearly, Stanford had a lot of wiggle room to reduce its charges for Winston's treatment.

Hospitals rarely receive their chargemaster rates because they nego-tiate procedure-specific payments directly with commercial health insurance companies. These commercial rates vary dramatically by insurer and usually exceed Medicare payment rates by a wide margin. In this way, commercial insurance premiums subsidize provider operations. As we shall see later, the level of that subsidy has increased substantially in the last 20 years. Differential pricing enables hospitals to shift costs, offsetting lower governmental payments by charging insurance compa-nies and individuals more for identical treatments.

The chargemaster rate is somewhat similar to a car's list price, except the markups are multiples higher. Buying a car from a dealer can require skillful negotiation. With some wheeling and dealing, the list price can go down. Once that new deal is struck, however, it's not the end of the haggling. Instead, a new set of negotiations begins. The dealer offers a variety of options (features, financing rates, etc.) that put the price back into flux. By the time the dealership's finance department calculates monthly payments, even savvy car buyers may not know whether they are getting a good deal or not.

At least car buyers and dealers start with a transparent list price. Health systems don't. They believe their chargemaster prices offer competitive advantage, so they keep them secret. A 2018 regulatory pro-nouncement by the Centers for Medicare and Medicaid Services (CMS) may change this behavior. Beyond negotiated payments, payers inflate treatment bills by performing additional procedures, employing out-of-network professions, and doing unnecessary diagnostic tests.[4] The bottom line is that consumers have little or no clue how much healthcare treat-ments cost and what their share of the payment will be.

As Janet Winston experienced, this mind-numbing game of revenue cycle roulette is time consuming, emotionally draining, and devoid of logic. When disputes occur, each side on the payer-provider divide mar-shals armies of technocrats to settle medical claims. Consumers too often end up in the middle even as their bills are sent to collection agencies. If you have spent hours on the phone going back and forth between a collec-tions agency, a hospital claims department, and an insurance bureaucrat to sort a disputed claim, then you are part of an unpaid involuntary army of frustrated consumers sucked into the System's vortex.

HEALTHCARE'S UNAFFORDABILITY

In November 2017, Dr. Ezekiel Emanuel, Aaron Glickman, and I published an article in the *Journal of the American Medical Association* (*JAMA*) that introduced the Healthcare Affordability Index (the Index). *JAMA* included editorial critiques from respected economists Ewe Reinhardt of Princeton and Joseph Antos of the American Enterprise Institute. Our article was widely read and heavily commented upon.

For decades, when Americans thought about healthcare, they worried primarily about access to necessary care services. According to a 2018 Gallup survey, 23 percent of Americans now cite care affordability as their biggest fear. More than 25 percent of people put off getting care because of financial concerns. More than 60 percent of people think that rising prescription drug prices should be a top national priority.[5]

The Healthcare Affordability Index is a simple and powerful metric for assessing the impact of rising healthcare costs on American living standards (Figure 3.2). The Index measures the relationship between the total cost (employer and employee portions) of a commercial family health insurance policy relative to median household income (MHI).

$$\frac{\text{Family Health Insurance Cost}}{\text{Median Household Income}} = \text{HEALTHCARE AFFORDABILITY INDEX}$$

FIGURE 3.2 The Healthcare Affordability Index provides a straightforward metric for tracking the relative healthcare costs for average families over time.

Since 1999, the Kaiser Family Foundation has published an annual survey of employer health benefits.[6] Employer-sponsored health insurance covers approximately 152 million nonelderly Americans, largely through private commercial health insurance plans. The average cost of a family health insurance policy in 2018 was $19,616.

The Census Bureau has tracked nominal and real median household incomes since 1984. It is a widely used measure of middle-class incomes. On an inflation-adjusted basis, median US household incomes peaked in 1999 and have stagnated since. Median US household income in 2017, the latest year reported, was $61,372. A Sentier Research report found US median household income to be a record $62,175 in June 2018.[7]

Measuring the numerical relationship between these credible, widely available metrics creates a framework for assessing the financial burden imposed by health insurance on middle-income families. Figure 3.3 measures healthcare affordability between 1999 and 2018 through the Healthcare Affordability Index.

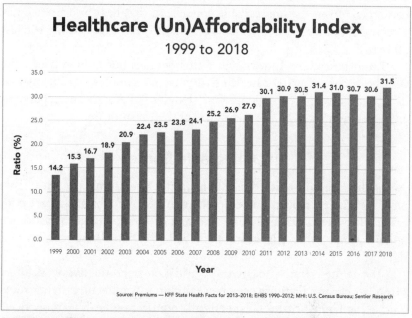

Healthcare (Un)Affordability Index
1999 to 2018

Source: Premiums — KFF State Health Facts for 2013–2018; EHBS 1990–2012; MHI: U.S. Census Bureau; Sentier Research

FIGURE 3.3 **The cost of employer-sponsored healthcare as a percent of household income has more than doubled since 1999.**

The Index more than doubled between 1999 and 2018, from 14.2 percent to 31.5 percent. Our belief is that increasing health insurance costs have contributed to stagnant income growth for workers as employer-paid health insurance premiums have become a greater percentage of employees' total compensation.

Interestingly, the Index plateaued at roughly 30 percent from 2011 to 2017. This may indicate that health insurance costs are approaching a natural ceiling relative to family incomes. Consistent with this conclusion, the calls for restraining healthcare cost growth have magnified during this period. This is a disturbing trend.

The academic reaction to the Index largely focused on defining affordability and income. Some suggested our formula was misleading because it did not include employer health insurance contributions as a component of family income. Adding employer-paid health insurance premiums to income lowers the Index score modestly but does not change its upward trajectory during the 1999–2018 measurement period.

While these criticisms have validity, they miss the more important trend relationship over time between health insurance costs and middle-class incomes. Defining affordability and income creates a smokescreen. It distracts from the unassailable conclusion that health insurance has consumed an ever-greater percentage of family resources during the last 20 years.

Importantly, the Index reveals this obvious but hidden truth: the very high cost of private health insurance contributes significantly to middle-class wage stagnation. More than half of Americans depend on employer-sponsored health insurance for their healthcare.

An Unbearable Burden

As healthcare costs rise, health insurance premiums also rise. This requires both employers and employees to pay more for healthcare coverage. Between 1999 and 2018, the cost of a family health insurance policy has more than tripled from $5,791 to $19,616. These are alarming figures.

The United States boasts the world's most productive workforce. High worker productivity creates wealth and sustains high living standards. The United States outspends all countries on healthcare services. Logic suggests that generous health spending enhances national productivity, competitiveness, and wealth creation. The opposite is true. American's health status is lower than that in other developed economies. While all Americans bear the burden of increasing health insurance premiums, that burden falls disproportionately on lower-income communities and families who suffer stagnant wages and increasing health disparity.

Historically, there has been a tight correlation between improving productivity and median household income. This is wealth creation in action. The benefits of higher productivity flowed directly to American workers in the form of higher wages. This historic pattern changed for the worse as America entered the new millennium.

Despite increasing productivity, wages for American workers have stagnated since 2000 on an inflation-adjusted basis (see Figure 3.4). There are multiple reasons for this depressing reality. These include two major

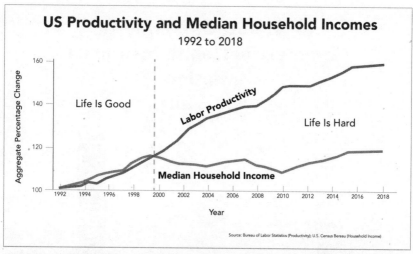

FIGURE 3.4 While US productivity has continued to rise, median household income has been stagnant. Workers aren't seeing the benefits of their increased productivity.

recessions and increasing competition from a lower-cost globalizing workforce. Healthcare's rising costs, however, are an underappreciated component of the wage stagnation afflicting US workers. Increasing health insurance premiums reduce monies available for wage increases.

Rising health insurance premiums act like a tax on worker incomes. Unfortunately, the System has become more dependent on this "tax" to fund its profligacy. Employer-sponsored health insurance subsidizes America's inefficient and exceptionally high-cost healthcare delivery system. As Figure 3.5 illustrates, commercial health insurance premiums have risen more than three times the rate of inflation (as measured by the Consumer Price Index) and almost double the rate of medical inflation.

High-cost healthcare could not exist in America without very high-cost private health insurance. Importantly, the US healthcare system has become increasingly dependent upon high-cost commercial premiums to fund increasing healthcare expenditures. My biggest disappointment with US healthcare is that employers haven't demanded more value for their healthcare purchases.

Educating Americans on the direct connection between healthcare expenditures and the all-in costs of health insurance is a national priority.

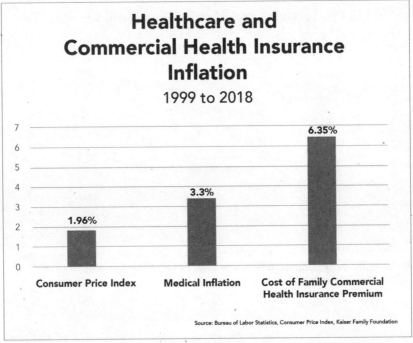

Healthcare and Commercial Health Insurance Inflation
1999 to 2018

Consumer Price Index: 1.96%
Medical Inflation: 3.3%
Cost of Family Commercial Health Insurance Premium: 6.35%

Source: Bureau of Labor Statistics, Consumer Price Index, Kaiser Family Foundation

FIGURE 3.5 **The System is more dependent than ever on subsidies from commercial insurers.**

The Index is an effective tool for making this connection understandable. Here are several salient observations regarding the Healthcare Affordability Index:

- Increasing health insurance costs exert a substantial and depressing influence on wage growth. Health insurance premiums increased 4.5 times faster (239 percent vs. 53 percent) than workers' earnings between 1999 and 2018.

- All other things being equal, a constant 14.2 percent Index would translate into a 2018 median household income of $72,943, which is a meaningful $10,768 (17.3 percent) increase over the current level of $62,175.

- Adding deductibles and co-pays increases the cost of health care coverage for Americans beyond the Index. This is particularly true for the increasing numbers of Americans with high-deductible health plans.

Consumers Disconnected from Rising Healthcare Costs

Americans understand that healthcare is expensive, but they generally do not recognize the direct connection between health insurance premiums, healthcare costs, and incomes. The following factors contribute to this perception failure that discourages optimal consumer purchasing behaviors:

- **Employers and governments cover the lion's share of health insurance costs.** This benefit insulates consumers from actual healthcare expenditures.

- **Consumers experience the healthcare marketplace through the purchase and use of health insurance products.** Their relevant measures are not healthcare costs, but rather the costs of insuring against adverse health expenditure (employee health insurance premiums, deductibles, and co-pays).

- **Employees focus on income, while employers focus on total compensation.** Consequently, workers underappreciate the negative impact rising healthcare and health insurance costs exert on their take-home pay.

Increasing healthcare and related employer-sponsored health insurance costs exert a double whammy on wages. Workers pay more for health insurance, decreasing out-of-pocket spending. Meanwhile, escalating health insurance costs limit employers' ability to increase wages. The net result: workers pay more for health insurance *and* receive lower pay.

It gets worse. While total employer health insurance is heavily subsidized, combined spending for average employee premiums and potential spending for deductibles has increased dramatically—from 7.8 percent in 2007 to 11.7 percent in 2017.[8] Heathcare's burden on middle-class families grows ever larger.

STATE-SPECIFIC HEALTHCARE AFFORDABILITY

The state-specific Healthcare Affordability Index scores vary dramatically, from a low of 22.9 in Utah to a high of 44.6 in West Virginia. The heat map in Figure 3.6 displays the Index in thirds: high, average, and

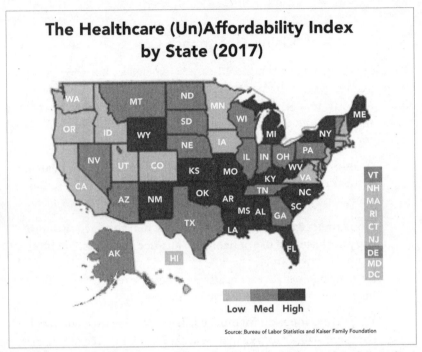

The Healthcare (Un)Affordability Index by State (2017)

Low   Med   High

Source: Bureau of Labor Statistics and Kaiser Family Foundation

FIGURE 3.6   **The variance in healthcare affordability does not just follow the median household income.**

low. The darker the color, the higher the Index and the greater the ratio of health insurance costs to family incomes.

As described above, the Index measures the percentage relationship between total family health insurance premiums and median household income (MHI). Of the two components, there is far greater variation in MHI than in health insurance premiums. Washington, D.C.'s MHI of $83,382 is almost double Mississippi's MHI of $43,441. The high variation among states in median household income gives MHI greater weight in explaining state-specific Index scores. MHI explains roughly 80 percent of an individual state's ranking.

By contrast, the differential between the highest and lowest health insurance policies is only 37 percent. At $16,350, Utah's premiums are the lowest. At $22,417, Alaska's premiums are the highest. With significantly lower variation, total insurance premiums have less influence than MHI in calculating state-specific Index scores.

Here's the rub. The lower a state's median household income, the higher the burden of paying for commercial health insurance. Figure 3.7

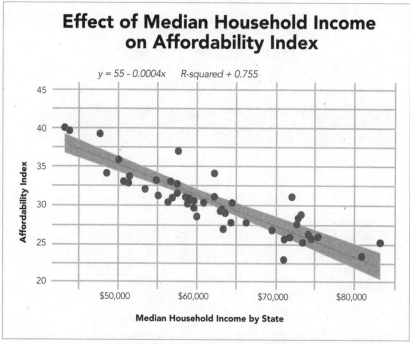

Effect of Median Household Income on Affordability Index

$y = 55 - 0.0004x$ R-squared + 0.755

FIGURE 3.7   **The poor get poorer: the lower a state's median household income, the higher the burden of paying for commercial health insurance.**

depicts the tight correlation between a state's MHI and its Affordability Index.

As depicted above, the Affordability Index correlates inversely with median household income. States with higher Index scores have lower MHI and vice versa. Figures 3.8 and 3.9 identify the 10 states with the most and least affordable Index scores.

The two outlier states are New York and Wyoming. Ranked twenty-second with $62,447 in MHI, New York achieves the seventh least affordable Index score (34.1) because its residents pay very high health insurance premiums, $21,317 for an average family policy. This premium level ranks third nationally. At $21,355, Wyoming residents pay even more for health insurance than New Yorkers. This propels Wyoming to the fifth least affordable Index score.

The 10 states with the most affordable Index scores come from the group of 14 states with the highest median household incomes. Relative rankings within this group result from the cost of health insurance policies within each state. States ranked 11–14 in MHI (Minnesota, Utah,

Least Affordable
Healthcare States
Highest 10 Index Scores in 2017

State	Affordability Index Scores	Income	Rank
West Virginia	44.6	$45,392	49
Mississippi	39.9	43,441	51
Louisiana	39.6	43,903	50
New Mexico	39.2	47,855	48
Wyoming	36.9	57,837	33
North Carolina	36.0	50,343	46
New York	34.1	62,447	22
Arkansas	34.1	48,829	47
Maine	33.7	51,664	43
South Carolina	33.2	54,971	41

Source: 4sight Health Affordability Index; Median Household Income: U.S. Census Bureau, 2017 Current Population Survey, Annual Social and Economic Supplements Data Tables. Historical Household Income

FIGURE 3.8   Health insurance is least affordable in low-income states.

Virginia, and California) generated more affordable Index scores because family health insurance in these states costs less than $18,750.

States that ranked 7–10 in median household income (Massachusetts, New Jersey, Connecticut, and Alaska) did not qualify among the 10 best because health insurance in these states is expensive. Family health insurance policies in these states cost more than $20,000.

Interestingly, the size of a state's population and economy (as measured by state gross domestic product) had no correlation with Index scores. Scale doesn't matter. Health insurance is less affordable in the states with the second, third, and fourth largest populations and economies (Florida, New York, and Texas). By contrast, health insurance is more affordable in several small states (Hawaii, Idaho, New Hampshire, Rhode Island) and Washington, DC. With the exception of the Southeast, geography does not seem to predict the Index scores. A high percentage of low-income states with below-average Index scores concentrate in the Southeast.

Most Affordable
Healthcare States
Lowest 10 Index Scores in 2017

State	Affordability Index Scores	Income	Rank
Utah	22.9	$71,319	12
Maryland	23.3	81,084	2
Washington D.C.	25.1	83,382	1
Hawaii	25.2	73,575	6
Virginia	25.6	71,293	13
New Hampshire	25.7	74,801	4
Minnesota	25.7	71,920	11
Washington	25.8	75,418	3
Colorado	26.1	74,172	5
California	26.8	69,759	14

Source: 4sight Health Affordability Index; Median Household Income: U.S. Census Bureau, 2017 Current Population Survey, Annual Social and Economic Supplements Data Tables. Historical Household Income

FIGURE 3.9 **Higher-income states have more affordable health insurance.**

Crueler Still: "Premium" Employee Premiums in Some Low-Income States

There also is remarkable state-specific variation in the percentage of the total health insurance premium paid by employees. Wisconsin is the lowest at 15.1 percent. Louisiana is the highest at 34.4 percent, more than twice the Wisconsin level.

Many low-income states with below-average Index scores, notably Florida, Louisiana, North Carolina, and Oklahoma, also require their workers to pay higher employee health insurance premiums. This is a form of double jeopardy:

1. Lower-income workers have less affordable healthcare as measured by the Affordability Index; and
2. These workers also must cover a higher percentage of their total health insurance costs from wages.

It's no wonder that high costs now represent Americans' greatest healthcare concern. It used to be access to high-quality healthcare services.

The West Virginia Anomaly

The most intriguing state is West Virginia. At $45,392, West Virginia has the nation's third-lowest median household income. Only Mississippi and Louisiana are lower. Somewhat surprisingly, West Virginia has the nation's seventh-highest cost, $20,252, for family health insurance. The result is a staggering Healthcare Affordability Index score of 44.6, almost five points higher than the next highest score (Mississippi at 39.6).

Here's where it gets really interesting. Despite operating in a low-income state, West Virginia's employers pay more for health insurance ($16,494) than employers in any other state. As a result, West Virginia employees contribute the second-lowest percentage (18.6 percent). Only Wisconsin is lower at 15.1 percent.

It's a good thing that West Virginia's employers pay generously for health insurance benefits. The state has the highest percentage of people with preexisting medical conditions.[9] At the same time, West Virginia's high healthcare costs relative to other low-income states inhibit its ability to attract new employers to the state.

There is a powerful understory to these West Virginia figures. A multiyear investigation by National Public Radio and *Frontline* released in December 2018 reveals that coal mining companies and government regulators did not act upon well-established evidence linking silica dust with black lung disease.[10] As a result, thousands of coal miners contracted the preventable deadly disease. Scott Laney, an epidemiologist at the National Institute for Occupational Safety and Health, describes the human dimensions of the tragedy:

> It's an epidemic and clearly one of the worst industrial medicine disasters that's ever been described. We're counting thousands and thousands of black lung cases. Thousands of cases of the most severe form of black lung. And we're not done counting yet.

Former mine safety regulator Celeste Monforton reviewed the investigation's findings and offered these sobering comments:

> We failed. Had we taken action at that time [in the 1990s], I really believe that we would not be seeing the disease we're seeing now. Having miners die at such young ages from exposures that

happened 20 years ago . . . I mean this is such a gross and frank example of regulatory failure.

Inadequate safety practices by mining companies combined with pro-business (as opposed to pro-market) regulatory policies and lax enforcement have caused unnecessary disease and death in Appalachian communities. These communities also bear the high treatment and social service costs related to the disease. As with the American-made opioid crisis, "iron triangle" behaviors have fostered needless despair, diminished human potential, and increased economic hardship.

Healthcare emerged as the top issue in West Virginia's hotly contested 2018 Senate race between incumbent Democrat Joe Manchin and Republican Attorney General Patrick Morrisey. President Trump was very popular in West Virginia, carrying the state by 42 percent in the 2016 election. The president campaigned vigorously for Morrisey, but his magic didn't work. Voters concerned about healthcare voted overwhelmingly for Manchin and carried him to victory.[11]

OUTLIERS AND CONSEQUENCES

The Healthcare Affordability Index illuminates the relationship between commercial health insurance costs and median household incomes. In the United States, high-cost health insurance funds a very high-cost healthcare delivery system. Despite the high healthcare expenditure, the United States ranks only twenty-sixth in life expectancy at birth among higher-income countries.[12] Healthcare spending doesn't buy longevity.

As with Index scores, there is remarkable variation between individual states in life expectancy. Hawaiians live the longest lives at 81.3 years, while people in Mississippi live the shortest lives at 75.0 years. This creates a sizable life-expectancy gap of 6.3 years.[13] Interestingly, there is correlation among individual states between life expectancy and Index scores. People in states where the Index scores are more affordable live longer and vice versa. People in Hawaii and Minnesota live the longest and have among the most affordable Index scores. People in Mississippi, Alabama, and West Virginia experience the opposite.

Correlation is not causation. Poverty is the primary cause of life expectancy differences, and very poor people do not purchase commercial health insurance policies. Still, higher state-specific "burden" in funding commercial health insurance corresponds with shorter lifespans. Here is the dismal reality. America makes it harder for workers in low-income states to fund health insurance, and therefore lowers health status results. The poor get poorer, and the sick get sicker.

In good and bad ways, the United States is an "exceptional" nation. Overpaying for healthcare while tolerating subpar health outcomes and health status exacts an enormous tax on the nation and its people. This unbearable burden grows heavier each year.

Healthcare costs are strangling middle-class incomes. "We the People" fund America's bloated healthcare system, and its costs fall disproportionately on low- and middle-income Americans through wage stagnation and declining health status. This negative cost shift deprives American workers of vitally needed income.

Funding America's highly expensive, inefficient, and often ineffective healthcare delivery system through high-cost private health insurance plans has consequences. It weakens the American economy. It reduces the global competitiveness of US companies. It robs workers of higher wages and lowers living standards. It also siphons investment from more productive industries. Remarkably, the overall US economy achieves high productivity despite the System's underperformance and exceptionally high costs. That cannot last forever.

IT'S A DRAG

Healthcare is not only an economic concern for individuals and families, it's consuming an ever-larger share of the federal budget as well as exerting a negative drag on the overall economy.

In his insightful book *After the Music Stopped*, about the financial crisis and its aftermath, noted Princeton economist Alan S. Blinder examines the 2012 Congressional Budget Office's (CBO) long-term forecast and concludes controlling healthcare spending is the US government's central fiscal challenge. The forecast projects 75 years into the future, through 2087. This isn't really a forecast but an extrapolation of current spending patterns.

During this time period, interest payments to service the national debt soar. Revenues at current tax rates are woefully insufficient to cover government spending on defense, healthcare, social security, and all other noninterest expenditures. The government terms this *primary spending*. As a result, the increasing primary-spending deficit, in combination with increasing interest payments, pushes the overall national debt ever upward to almost 80 percent of GNP from 20 percent today. Even more terrifying, increasing healthcare expenditure fundamentally redistributes primary spending in the following two ways:

1. Primary spending rises to greater than 30 percent of GNP, fueled by increasing healthcare expenditure.
2. All non-healthcare primary spending (defense, social security, and everything else) *declines* to just over 10 percent of GNP. By the end of the forecast period, healthcare is *double* the cost of all other government activities combined.

Blinder concludes his analysis with this providential warning:

The implication for budgeteers is clear: If we can somehow solve the health care cost problem, we will also solve the long-run deficit problem. But if we can't control health care costs, the long-run deficit problem is insoluble. Simple, right? Impossible? We'd better hope not.[14]

Blinder's analysis focuses only on the federal government's healthcare expenditures. Private employers, individuals, and state governments confront the same runaway healthcare costs. Published in February 2018, CMS's 2017–2026 national health-expenditure forecast projects that overall health spending will be $5.7 trillion and consume almost 20 percent of national GNP (versus $3 trillion and almost 18 percent of GNP today).[15] How bad can it get? If you believe these forecasts, it could get really, really, really bad.

The global economy is experiencing unprecedented redistribution between developed and developing nations. As chronicled by the World Bank, global GNP more than doubled from $32.2 trillion in 2001 to $80.7 trillion in 2017. US GNP grew 83 percent during this same period, but the American share of global GNP shrank from 32 to 24 percent (Figure 3.10).

This economic repositioning occurred within a short 16-year period. With roughly 4.5 percent of the world's population, it's logical that the US percentage of the global economy will shrink as developing economies, particularly China and India, advance. An expanding global economy is good news. New markets for American products create new jobs in export-oriented industries, but achieving competitive advantage in a "flat world" is hard. The United States no longer has the luxury of being so wealthy that it can absorb the cost of underperforming industries and inefficient government programs.

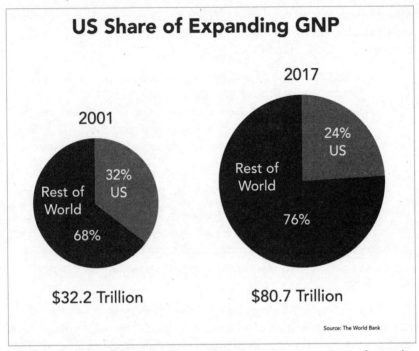

US Share of Expanding GNP

2001

2017

$32.2 Trillion

$80.7 Trillion

Source: The World Bank

FIGURE 3.10 **The United States is becoming a smaller percentage of a much larger, interconnected global economy.**

To maintain our living standard, the United States must excel within a much larger, more efficient global economy. Coming to terms with this new economic reality will force Americans to rethink tax policy, infrastructure investment, defense spending, social welfare benefits, education, and, of course, healthcare.

A more efficient, globalizing economy presents two profound challenges for the US healthcare system. First, healthcare must become more competitive. It needs to cost less while delivering comparable or superior treatment outcomes. To the extent the US healthcare system is less productive than healthcare systems in other countries, it exerts a negative drag on the overall US economy. Secondly, America's obesity and chronic-disease epidemics diminish labor force productivity. In a globalizing economy, the United States requires a healthier, fitter workforce to advance national living standards.

Our ability to gain control over healthcare spending and direct it to achieve better health outcomes will shape the nation's future prosperity. The nation's future economic health depends upon slower healthcare expenditure growth and improving health status. That's not happening now.

FOR PETE'S SAKE

It's not just about the money. In healthcare, it never is. Healthcare's purpose should be to deliver kinder, smarter, affordable care for all Americans.

In mid-October 2017, I toured a pediatric transitional care facility. For almost 20 years, this facility has provided transitional care services in homelike settings for children and their families as patients move from ICU/hospital care to home-based care.

Suffering from complex medical conditions, the facility's patients require ongoing care to live their best lives possible. Stays often extend for several months as children stabilize and family members learn how to provide home-based care. The facility also provides respite services for families needing a break from 24/7 caregiving responsibilities.

During the tour, I met a feisty, big-cheeked one-year-old with a magnetic personality named Pete (not his real name) who was wearing what looked like an old-fashioned leather football helmet. Pete suffered from multiple chronic conditions and was on a ventilator. I asked why Pete was wearing the helmet. The answer was devastating.

A low birth weight baby, Pete spent his early months in a neonatal intensive care unit (NICU) to gain weight before going home. Unfortunately, Pete experienced limited human interaction during his time in the NICU. As a result, he lay on his back those several months before being transferred into transitional care. All that time on his back deformed Pete's head. The helmet was working to reshape his head to normal proportions. Unfortunately, Pete's limited human contact in infancy will likely cause severe developmental challenges.

Joseph Stalin, the Soviet Union's brutal dictator, understood the calculus of sympathy. He said, "When one man dies, it's a tragedy. When thousands die, it's a statistic." At the height of the Syrian refugee crisis, the photo of Aylan Kurdi, a young boy washed up dead on a beach, had a greater impact on fund-raising for Syrian refugees than hundreds of thousands of deaths.[16] Likewise, the story of someone like Pete can touch the heartstrings in the way that statistics fail to do. Nevertheless, the aggregated statistics regarding children with complex medical conditions portray immense tragedy.

There are hundreds of thousands of children nationwide who could benefit from transitional care services. Why don't they get access to such care? It's not the cost. A patient day costs less than $1,000, including all services and therapies. NICUs can cost $10,000 per day and even more for infants on ventilators.

The horrific truth is that many NICU children receive inferior but high-cost care because neonatal and pediatric intensive care services are lucrative for hospitals. They have no financial incentive to explore better, lower-cost treatment alternatives. Once again, the System prioritizes revenues over outcomes. Kids like Pete suffer unnecessary physical and emotional harm from high-cost institutionalized care.

Like Pete, there are countless others who suffer under the System's care. Impoverished diabetics become amputees because it's more profitable to cut off a foot than manage their diabetes. Stressed-out mothers struggle to arrange care for their children in the face of an indifferent bureaucracy. Families have less money for college or vacations or monthly bills because healthcare consumes an increasing percentage of their disposable income. Millions could live healthier, longer, more productive lives if only they received better primary care before life-changing health problems arise.

The System has acted against the interests of the American people for decades. Reasonable attempts at reform have failed. The System's powerful incumbents maintain their privileged positions through regulatory manipulation, legislative fiat, and anti-competitive market behaviors.

The System taxes the American public without delivering commensurate value. It threatens national productivity, prosperity, and quality of life. The status quo cannot stand. Descendants of revolutionaries, Americans are not afraid to confront the System's tyranny. Stakes are high. Solutions are complex. Once unleashed, the customer revolution in healthcare will not cease until it delivers the healthcare the American people want, need, and deserve.

CHAPTER 4

America's Self-Created Opioid Tragedy

The saga of America's opioid crisis reads like *The Godfather*, except that organized crime never caused this level of chaos, community devastation, and death. The Healthcare Industrial Complex (the System) created and turbocharged the opioid crisis on an unsuspecting public. Nefarious collaboration between Congress, industry, and government agencies makes the System complicit in dealing dangerous drugs to vulnerable populations for gargantuan profits.

The opioid epidemic is devastating communities across the country. The human toll is catastrophic. In September 2017, the *Cincinnati Enquirer* released "Seven Days of Heroin: This Is What an Epidemic Looks Like," which chronicles an ordinary week of addiction misery in metro Cincinnati.[1] In their investigative report, more than 60 *Enquirer* reporters, photographers, and videographers bring to life the heartbreaking stories of a region ravaged by opioid addiction. The one-week statistics are breathtaking, gruesome, and mind-numbing:

- 18 deaths

- 180+ overdoses

- 200+ heroin incarcerations

- 15 heroin-addicted babies born

Crony capitalism created and sustains the opioid crisis. A predatory drug company designed an addictive painkiller, then marketed it heavily. Government regulators failed to guarantee the drugs' safety and efficacy. Doctors accepted gifts and payments that encouraged excessive prescribing. Distributors and pharmacy benefit managers (PBMs) fulfilled massive orders to suspect clinics and pharmacies. Pharmacists filled prescriptions with high-probability knowledge that they would be resold or abused. As a result, millions of patients became addicted to drugs they believed would heal them. Hundreds of thousands have died from overdoses.

Opioid use has spread addiction far beyond patients. Opioid-related addiction, crime, social service needs, human suffering, and loss of life have devastated families and communities throughout America, particularly in rural areas.[2] The Healthcare Industrial Complex (aka the "System") has unleashed a modern plague upon an unsuspecting American public.

AMERICA'S NEW ADDICTION

The sudden death of superstar musician Prince in April 2016 gave a face to a growing American tragedy. Prince's life was remarkable; his death was not.

Playing all his own instruments, Prince beguiled fans for almost 40 years and had 13 Top 10 songs. His unique musicology combined soul, funk, gospel, and rock genres. Still going strong at age 57, Prince succumbed to an overdose of fentanyl, an opioid commonly prescribed for chronic pain. Fentanyl is up to 50 times more powerful than heroin.[3]

Opioids are synthetic derivatives of heroin. They are highly addictive. Nearly 4,000 people become addicted to opioids every day. Almost 1,000 of those opioid addicts, 23 percent, also become heroin addicts.[4]

According to the US Surgeon General, 78 people die from opioid overdoses every day.[5] The mounting death toll from opioid overdoses is horrific (Figure 4.1).[6] In 2016 alone, 42,259 people died from overdosing on opioids according to the CDC. This represented two-thirds of all drug overdose deaths.[7]

Despite this all-too-common tragedy, opioids are still mainstream American medicine. Pharmaceutical companies develop and market opioids. The US Food and Drug Administration approves and regulates them. Physicians prescribe opioids abundantly to football players, military veterans, cancer patients, and others suffering from chronic pain.

Support in the American medical community is a principal reason the United States prescribes far more opioids for pain relief than any other country—for example six times more than France. Moreover, the

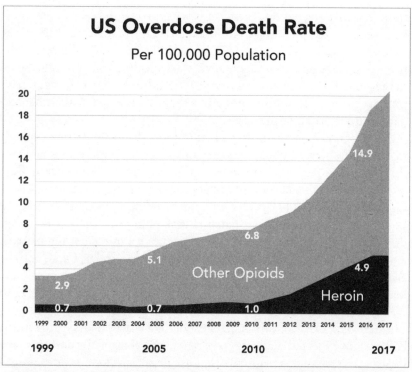

FIGURE 4.1 Skyrocketing opioid and heroin overdose deaths go together like crime and punishment. Between 1999 and 2010 most of the increase in opioid overdose deaths was from synthetic opioids, not heroin.

United States accounts for 99 percent of the powerful and highly addictive hydrocodone (better known by brand names Vicodin, Norco, Lorcet, etc.).[8] The opioid crisis is a uniquely American creation. Opioids are non-discriminatory in devastating lives and communities. Addicts cut across societal ranks—rich, middle class, and poor. Opioid abuse and addiction inflate healthcare costs, increase criminal activity, and overburden social services.

ILLICIT ORIGINS

Early studies suggested that opioid painkillers were not addictive. In the mid-1990s, the American Pain Society emerged and embraced these findings. They stressed the need to treat pain as the fifth vital sign (along with temperature, pulse, blood pressure, and breathing rate) even though clinicians cannot measure it with precision. As the new millennium arrived, the Joint Commission for Hospital Accreditation, the Veterans Administration, and other medical organizations stressed the need to manage pain more aggressively.[9] Medical training promoted pain management with opiates as a best practice, driven in part by aggressive pharma-funded "education" programs that often included all-expenses-paid conferences at plush resorts.[10]

Until OxyContin came to market in 1996, doctors prescribed opioids in limited fashion to manage severe pain associated with serious injury or illnesses. OxyContin is a formulation of oxycodone developed by Purdue Pharma, a privately held pharmaceutical company based in Stamford, Connecticut. OxyContin offered longer-lasting pain relief—up to 12 hours per pill. Prior to Oxy, patients took pain pills, such as Percocet, every four to six hours. Marketed by Purdue as a miracle drug, patients and physicians hopped on board the Oxy Express. Today, OxyContin is America's bestselling painkiller. Purdue Pharma has aggressively marketed the drug and reportedly achieved $35 billion in sales from 1997 to 2016.[11]

In reality, OxyContin's pain relief does not last 12 hours. Pain returns earlier than expected. Patients crave relief.[12] By continually dosing, many deplete their supply prematurely. They ask physicians for more drugs until refused. They hide their addiction, seek drugs elsewhere, and lose control of their lives.

In 2007, Purdue Pharma pled guilty to criminal charges that it misled doctors, regulators, and patients about OxyContin's potential for abuse. The company paid $600 million in fines and legal fees. Purdue's president, medical director, and top lawyer pled guilty to related fraud charges and paid a $34.5 million fine.[13]

Purdue is not alone in conducting questionable and/or illegal opioid marketing. The FBI arrested INSYS Therapeutics executives in December 2015 for bribing doctors and defrauding insurance companies to increase fentanyl sales.[14]

While awareness of the dangers of abuse and addiction has improved, overprescribing continues to be a major problem. Each year, doctors prescribe the equivalent of one bottle of opioids for every American.[15] Patients with temporary postsurgical pain typically receive 30-pill prescriptions when 3 or 4 pills would suffice.

Deadly addictive opioids fill the nation's medicine cabinets as a result, and these drugs are difficult to track and control. Opioid addiction usually starts when individuals experiment with painkilling drugs prescribed for themselves or someone they know. Big Pharma provides that initial fix and feeds the addiction by flooding American communities with oxycodone, hydrocodone, fentanyl, and other opioid-based drugs. Most opioid addicts get their first pills from relatives and friends versus doctors. Excessive prescribing has created a black market for resale of surplus opioids. Addicts buy opioids when they can. Many switch to less-expensive heroin when they can no longer afford or acquire prescription painkillers.

A December 2016 article in the *Charleston Gazette-Mail* reported that drug distributors delivered 780 million oxycodone and hydrocodone pills to West Virginia pharmacies between 2007 and 2012.[16] That translates into 433 opioid pills for every man, woman, and child in the state. During that period, 1,728 West Virginians died from overdosing on those drugs.

In a 2016 report, the US Surgeon General stressed that substance abuse and addiction are symptoms of chronic illness:[17]

> For far too long, too many in our country have viewed addiction as a moral failing. This unfortunate stigma has created an added burden of shame that has made people with substance use disorders less likely to come forward and seek help.
>
> It has also made it more challenging to marshal the necessary investments in prevention and treatment. We must help everyone see that addiction is not a character flaw—it is a chronic illness that we must approach with the same skill and compassion with which we approach heart disease, diabetes, and cancer.

It wasn't enough for the System that opioids were killing Americans at alarming numbers, particularly in rural areas. When the DEA undertook an aggressive campaign to close down overprescribing pharmacies or "pill mills," Big Pharma and their friends in Congress and government used their clout to curtail the DEA's enforcement efforts. This case study illustrates how the Healthcare Industrial Complex plies its trade.

BIG PHARMA SQUELCHES THE DRUG ENFORCEMENT ADMINISTRATION (DEA)

Talk about bombshells. On October 15, 2017, the *Washington Post* and *60 Minutes* released a detailed and damning investigative report titled "The Drug Industry's Triumph Over the DEA."[18] The report chronicles how Big Pharma and its congressional allies orchestrated passage of legislation that has severely weakened the DEA's ability to curtail illegal distribution of opioid drugs. Here's what happened.

The Drug Enforcement Administration (DEA) intensified its investigation of drug distribution companies in 2006 as the opioid epidemic was worsening. An aggressive enforcement effort led by Joseph Rannazzisi (investigation) and Linden Barber (litigation) began targeting wholesale drug distributors servicing "pill mills." The "big three," McKesson, Cardinal Health, and AmerisourceBergen, distribute 85 percent of the nation's drugs.

Under the 1970 Controlled Substances Act, distributors have a legal and ethical obligation to report suspicious opioid deliveries. The DEA had two enforcement mechanisms for stopping suspicious sales: (1) issue an "order to show cause" that gives companies 30 days to respond to allegations of wrongdoing; and (2) issue an "immediate suspension order" where the DEA immediately halts commerce from that company in targeted substances.

Many Big Pharma companies, including the big three mentioned above, have paid large fines for improper opioid distribution. These fines represent a small percentage of the billions of dollars earned by pharmaceutical companies selling, distributing, and dispensing opioids. For the record, the Drug Enforcement Administration collected $425 million in fines over a 10-year period beginning around 2006.[19]

Even though the fines were a relative pittance, Big Pharma objected to the DEA's aggressive enforcement approach and fought back. Collectively, the pharmaceutical industry hired 56 former DEA and Justice Department officials, including Linden Barber, to execute their attack on the DEA. Their goal was to limit the DEA's stepped-up enforcement against drug distribution companies.

Big Pharma lobbyists worked behind the scenes with select members of Congress to draft legislation to curtail the DEA's enforcement powers. Money talks. Between 2014 and the law's 2016 passage, Big Pharma spent $106 million lobbying for the Drug Enforcement Act. Barber testified as an expert witness, explaining why the new legislation was necessary. His testimony had an Orwellian ring to it:

> As a supporter of DEA's mission, I urge the committee to take legislative action that clarifies the definition of imminent danger.

Barber's statement is reminiscent of the Vietnam-era Pentagon press quote that "it became necessary to destroy the town (Ben Tre) to save it."[20] With Big Pharma's drafting help, Congress "clarified" the definition of "imminent danger" to an extent that made Drug Enforcement Administration's use of imminent suspense orders almost impossible to justify.

Starting in 2015, new leadership at the DEA (Chuck Rosenberg) and the Justice Department (Loretta Lynch) committed to "working more closely" with the pharmaceutical industry. Reflecting the new, more cooperative approach, Lynch's office informed Congressman Tom Marino that the DEA had met with 300 pharmaceutical industry representatives since she had taken the helm at Justice. By contrast, Lynch's predecessor (Eric Holder) took the unusual step of publicly opposing the Drug Enforcement Act.

After industry complaints regarding Rannazzisi's forceful investigative style, the Drug Enforcement Administration relieved him of managerial responsibility for its 600-person investigative unit and began an internal investigation. In response, Rannazzisi retired in 2015 after a 30-year career with the DEA.

For several years in a row, Pennsylvania Representative Tom Marino sponsored legislation to weaken the DEA's enforcement powers. The "2016 Ensuring Patient Access and Effective Drug Enforcement Act" gutted the DEA's ability to halt questionable sales of prescription pain pills. As a result, the DEA's number of "immediate suspension orders" against suspect doctors, pharmacies, and drug companies plummeted from 65 in 2011 to just 8 in 2016.

Notice the irony that the "Drug Enforcement Act" actually made it harder for the Drug Enforcement Administration to stop and punish behaviors that fueled the opioid industry—and crisis. It took four tries, but Marino finally passed the 2016 Drug Enforcement Act with unanimous voice votes in the House and Senate. President Obama signed Marino's bill into law on April 19, 2016.[21]

Passage of the 2016 Drug Enforcement Act capped a multifaceted, multiyear effort by the pharmaceutical industry to diminish the DEA's ability to interfere with its commercial interests. The Drug Enforcement Administration and the Justice Department had fought against the legislation for years but ultimately chose to accept it. Big Pharma won. Society lost.

CRONY CAPITALISM ON THE RISE

Reaction to the *Washington Post* and *60 Minutes* report was swift and consequential. Pennsylvania Representative Tom Marino, the principal sponsor of the 2016 Drug Enforcement Act, withdrew his name from consideration for becoming President Trump's drug czar. Missouri Senator Claire McCaskill immediately introduced legislation to restore the DEA's ability to execute more aggressive suspension orders.

The 2016 Drug Enforcement Act is what crony capitalism looks like. Powerful industry lobbyists capture the government's policy-making apparatus to advance their own interests. In 2018, drug manufacturers and pharma supply-chain companies employed more than 1,100 lobbyists—almost two for every member of Congress.[22] In 2016, pharma spent almost $100 million more on lobbying than the next highest-spending industry group.[23] Big Pharma's ability to manipulate market supply and demand for dangerous opioid drugs makes an already dire situation worse.

Industry capture of the government's policy-making apparatus is dangerous to democracy. Big Pharma's ability to pass the Drug Enforcement Act is a textbook example of a powerful industry hijacking public policy and limiting government's policing power. Senator McCaskill's description of the 2016 act's passage reveals crony capitalism at play in the halls of Congress:

> But it's really insidious in that, you know, these drug distributors hired people out of the DEA, and then they went to work trying to wear down the DEA as it relates to changing this law. Members of Congress who were pressing this law, you know, tried to keep saying, you don't have a good working relationship with the distributors.
>
> Meanwhile, these distributors were sending 9 million pills into a small community in West Virginia that had fewer than a thousand people. Obviously, they were not trying to do their best job in terms of making sure these products were [not] diverted to the black market. So, I think this was Congress not paying close enough attention, pharma and the drug industry having too much influence and the revolving door that so often helps industries get their way.[24]

This is the System at work, pushing unneeded and addictive opioid drugs on an unsuspecting and trusting public. Public outcry has driven efforts to reduce opioid prescriptions, address addiction, and increase distribution of lifesaving naloxone, which reverses opioid intoxication or overdose.

Like epinephrine (the drug used in EpiPens), naloxone is a readily available, low-cost, off-patent drug with proven efficacy. Like EpiPen manufacturer Mylan Pharmaceuticals, naloxone manufacturers generate their massive profits by creating easy-to-use (and easy-to-replicate) delivery mechanisms that receive FDA patent protections. The *New England Journal of Medicine* reports that naloxone manufacturers, not missing a massive profit opportunity, are dramatically raising prices as demand for their products increases (Figure 4.2):

> Each formulation of naloxone—two injection doses, Narcan nasal spray, and Evzio auto-injector—essentially has one supplier. Though there are three manufacturers with FDA approval for 0.4-mg-per-milliliter-dose injections, the vast majority are sold by Hospira, which has increased the price by 129% since 2012. . . . Only Amphastar manufactures 1-mg-per-milliliter injections, the dose used off-label as a nasal spray, which currently costs $39.60 after a 95% increase in September 2014. Newer, easier-to-use formulations are even more expensive. Narcan costs $150 for two nasal-spray doses. A two-dose Evzio package was priced at $690 in 2014 but is $4,500 today, a price increase of more than 500% in just over 2 years.[25]

Recent and Current Prices for Naloxone

Naloxone Product	Manufacturer	Previous Available Price (yr)	Current Price (2016)
Injectable or intranasal, 1 mg-per-milliliter vial (2 ml) (mucosal atomizer device separate)	Amphastar	$20.34 (2009)	$39.60
Injectable			
0.4 mg-per-milliliter vial (10 ml)	Hospira	$62.29 (2012)	$142.49
0.4 mg-per-milliliter vial (1 ml)	Mylan	$23.72 (2014)	$23.72
0.4 mg-per-milliliter vial (1 ml)	West-Ward	$20.40 (2015)	$20.40
Auto-injector, two-pack of single-use prefilled auto-injectors (Evzio)	Kaleo (approved 2014)	$690.00 (2014)	$4,500.00
Nasal spray, two-pack of single-use intranasal devices (Narcan)	Adapt (approved 2015)	$150.00 (2015)	$150.00

Source: Medi-Span Price Rx (Wolters Kluwer Clinical Drug Information)

FIGURE 4.2 **The price of the two-pack of prefilled auto-injectors, which is most often used with children, has increased sevenfold.**

Unlike naloxone manufacturers, the Mission Health system has resisted the temptation to amplify profits by providing high-cost treatments for opioid addiction. Mission serves the people of largely rural western North Carolina. Twelve percent of the babies born in Mission hospitals are opiate addicted and require detoxification. Detox occurred in expensive neonatal intensive care units (NICUs) until Mission's physicians developed a more effective, home-based detox program. This procedure is significantly less expensive, it enhances the nascent mother-child relationship, and it also advances childhood development. Each day a baby spends in a NICU requires two days of recovery time with its mother.

For all its great work helping babies, Mission experienced $4 million in lost NICU payments for the less invasive detox treatments. Doing the right thing for mothers and children cost the health system money.

CRONY CAPITALISM HAS CONSEQUENCES

The System has the blood of the American people on its hands. Healthcare's "iron triangle" worked diligently over a long period to infect American communities with this scourge of opioid addiction. All component parts coordinated to achieve this conclusion:

- Medical researchers didn't qualify their findings.

- Manufacturers lied about opioid safety and benefits to turbo-charge sales.

- The FDA approved products without adequate review.

- Revolving-door professionals shuttled between government and industry, advancing industry interests with insider information and relationships.

- Interest groups spread propaganda on pain management.

- Medical professionals embraced pain as a fifth vital sign and accepted perks for prescribing opioids.

- Drug distributors resented DEA interference in their business operations and worked to eliminate it.

- Medical schools didn't challenge industry-led protocols.

- Members of Congress took Big Pharma's money to do their bidding.

This shameful behavior created a public health challenge that will require decades, resources, and funding to address. Ironically, Congressman Tom Marino would be leading this effort as President Trump's drug czar if the *Washington Post* and *60 Minutes* hadn't exposed his leading role in limiting the DEA's enforcement capabilities.

One final note. In November 2018, then FDA Commissioner Dr. Scott Gottlieb (he resigned his position in April 2019) announced that the FDA had approved Dsuvia.[26] Dsuvia is an opioid drug manufactured by AcelRx Pharmaceuticals that is 10 times more powerful than fentanyl (the drug that killed Prince). This approval was highly controversial. The FDA granted it despite vocal opposition from four US senators and the FDA advisory panel chair. Opponents worry about Dsuvia's addictive potential, its easy-to-divert pill delivery mechanism, and its lack of unique medical properties.[27]

The American people should be afraid, very afraid.

Declaration of Independence

After its stirring opening paragraphs, the Declaration of Independence presents a detailed list of grievances that justify the separation of the colonies from King George III and Great Britain along with the efforts undertaken to address these grievances peacefully (Figure CI.1). Our Founding Fathers had clearly had enough. At the end of the Declaration they conclude that

> these united Colonies are, and of Right ought to be Free and Independent States, that they are Absolved from all Allegiance to the British Crown, and that all political connection between them and the State of Great Britain, is and ought to be totally dissolved.[1]

Fast-forward from 1776 to the current day. The United States has suffered under the tyranny of the Healthcare Industrial Complex (the System) for decades. The System's decadence and profligacy are increasing. Efforts to reform meet with repeated injury. There is no reason to believe continued attempts to reform the System gently will succeed.

Therefore, it is time for the American people to declare independence from the System and initiate a healthcare revolution to blow it up and replace it with a new American healthcare that serves the people. Here are the compelling grievances that impel the separation:

- **The System's ravenous appetite for growth is stealing resources from essential segments of American society.**

- **The System's fragmented approach to health and healthcare delivery fails to treat the whole person.** It doesn't listen and lacks compassion. It overtreats and undertreats without regard to outcomes. It makes too many mistakes and harms far too many people.

FIGURE CI.1   United States Declaration of Independence

- **The System demonstrates no willingness to change its behaviors.** It continues to invest in the high-cost and overbuilt acute/specialty care segment while underinvesting in vital primary and behavioral health services.

- **The System has been captured by special interests and industry incumbents** that pursue revenue/profit maximization for their benefit without delivering commensurate value to customers.

- **The level of waste in the System is both unacceptable and growing.**

- **The System cannot improve incrementally.** American healthcare requires radical transformation and disruption to align industry, customer, and consumer interests.

PART II

Revolutionary Forces

BLITZKRIEG

In the longest and largest World War I battle, France went toe-to-toe with Germany for 10 months at the Battle of Verdun (Figure PII.1). France's victory came at enormous cost. Verdun was the deadliest battle in human history with over 715,000 casualties. By contrast, the bloody US Civil War had 620,000 casualties over four years.

With a rearming Germany and the memories of Verdun's carnage still fresh, France began building an impregnable series of fortifications in 1930 along its border with Germany. The Maginot Line took five years to construct at a cost of over 3 billion francs during a period of global economic depression. French military commanders believed the Maginot Line would slow any German invasion, facilitate troop mobilization, and place their troops at strategic advantage should hostilities erupt.

The Maginot Line was the perfect defense for World War I. But between the wars, the speed, agility, and durability of German tanks and aircraft improved markedly. When combined with aggressive combat tactics, the German army became a deadly attacking force. On May 10, 1940, German panzer tanks, with close air support, raced around the Maginot Line and entered France through Belgium. Within six weeks, the German army was parading down the Champs-Élysées and the Nazi flag flew above the Arc de Triomphe.

FIGURE PII.1 Germans avoided the impregnable Maginot Line by going around it. France's apparent strength masked its vulnerability. Entrenched, asset-heavy health companies are also vulnerable.

France's apparent strength, the Maginot Line, masked vulnerability. Traditional health companies confront a similar strategic dilemma. Their asset-heavy, volume-based business models provide competitive advantage in marketplaces where fee-for-service (FFS) payment predominates. Their apparent strength masks vulnerability to nimble, consumer-oriented health companies that can deliver better care outcomes at lower costs with greater convenience.

Invasions rely on force multipliers to overcome entrenched adversaries. Force multipliers are tools and tactics that amplify productivity and effectiveness. Guerilla warfare tactics amplify the effectiveness of small armies. German blitzkrieg (lightning war) tactics overwhelmed a protected but immobile French army.

As with all successful revolutionary movements, force multipliers are turbocharging America's healthcare transformation. The most important is empowered healthcare buyers (aka customers). They are using their purchasing power, most notably through full-risk contracting, to demand higher-value healthcare products and services.

Revolutionary new companies are emerging to meet the increasing demand for value-based care delivery. Powered by liberated data, they're solving customers' jobs-to-be-done in real time with energized and engaged clinicians. They're winning market share by delighting one customer at a time. Empowered buyers amplify their success by purchasing their services.

Full-risk contracting is the transformative force driving organizations to adopt strategies that align payment incentives with customer need. Status quo-busting payment mechanisms include "bundled payments" with outcomes guarantees for episodic care, and "capitated payments" for ongoing care are growing fast and gaining critical mass in select markets.

America will not change the way it delivers healthcare until it changes the way it pays for healthcare services.

However, payment reform is not sufficient to break the System's stranglehold on the mechanics of healthcare expenditure. Enlightened regulatory reform and eliminating the capture of healthcare agencies by special interest groups must augment payment reform to create the healthcare system the American people deserve.

Part II addresses the Revolutionary Forces that are propelling a customer-led revolt by the American people against the System:

- **Chapter 5, "Empowered Customers (Buyers),"** describes how the combination of empowered customers and full-risk contracting is fundamentally changing healthcare's supply-demand dynamics and tipping individual markets toward value. Demand-driven change generates revolutionary results.

- **Chapter 6, "Liberated Data,"** details how liberated Big Data in combination with dynamic organizational models empower frontline staff. And liberated data arms clinicians and consumers with the information they need to make the right decisions in real time. Liberated data spreads knowledge and saves lives.

• **Chapter 7, "Pro-Market Regulation,"** explains the role balance plays in establishing enlightened regulatory policies and enforcement that sustain level-field competition without unduly burdening market participants. Revolutionary Healthcare is always pro-market, not always pro-business.

CHAPTER 5

Empowered Customers (Buyers)

Walmart knows its customers. Store greeters welcome shoppers when they arrive and smile goodbye when they leave. Walmart's folksy charm is just one component of the company's laser focus on delighting its customers. Walmart intensely tracks customer purchases and behaviors, as does its only true rival Amazon. This data-driven awareness leads to new insights and business ideas that delight customers.

For example, Walmart noticed its customers were spending less per store visit. After intense research, the company discovered why. Its customers were allocating more discretionary income to healthcare, so they had less to spend on other things. In December 2018, the Commonwealth Fund issued a white paper titled "The Cost of Employer Insurance Is a Growing Burden for Middle-Income Families."[1] It reports that the percentage of median income consumed by employee health insurance premiums and potential deductible spending rose from 7.8 percent in 2007 to 11.7 percent in 2017. The burden is highest in Louisiana and Mississippi, where these healthcare costs consume more than 15 percent of median income.

Rather than fight the trend, Walmart is finding ways to help both these customers and its own employees get more value from their healthcare purchases. It turns out that what's good for Walmart customers and employees is also good for Walmart itself.

Walmart executive Lori Flees explained the company's logic at a Minneapolis conference in October 2018.[2] Walmart is the nation's largest employer. Providing health insurance for Walmart's 2.2 million workers is the company's second-highest cost (after wages). Rather than complain,

Walmart decided to become a better purchaser of healthcare services and work with health companies that deliver better outcomes at lower prices. This value-first mindset is transforming American healthcare. As Flees summarized,

> So these are the things that drive us to be interested in health care: Our customers need help. Our associates need and want to be healthy. And it's good for our business.[3]

Like growing numbers of Americans, Walmart's customers don't just worry about health, they also worry about accessing and paying for healthcare services. Walmart's motto, "Save Money. Live Better," guides the company's strategic thinking and market positioning. Renowned for finding affordable solutions to customer challenges (e.g., access to affordable banking services), Walmart sees opportunity in healthcare.

Toward that end, Walmart pursues innovative strategies that improve health and reduce healthcare costs for employees and customers. It contracts directly for specialty care procedures at fixed prices (through full-risk "bundled" payments) for the entire episode of care. For example, Walmart has signed agreements with designated "centers of excellence" for lower-cost, higher-quality spinal surgery, while slashing payments for similar procedures with other providers. Most spinal surgery is unnecessary, so Walmart incentivizes its associates to explore noninvasive treatments for their back pain before going under the knife.[4] Ironically, physicians at Walmart's orthopedic centers of excellence disproportionately recommend noninvasive procedures. Too bad the local providers didn't do that in the first place.

To promote wellness, Walmart markets "Great for You" healthier foods to its customers. It also operates in-store clinics, pharmacies, and vision centers to improve access to those services. It even hosts in-store health screening events to catch "patients" while they go about their normal lives. Since 2006, the retail giant has sold $4 generic prescriptions and has partnered with Humana to offer lower-cost drugs to Medicare patients.

The bottom line is that Walmart wants to bring "everyday low prices" to healthcare. It's not alone—so do Amazon, CVS, Walgreens,[5] and even Best Buy.[6] Imagine that, big retailers see opportunity in providing value-added healthcare to customers.

Incumbents should beware. Healthcare is under siege. Big retailers are attacking the System's soft underbelly and winning market share by delighting customers. It turns out that retailers know a thing or two about understanding and fulfilling customer needs.

Clay Christensen's
Fundamentals of Jobs-to-Be-Done Theory

As Theodore Levitt said, "People do not want a quarter-inch drill, they want a quarter-inch hole." It is true. People buy products and services to get jobs done; and while products come and go, the underlying job-to-be-done does not go away.

Instead of improving an existing product or service (creating a better quarter-inch drill), focusing on trying to find better ways to create a quarter-inch hole (to get the job done) will deliver actual innovation.

In relation to healthcare, people have three primary jobs-to-be-done: fix me when I'm broken; keep me as healthy as possible; and teach me to make lifestyle choices for improved health. I'll discuss these more in Chapter 8.

MEETING CUSTOMERS'
JOBS-TO-BE-DONE

Management guru Peter Drucker distilled the essence of businesses as follows, "The purpose of a business is to create and keep customers." This simple statement has profound implications for healthcare as it moves into a pro-market, consumer-focused era. It serves as an orienting principle for identifying customers' jobs-to-be-done ("Jobs"),[7] designing service offerings, and building business models. The best companies relentlessly focus on solving customer needs, wants, and desires. This is the power of demand-driven change. It delivers revolutionary outcomes to consumers. Just consider how customer-centric Walmart is.

The flip side of this equation is that customers must have the knowledge, inclination, and wherewithal to select the products and services that fulfill their "Jobs." When they do, customers engage with companies that solve their problems and disengage from those that don't. As customers increasingly exert their purchasing power in healthcare, they will transform the industry's supply-demand relationships. This emerging market dynamic is the foundation for the customer revolution in healthcare.

Fulfilling customers' "Jobs" is no small challenge for health companies. In Chapter 3, I observed that healthcare principals routinely execute transactions without customers. Instead, they strive to increase revenues and profits by optimizing service volume and payment formularies. Quality, outcomes, and great customer service (i.e., value) are not prerequisites for success in fee-for-service medicine. This payment reality and the managerial orientation supporting it block health companies from reading the market signals customers send through their purchasing decisions. Customer-centric businesses rely upon these market signals to adjust prices, services, and product quality to optimize sales and profits.

Peter Drucker also noted, "If you [health companies] want to do something new [solve customers' "Jobs"], you have to stop doing something old [clinging to FFS business models]."

Part III, "Revolutionary Healthcare," will dissect the many "somethings new" that health companies are doing to succeed in the post-transformation marketplace. The essential message here is that empowered buyers are the "revolutionary force" driving the industry into "Revolutionary Healthcare." Health companies that fail to understand this emerging reality and adjust their business models accordingly will lose market relevance.

Interestingly, Walmart is both a customer and a competitor to health companies. There are two basic types of business models with two categories of customers:

- Business-to-business (B2B)

- Business-to-consumer (B2C)

As a self-insured company for its employees' health expenditures, Walmart is a major purchaser of healthcare products and services (a customer). Its decision to contract directly with select health companies for care services makes it a sophisticated B2B customer.

When fulfilling customers' jobs-to-be-done, it's essential to understand what "Job" the customer is hiring the company to do. In direct contracting for its employees' healthcare, Walmart's "Job" is finding affordable, high-quality healthcare service providers to deliver appropriate care to employees. Health companies that want to attract Walmart and like-minded companies will organize their business models to solve this "Job."

Walmart also competes with health companies, particularly in B2C products and services. Already a major pharmacy, Walmart now offers clinic services, wellness education, eyeglasses, and healthy food. Expect it to expand the range and scale of its health and healthcare offerings. It understands its customers' healthcare "Jobs." Its trusted brand with price-conscious consumers positions it well for a disrupting healthcare marketplace where consumers seek affordable solutions to routine health and healthcare problems.

Health companies that want to compete in the B2C healthcare marketplace will likewise need to develop business models that solve consumers' healthcare "Jobs." In doing so, they will encounter formidable competition from retail companies like Walmart that have well-developed consumerism experience and instincts.

As B2B and B2C channels mature in healthcare, customers will search for and discover better ways to solve their healthcare "Jobs." They will redefine and transform the healthcare industry through their purchasing decisions. This type of demand-driven change is well known outside healthcare, but alien to incumbent health companies.

What distinguishes this demand-driven period of market reform from other attempts to reform the System is that the buyers of health and healthcare services (customers) now have ways to pay for health and healthcare services that align with their "Jobs." Full-risk contracting for healthcare services shifts the power dynamic from healthcare service providers to healthcare service purchasers. It is the unstoppable force that pushes Revolutionary Healthcare forward.

FULL-RISK CONTRACTING: THE TRANSFORMATIVE CATALYST

Although forms of full-risk contracting have existed for decades, they are now gaining sufficient critical mass in select markets to change payer and provider business models. Before digging into that trend and its implication, let's first examine the current distribution of payers and payment vehicles.

There are three categories of healthcare purchasers who either pay for healthcare directly (through self-insurance mechanisms) or buy health insurance to cover that risk. I list them below with the 2017 figures for the percentages covered within each category:[8]

- Employers (companies)—49 percent of Americans

- Governments (federal, state, and local)—36 percent of Americans

- Individuals (insured and uninsured)—16 percent of Americans

Employer-sponsored health insurance programs cover roughly half of all Americans. Governments purchase healthcare through Medicare, Medicaid, government agencies, and employee insurance programs. Individuals who pay for their own healthcare either directly or through a state exchange are far fewer in number. Nine percent of Americans do not have any health insurance coverage.

Healthcare coverage and healthcare expenditure are not correlated. Even though half of Americans have private health insurance and they pay disproportionately more for individual healthcare transactions, private insurance accounts for only 34 percent of total health expenditure (2017 figures). Public insurance (Medicare, Medicaid, Veterans Administration, Defense Department, and the Children's Health Insurance Program or CHIP) account for 41 percent of total expenditure. The conclusion is obvious. Publicly insured individuals disproportionately consume healthcare services, but governmental payers pay less (often substantially less) per transaction. "Out-of-pocket" expenditures account for 10.5 percent of healthcare expenditure.[9]

As discussed in Chapter 2, complex fee-for-service payment formularies dominate healthcare transactions. Figure 5.1 details the FFS and value-based payments received by large health systems. FFS payment remained above 80 percent of total payment between 2014 and 2017 but dropped to 77 percent in 2018.

Although the 2018 decrease in FFS payments is laudable, the vast majority of value-based payments are in shared savings contracts with no downside risk. That is, providers are not at risk if they do not achieve the targeted savings level. A simple example will illustrate.

A hospital contracts with an insurance company to conduct knee replacement surgery. Historically, the insurance company has paid the hospital $25,000 for this surgery. In a shared savings agreement, the hospital and insurance company agree to equally split any savings below the historic $25,000 payment level. There is no penalty to the hospital if it does not achieve any savings (hence, no downside risk).

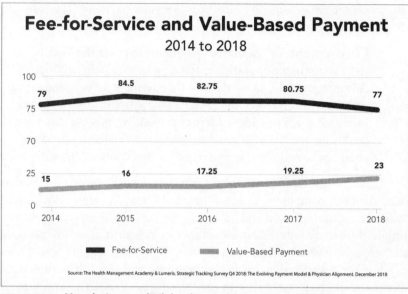

Fee-for-Service and Value-Based Payment
2014 to 2018

Source: The Health Management Academy & Lumeris. Strategic Tracking Survey Q4 2018: The Evolving Payment Model & Physician Alignment. December 2018

FIGURE 5.1 **Hospitals are still living in a fee-for-service world.**

These upside-only payment arrangements are an intermediate step toward true value-based payment and delivery. US healthcare will not achieve true value-based healthcare until health companies accept full risk (upside and downside) for delivering targeted high-quality outcomes with great customer experience.

In full-risk contracting, health insurance companies pay a fixed amount to providers for procedures, say $20,000 for knee replacement surgeries. Providers profit if they perform the surgery at a cost below $20,000 while meeting quality and service standards. However, providers lose money if their costs to perform the surgery exceed $20,000 and/or they fail to meet quality and service standards.

Full-risk contracting achieves radical payment reform by making health companies fully accountable for care outcomes, quality, and costs. It comes in two basic forms:

- **Predetermined "bundled" payments for episodic care** like the knee replacement surgery described above. Under bundled payment contracts, providers receive a predetermined payment to cover the total treatment cost for a specific episode of care (from admission through treatment, discharge, and recovery) over a defined period. Bundled payment procedures must meet predetermined quality measures to receive payment. The contracts generally carry 90-day performance guarantees.

- **Fixed monthly or "capitated" payments to cover the health risk for distinct populations.** These programs, such as Medicare Advantage (MA), adjust the monthly payment for each individual's perceived health risk. Going full risk for a patient's overall health incentivizes the provider to deliver preventive and other low-cost healthcare services that avoid costlier services later. It motivates providers to make and keep a population of consumers healthy.

In healthcare's most overused metaphor, health companies' leaders describe their companies as straddling between a "volume" dock and a "value" boat as the boat drifts into the lake. Leaders using this metaphor implicitly acknowledge their acceptance of suboptimal performance in exchange for FFS payment.

Fee-for-service payment is transactional and rewards activity, not outcomes. By contrast, full-risk contracting is exactly the opposite. It pays for outcomes and rewards providers that deliver them efficiently. It is almost impossible for health companies to practice activity-based FFS medicine and outcomes-based full-risk contracting simultaneously. This explains why most providers and payers do not participate in full-risk contracting or suffer significant losses when they do.

In essence, full-risk contracting shifts care-management risk from governments, employers, and individuals to payers and providers. Full-risk contracts incorporate both business-to-business and business-to-consumer customer segments. Governments and large employers can establish full-risk contracts with health plans and/or health systems. Individual plans bought on public health exchanges are full-risk contracts. In addition, health plans can enter into full-risk contracts directly with consumers through the Medicare Advantage (MA) program. Increasing numbers of states are pursuing forms of direct contracting for their Medicaid populations.

As noted at the beginning of this chapter, Walmart has negotiated full-risk bundled payment contracts for select specialty treatments with designated centers of excellence. They are not alone in pursuing full-risk contracting to improve outcomes, lower costs, and eliminate unnecessary treatments. Here are three notable examples:

- **In November 2018, the Trump administration reversed course and embraced mandatory bundles for select orthopedic,**

cardiac, and oncology treatments. When making the announcement, Secretary Azar observed that mandatory models (full-risk
bundled payments) are "the most effective way to . . . save money
and improve quality."[10]

- **In August 2018, General Motors signed a five-year agreement
  with Henry Ford Health System to provide comprehensive
  healthcare services for GM's salaried employees in Southeast
  Michigan.** This is a landmark transaction that moves GM away
  from pure fee-for-service (FFS) payment while holding Henry
  Ford accountable for care delivery cost, quality, outcomes, and
  service levels.

  The GM–Henry Ford agreement will be Michigan's first
  direct-care contract. It reflects changing market dynamics and a
  maturing relationship between large self-insured employers and
  large integrated healthcare systems.[11]

- **In March 2018, the state agency Massachusetts Medicaid
  (MassHealth) began contracting with 17 health systems to
  manage the care for 850,000 Medicaid enrollees based on predetermined monthly payments for each individual.**

  The program assigns members to health systems. In return,
  the health systems assume financial risk for all their expenditures caring for those individuals in exchange for predetermined
  monthly payments that are based on individual health status.
  The program will monitor costs, quality, outcomes, and member
  experience.

  In announcing the program, Governor Charlie Baker
  stressed that the agreements with health systems "will directly
  lead to better and more coordinated care for MassHealth members across the Commonwealth."[12]

As illustrated above, governmental and commercial payers are
embracing full-risk contracting. Adam Boehler, President Trump's director of the Center for Medicare and Medicaid Innovation (CMMI) since
August of 2018, proclaimed during a November 2018 interview that "one
of our prime goals is to get rid of fee for service [payment]." This is a
bipartisan position. Patrick Conway, Boehler's Obama-appointed predecessor (now CEO of Blue Cross Blue Shield of North Carolina) is equally
adamant. At an October 2018 conference, Conway said, "I want fee-for-
service, volume-based care to die, and I want to kill it as fast as possible."[13]

Like rock and roll, full-risk contracting is here to stay. Medicare Advantage plans are just the most prominent form of full-risk contracting. Given its transformative potential, it's time to examine Medicare Advantage more closely.

ADVANTAGE MEDICARE ADVANTAGE

The System's unforgivable failure to coordinate care, manage chronic disease, and promote health increases human suffering and treatment costs. In stark contrast, high-performing Medicare Advantage (MA) programs accomplish these objectives through focused medical management. MA works because its payment and performance incentives reward comprehensive and holistic care delivery. Its shifts the government's care management risk to MA health plan sponsors. In this sense, MA represents successful public-private partnerships that advance value-based reform.

Full-risk contracting arrangements, including Medicare Advantage, are the transformative force challenging conventional healthcare business models. Under full-risk contracting, payers and providers need new capabilities to improve patient-centric health outcomes. MA plans that cannot manage their members' care within fixed revenue parameters lose money. The Centers for Medicare and Medicaid (CMS) provides funding within predefined parameters to MA plan sponsors.

Commercial health insurers develop, market, and administer Medicare Advantage plans that compete for members in the public marketplace. Customers select MA plans with the benefits they want at prices they're willing to pay. Successful MA plans attract members, meet their health needs efficiently, and receive high quality scores.

Medicare Advantage is gaining sufficient critical mass in many markets to stimulate vertical integration of care payment and delivery. A third of Medicare beneficiaries are now enrolled in MA programs. That percentage could grow to as high as 50 percent by 2025 as record numbers of baby boomers age into Medicare beginning in 2019. Properly executed, MA has the scale to transform US healthcare delivery by aligning payment incentives with desired health outcome objectives. A recent study by Avalere found compelling evidence that MA plans manage the health of sicker Medicare beneficiaries more cost effectively than traditional FFS Medicare. Key findings from the Avalere study include the following (as a reminder, FFS = fee-for-service):

- Medicare Advantage had a higher percentage of beneficiaries with chronic conditions who enrolled in Medicare due to disability (36 percent versus 22 percent FFS) and who are dual-eligible/low-income beneficiaries (23 percent versus 20 percent FFS) than FFS Medicare.

- Medicare Advantage beneficiaries, compared to FFS Medicare beneficiaries, had a 57 percent higher rate of serious mental illness (9 percent versus 5 percent of FFS) and a 16 percent higher rate of alcohol/drug/substance abuse (7 percent versus 6 percent of FFS).

- Utilization of costly healthcare services was lower for Medicare Advantage beneficiaries, including 23 percent fewer inpatient stays (249 versus 324 per 1,000 beneficiaries in FFS Medicare) and 33 percent fewer emergency room visits (511 versus 759 per 1,000 beneficiaries in FFS).

- Average annual Medicare Advantage beneficiary costs were not significantly different from average costs for FFS Medicare beneficiaries, but annual spending per beneficiary on preventive services and tests was 21 percent higher in Medicare Advantage ($3,811 versus $3,139 in FFS Medicare); FFS Medicare had 17 percent higher spending on inpatient costs ($3,477 versus $2,898 in Medicare Advantage); and FFS Medicare had 5 percent higher spending on outpatient/emergent care services ($2,474 versus $2,359 in Medicare Advantage).

- Medicare Advantage outperformed FFS Medicare on several key quality measures, including a nearly 29 percent lower rate of all potentially avoidable hospitalizations (17 percent versus 24 percent in FFS); 41 percent fewer avoidable acute hospitalizations; 18 percent fewer avoidable chronic hospitalizations; and higher rates of preventive screenings/tests, including LDL testing (5 percent more) and breast cancer screenings (13 percent more).

- Relative to FFS Medicare, Medicare Advantage beneficiaries in the clinically complex diabetes cohort experienced a 52 percent lower rate of any complication (8 percent versus 17 percent of FFS and a 73 percent lower rate of serious complications (2 percent versus 6 percent of FFS).[14]

By any measure, these are impressive results. The Avalere study summarizes the results of its analysis as follows:

> These results indicate that, compared to FFS Medicare, Medicare Advantage provides more preventive services and utilizes interventions designed to better manage chronic conditions, which may avert preventable complications and result in lower overall costs. This was especially true among the most clinically complex and dual-eligible/low-income beneficiaries.
>
> Despite Medicare Advantage beneficiaries having more social and clinical risk factors, they had similar costs to those in FFS Medicare overall, indicating that Medicare Advantage's focus on coordination of care may lead to more efficient treatment patterns and care delivery. Medicare Advantage has inherent incentives to coordinate care and deliver preventive services that do not exist in the FFS Medicare program.
>
> The study findings show that Medicare Advantage beneficiaries with chronic conditions experience better outcomes, fewer adverse events at similar or lower costs, and suggests a better quality of life for beneficiaries with chronic conditions in Medicare Advantage.

The marketplace sees enormous investment potential in Medicare Advantage companies. In October 2018, Devoted Health raised $300 million in private equity financing led by Andreesen Horowitz with a company valuation of $1.8 billion.[15] Founded in 2017 by health tech entrepreneurs Ed and Todd Park, Devoted is a nationwide Medicare Advantage company offering customer-focused, relationship-based, easy-to-use health plans that deliver the right care at the right time.

Addressing Medicare Advantage's Structural Flaws

Medicare Advantage plans require two core competencies to succeed financially. The first is the medical management of the plan's enrollees. As described in the Avalere study, everything good in MA results from the active management of MA plan enrollees. Enhancing MA plans' collective ability to manage members' health is America's last, best hope for transforming healthcare delivery.

The second core competency is managing revenue flows in and out of the health insurance plan. Everything bad in Medicare Advantage results from the design and application of CMS payments to MA health plans.

"Fixing" these flaws would dramatically improve MA's performance and speed health system transformation.

The following four structural flaws distort the proper functioning of MA plans.

1. Risk adjustment
2. Baseline variation in FFS payment rates
3. Contracting friction between MA plans and providers
4. Release mechanism for high-cost enrollees

Let's address them individually.

1: Risk Adjustment

Risk adjustment is the mechanism through which CMS calibrates the payments it makes to Medicare Advantage plans for the expected care cost of MA plan enrollees. CMS employs a complex formulary employing demographic and diagnostic information for each beneficiary. Sicker enrollees generate higher monthly payments for MA plans.

The marketplace is always smarter than central planners. MA plans have become adept at identifying additional diagnoses that increase monthly premiums separate and apart from the enrollee's true health status. For this reason, risk scores are 8 percent higher and have risen 1.5 percent faster for MA enrollees than for traditional Medicare enrollees.[16]

Higher payments for specific beneficiaries inflate MA plan revenues and profits. In a February 2017 *Health Affairs* article, Richard Kronick projects this "coding intensity" could increase MA spending by more than $200 billion over 10 years.[17]

CMS could eliminate much of this "diagnosis gaming" by assuming the demographic and diagnostic characteristics of MA and traditional Medicare populations are equivalent. Even better, CMS could move away from risk adjustment altogether and apply experience ratings to specific MA populations. Experience ratings assign premiums based on the actual healthcare use of similar populations. The larger the populations, the more accurate the assessments.

2: Baseline Variation in FFS Payment Rates

The complexity of Medicare's payment formularies makes them vulnerable to manipulation and results in remarkable payment variation across the nation. For example, the 2016 per capita cost in Miami/Dade County was $14,133. That figure was 76 percent higher than the 2016 per capita cost of $8,054 for Seattle/King County.[18]

Physician practice patterns are the primary factor driving fee-for-service payment differentials exhibited in Miami and Seattle. Medicare patients get more care in Miami (much of it unnecessary) than in Seattle. These payment differentials exist despite Seattle's higher cost of living.[19]

No good deed goes unpunished. It's unfair that more efficient healthcare markets like Seattle receive lower per capita payments for generating the same or better care outcomes. Lower payment levels also make it harder for Seattle-based MA plans to generate profits by eliminating unnecessary healthcare expenditures. It's a lose-lose proposition.

Medicare should decouple Medicare Advantage plan per capita payments from fee-for-service-driven payment formularies and replace them with national, experienced-based rates. Over time, this would shift payments from higher-premium markets to lower-premium markets and result in more effective and efficient care delivery across MA plans throughout the country.

3: Friction Between MA Plans and Providers

Medicare Advantage plan ownership is highly concentrated among three commercial insurance companies. UnitedHealthcare, Humana, and Blue Cross affiliates accounted for 57 percent of nationwide MA enrollment in 2017. Eight companies and affiliates accounted for 77 percent of enrollment.[20]

Commercial MA plans typically contract with providers on an FFS basis for specific treatments. The plans manage their members' care efficiently to generate higher profits. Better care management keeps medical expenditures low.

This payment model can become problematic when dominant MA plans exert price-setting pressure on providers. More commercial insurers offering MA plans levels competition within markets and establishes more balance in payer-provider price negotiations.

MA plans that contract with providers using sub-capitated rates for specific services (e.g., behavioral health services) align payment with desired outcomes in the same way capitated MA rates do for MA plans overall. More sub-capitated arrangements will improve plan performance by focusing those providers on value creation.

Concern with fair provider payment will grow as MA plans increase enrollment. Unfair payer or provider pricing power distorts market function and destroys value creation. The best way to address unfair payments by MA plans is to create more competitive MA marketplaces for both payers and providers. This will enable value-oriented health companies to differentiate, win customers, and gain market relevance for the right reasons.

4: Release Mechanism for High-Cost Enrollees

Medicare Advantage enrollees have the right to convert back to traditional Medicare at any time. This creates an incentive for MA plans to shift the financial risk of caring for their highest-cost enrollees by nudging them to convert their health insurance back to traditional Medicare. Typically, these high-cost enrollees require significant acute-care interventions.

The colloquial term for this cruel practice is "lemon dropping," equating sick elderly members with broken-down cars. In May 2017, Tampa-based Freedom Health settled a false claims lawsuit, which included allegations of lemon dropping, with the Justice Department for $31.7 million without accepting liability.[21] I have found no study that documents the scope and scale of this cost shift from Medicare Advantage plans to traditional Medicare, but the potential for abuse is enormous. The existence of this "release mechanism" creates a perverse incentive to place the company's financial well-being above that of chronically sick enrollees. Given MA's organic growth, eliminating this ability of MA programs to shift financial risk constitutes prudent regulatory policy.

MA's Bottom Line

At issue is whether Medicare Advantage will be the driving catalyst for industry transformation. To realize this potential, MA must amplify its medical management capacity and diminish the financial maneuvering that compromises its effectiveness.

The future of US healthcare and the health of the US economy hang in the balance. Former president Ronald Reagan famously quoted the Russian proverb "Trust but verify" in describing his approach to negotiating nuclear disarmament with his Soviet counterparts. Employing President Reagan's sensibility, CMS must enhance MA's regulatory framework, trust the marketplace will evolve toward efficiency, and verify that MA plans deliver value for customers. In that way, Medicare Advantage will truly provide advantage to the American people.

FULL-RISK CONTRACTING: GAINING MARKET TRACTION

Transformative innovations, like full-risk contracting, take time to scale and advance into the marketplace. In his pioneering book *Crossing the*

Chasm, Geoffrey Moore describes the sequencing of the following five customer groups adopting transformative innovation as it moves into the marketplace.

1. Innovators—first 2.5 percent of the market
2. Early adopters—next 13.5 percent
3. Early majority—next 34 percent
4. Late majority—next 34 percent
5. Laggards—final 16 percent

Moore identifies an adoption "chasm" between "visionaries" (innovators and early adopters) and "pragmatists" (early majority). These chasms emerge because visionaries and pragmatists have different purchasing motivations.

Visionaries want to lead innovative change and willingly take more risk. By contrast, pragmatists don't become buyers until they believe a transformative innovation is taking hold. That occurs when the transformative innovation captures 15–20 percent market share. Only then will pragmatists move to incorporate the transformative innovation into their business models.

The technology firm Gartner developed the "hype cycle" to describe the emotional roller coaster that accompanies transformative technologies as they move through the different buyer groups. The hype cycle rises quickly to "the peak of expectation" before falling dramatically into the "trough of disillusionment" as the innovation seeks to cross the adoption chasm (Figure 5.2).

As market share approaches and surpasses 20 percent, the transformative innovation enters "the slope of enlightenment" where pragmatists become active buyers. It settles into "the plateau of productivity" as the innovation earns widespread adoption. Many, perhaps most, transformative innovations do not develop enough momentum to cross the adoption chasm. They die in the "trough of disillusionment." That will not happen with full-risk contracting. It will "jump the adoption chasm," but do so unevenly. Local healthcare markets in the United States have distinctive supply-demand relationships that influence medical practice and business model configurations. Those factors will shape the pace at which individual markets shift to value-based payment.

As mentioned earlier in this chapter, the 2016 per capita total healthcare cost in Miami/Dade County was 76 percent higher than that in Seattle/King County.[22] Physicians in Miami provide more care (much

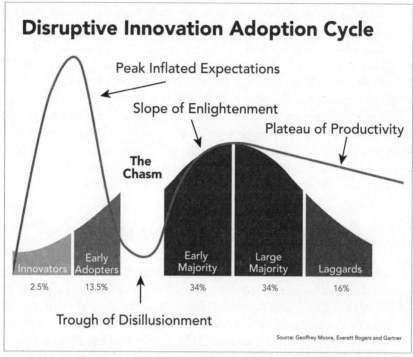

Disruptive Innovation Adoption Cycle

Peak Inflated Expectations

Slope of Enlightenment

Plateau of Productivity

The Chasm

| Innovators | Early Adopters | Early Majority | Large Majority | Laggards |
| 2.5% | 13.5% | 34% | 34% | 16% |

Trough of Disillusionment

Source: Geoffrey Moore, Everett Rogers and Gartner

FIGURE 5.2 **Adoption of transformative technologies often fails before hitting 20 percent market share because they cannot attract "pragmatic" early majority buyers.**

of it unnecessary) to Medicare patients than physicians in Seattle. These types of payment and practice variation determine an individual market's readiness for shifting to value-based payment and delivery.

Stuck in the "early adopter" stage for the last decade, full-risk contracting is making the leap into the "early majority" in select markets (e.g., Minnesota; Portland, Oregon; Orange County, California) as Medicare Advantage enrollment exceeds 50 percent of Medicare beneficiaries. In those markets, enlightened payers and providers understand that market dynamics are shifting toward value-based payment and delivery. They want to position for this market shift, so they are aggressively pursuing vertical integration strategies to manage the healthcare needs of MA enrollees as well as to accommodate other full-risk contracting arrangements with governments, self-insured companies, and individuals.

These "early adopting" markets illustrate how bottom-up market reform will spread throughout the broader healthcare landscape. As individual markets achieve a critical mass of full-risk payment vehicles (e.g., comprising 25 percent to 30 percent of revenues), "early majority" health companies will vertically integrate payment and delivery capabilities to manage episodic and ongoing care for their members.

The science fiction writer William Gibson astutely noted, "The future is already here—it's just not evenly distributed."[23] Gibson's observation captures the uneven adoption dynamic of full-risk contracting. It also captures the inevitability of healthcare's future "value-based" operating paradigm.

OLD MATH VS. NEW MATH

The combination of motivated healthcare buyers with full-risk contracting payment models creates a transformative force for revolutionary change in US healthcare. Without overstatement, this new demand-driven purchasing model for healthcare services is creating a "Copernicus" moment for healthcare. Copernicus presented the theory that the earth revolved around the sun, in opposition to established science that posited that the earth was at the center of the universe.

Despite rhetoric to the contrary, providers and payers have been at the center of the System's FFS universe. They have artificially controlled the economics of healthcare payment and delivery for their benefit, not for the benefit of customers and consumers. After decades of operating in this System-centric universe, health companies are discovering that the payment and delivery of health and healthcare services actually revolve around customers and consumers. Empowered buyers insisting on value for their healthcare purchases are turning the healthcare world upside down and inside out.

Healthcare needs a new math for this new age (Figure 5.3). Fee-for-service payment is healthcare's old math. Revenues are flexible. Managing expenses is relatively less important. "Getting paid" is the principal managerial goal. Overtreating patients and manipulating billing codes are proven strategies for optimizing reimbursement. The System wins. The American people lose.

In well-functioning markets, the supply of products and services offered adjusts to an intrinsic level of customer demand. Prices for commodity products and routine services are highly elastic. Higher

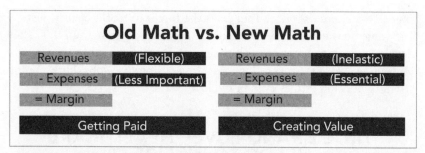

FIGURE 5.3 Health systems must change their focus from boosting revenues to controlling expenses and creating value.

prices reduce demand. Consequently, prices coalesce around fixed price points. In such markets, managing expenses effectively is essential for profitable operations. Robust cost accounting capabilities drive constant performance improvement, tight pricing algorithms, and efficient resource utilization.

In competitive markets, "creating value" distinguishes winning companies. They deliver high volumes of high-quality products and services at low prices with exceptional customer experience (think Amazon). Most healthcare services are routine. They occur frequently, have predictable outcomes, and invite standardization.

Under full-risk contracts, revenues are inelastic (generally fixed) and managing expenses is exceptionally important. Health companies participating in full-risk contracting must deliver necessary care within budgetary constraints or lose money. Since many full-risk programs incorporate customer choice, successful health companies also must deliver a great consumer experience to increase their market presence. This is healthcare's new math, and health companies must learn it to be competitive in the post-transformation marketplace.

The realization that full-risk contracts will define the post-reform marketplace has triggered significant repositioning by "pragmatists." The CVS-Aetna merger, the Advocate-Aurora merger, and the new Amazon, Berkshire Hathaway, JP Morgan (ABJ) health company reflect this emerging market dynamic. These companies recognize the need to enhance their full-risk contracting capabilities to accommodate increasing market demand among both buyers and sellers of healthcare services.

Revolutionary health companies aren't waiting to attack the System's inefficiencies. They're creating value and going directly to healthcare buyers. They're offering better healthcare products, competitive prices, and superior customer service. They have the forces of truth, beauty, justice, and value on their side. The best companies do even more than this. They develop a deep connection with their customers that reciprocates loyalty for solving their jobs-to-be-done. Meeting customers' "Jobs" builds brand strength and sometimes even brand love.

TRUE BRAND LOVE—HEALTHCARE NEEDS TO INSPIRE IT

Customer-centricity and meeting customers' "jobs-to-be-done" are the keys to retailing success. After all, business cannot exist without customers. While some companies do it better than others, meeting customers' needs is standard operating procedure for businesses in general. Except, of course, in healthcare, where embracing consumerism is a new phenomenon.

In March 2016, I participated in a consumerism conference in Florida attended by senior executives from leading health systems. The conference was a nice break from Chicago's winter weather and gave me an opportunity to gauge how health systems were approaching this brave new consumer-centric world.

Speaker after speaker noted increasing consumer frustration with healthcare delivery. These frustrations included high costs, poor service, poor communication, and constant administrative hassles. It was clear that health system executives in attendance understood that connecting with customers and improving customer experience are essential to building brand strength and organizational sustainability.

The conference included a riveting presentation on "brand love" by a global marketing director from Johnson & Johnson's Consumer Products Division. She described brand love as "loyalty beyond reason" and stressed the benefits of establishing true connection between customers and products. For example, J&J began marketing Listerine as a cure for halitosis ("the reason some women never marry") in the 1920s. From those modest beginnings, Listerine has developed full-out brand love with many of its customers. Customers' hearts beat faster when they see a bottle. They pay premium prices for the privilege of gargling with the antiseptic-tasting mouthwash and enthusiastically tell their friends about all its other beneficial uses.

Brand love is emotional, not rational. For some reason I prefer Energizer batteries to every other brand. It makes no sense. Other batteries

FIGURE 5.4 The brand love for the Energizer bunny differentiates the company even though it's selling a basic commodity.

work just as well or better. Maybe it's the Energizer Bunny (Figure 5.4). It just keeps on going!

Conventional marketing begins with "what" products companies sell. It then explains "how" those products differentiate from competitive offerings (why this car is better than that car) and concludes with a logic-based pitch for "why" customers should buy them. These rational appeals highlight product features and competitive prices. Yet, they rarely go viral and generate breakout sales. It's too easy for customers, thinking rationally, to switch products.

Simon Sinek, the author of *Start with Why*, describes conventional marketing as "outside in." This means starting with "What" the company is offering and "How" its product or service will make things better for the customer. For the marketer, "Why" the offering matters to customers is often little more than window dressing or an afterthought.

Sinek believes the best marketing starts with "Why" at its center and moves out to connect with "How" and "What." Human beings are hardwired to respond to appeals grounded in purpose, trust, belief, and stories. The "Why" matters to people. It connects the brand to what they think, believe, want, and desire. The brand becomes an extension of their self-image.

In a widely viewed TED Talk, Sinek uses Apple to highlight the power of "inside-out" appeals that generate intense brand love. In reality, Apple is one electronics manufacturer among many competing for global market share. Conventional marketing would showcase images of Apple's computers (the What) and highlight their elegant design, integrated operating system, and ease of use (the How) before making the Why sales pitch. Pretty boring.

Apple is anything but a conventional company. Apple's marketing starts with the Why and works outward. Apple wants to empower individuals to make the world a better place. Apple demonstrates this through its computers' elegant designs, integrated operating system, and ease of use. Same "How," different context. Customers respond and flock to buy Apple products.

During the 2015 holiday season, Apple ran the "Someday at Christmas" ad with singers Andra Day and Stevie Wonder to promote its latest iPad. Here's how iSpot.tv describes the ad:

Singer Andra Day joins the legendary Stevie Wonder to sing his classic 1967 holiday song "Someday at Christmas." Without a band, Wonder sets up his Apple computer to record both the piano he plays and the vocal track. As Day and Wonder sing together, their family plays games, makes crafts and spends time together. To bring the song to a close, the youngest member adds her voice to the mix and then the rest of the family joins in.[24]

My eyes teared up the first time I saw this ad. During the same holiday season, Microsoft ran nonstop ads for its competing Surface Pro tablet highlighting all its great new features. Total "What" advertising. Nobody cared.

In Sinek's words, people don't buy Apple for what Apple does. They buy Apple for why Apple does what it does. By using Apple products, customers align with Apple's values and project those values to the world. In so doing, customers begin to see themselves as they would like others to see them. Like all positive relationships, brand love increases self-esteem, confidence, and interconnectedness. It satisfies deeply human needs. People buy Apple products because Apple empowers individuals and enriches their lives. This enables premium pricing for commodity products.

Almost all advertising by health companies highlights great doctors, great technologies, and grateful patients. They feature the "what" and not the "why." It's hard to tell the companies apart. All health systems have great doctors, grateful patients, and believe in quality. That's not enough to differentiate and build true brand love.

Back at the consumerism conference, the 20 participating health systems detailed their early efforts to engage consumers. Their initiatives were basic and included call centers, consumer-facing apps, and focus groups. With spring training for baseball occurring nearby, many presenters described their consumerism strategies as "being in the early innings."

After the session, I joked with one of the J&J representatives that healthcare consumerism wasn't in the early innings, that it was still in spring training. Without missing a beat, he responded, "It's worse than that. They don't even know what game they're playing."

Imagine how great American healthcare could be if health systems adopted Simon Sinek's "start with why" philosophy and committed to making it an everyday reality. Brand love isn't clever. It reflects deep trust between companies and customers built over years of interactive, mutually beneficial experience.

Customers reward companies that meet their jobs-to-be-done, tailor services, and deliver on their promises. Delivering value to customers and exceeding customer expectations have pushed Amazon to the pinnacle of corporate success. All because their empowered buyers keep coming back to Amazon for more and more products and services.

THE BIG IDEA: PUTTING CUSTOMERS FIRST

This chapter began by profiling Walmart's healthcare strategies as both a customer and a seller of healthcare services. It ends by profiling Amazon, the digital retailer that is giving Walmart a run for its money. What both companies share is a relentless commitment to delivering value to customers.

Walmart became the retail juggernaut it is today by giving consumers more product choice, lower prices, and greater convenience. It pioneered big-box retailing, reinvented the supply chain, and gave customers exactly what they wanted. Amazon has challenged Walmart's retail supremacy by using digital platforms to give customers even greater choice and even greater convenience at exceptionally competitive prices.

> *The fox knows many things,*
> *but the hedgehog knows one big thing.*
> —Greek philosopher Archilochus, 700 BC

Amazon CEO Jeff Bezos is a classic "hedgehog" strategist. He runs his company according to one core principle: pursuing strategies that deliver value to customers no matter what. Every Amazon meeting contains an empty chair to represent the consumer. Bezos crystalizes Amazon's vision succinctly: "We've had three big ideas at Amazon that we've stuck with . . . Put the customer first. Invent. And be patient. They're the reasons we're successful."[25]

Amazon allows approved vendors to undercut its prices on its own website. Why? It generates better value for customers. Amazon will undercut these partner vendors if their profit margins become too high. Why? It generates better value for customers.

When Amazon entered the book publishing business, its worldview was both simple and devastating. The only irreplaceable components were authors and readers. Amazon's technology could diminish and even replace publishers, distributors, and bookstores. One by one, publishing's middlemen disappeared in multitudes.

Bezos wants Amazon to be the "earth's most customer-centric company." Amazon cultivates close and friendly relationships with its customers. Technology assists in personalizing services, but the culture of truly caring for customers has taken decades to nurture and grow. Consider the intimate way in which Bezos describes Amazon's customers:

> We see our customers as invited guests to a party, and we are the hosts. It's our job every day to make every important aspect of the customer experience a little bit better.

It's easy to love and trust the Amazon brand. Amazon delivers incredible value and overcorrects when it makes mistakes (which is rare). Imagine Amazon as an empowered buyer of health and healthcare services through its new partnership with Berkshire Hathaway and JP Morgan. Now magnify its impact as Amazon-like buying behaviors spread to other purchasers of healthcare services. It takes my breath away. It's a world turned upside down. It's revolutionary.

Empowered buyers with new full-risk payment models change everything in healthcare, and they should. Healthcare is deeply personal, intimate, essential, and sometimes scary. Consumers want to love and trust health companies. They want to believe payers and providers are on their side, acting in their best interest. With greater freedom to select health companies, consumers will gravitate to those that fulfill their jobs-to-be-done, make them feel special, and return their trust in equal or greater measure. Demand-driven change leads to Revolutionary Healthcare.

CHAPTER 6

Liberated Data

Combining big data with human savvy and know-how is a powerful engine for gaining new insights and advancing human betterment. The capture of a stone-cold killer illustrates the point.

From 1974 to 1986, an unknown assailant dubbed "The Golden State Killer" roamed northern California committing heinous crimes. They included 13 murders, 50 rapes, and at least 100 break-ins. He was careful but sadistic, sometimes calling rape victims to say he was coming back to kill them. It took investigators decades, some luck, and breakthrough DNA forensics to identify and capture the elusive predator. DNA forensics is now a validated, accessible source of data that exponentially advances law enforcement's capabilities.

More than 30 years after the trail went cold, a retiring Sacramento police detective decided to look into the investigation one last time. Using the Golden State Killer's DNA, the detective submitted a fake ancestry request to GEDmatch, an open-source genomics website that helps researchers and genealogists identify potential relatives.

GEDmatch operates out of the small bungalow home of octogenarian Curtis Rogers, a retired Quaker Oats executive with a profound interest in genealogy. The database stores over a million DNA profiles. It leverages Google Cloud Platform's massive computing power to search for genetic matches.

After receiving their GEDmatch report, the Sacramento police hired a forensic genetic genealogist, CeCe Moore, to use that information to identify potential suspects. From partial family matches, Moore began building a family tree. She augmented genetic matches with publicly available information including obituaries, marriage licenses, and even Facebook accounts to refine her search. Before long, Moore had her man.

On April 25, 2018, the Sacramento district attorney announced the arrest of James Joseph DeAngelo for crimes committed as the Golden State Killer. It turned out DeAngelo had been hiding in plain sight all along. A 72-year old former police officer, he was arrested by authorities at his suburban Sacramento home, where he lived with his daughter and granddaughter.[1]

Since then, police departments across America have made at least a dozen more cold-case arrests using genealogy data. Hundreds more cases await follow-up.

When combined with forensics, genetic genealogy is a powerful application of big data.

Big data's big potential emanates from its remarkable ability to collect, curate, and analyze massive quantities of information quickly and efficiently. In doing so, it propels human problem-solving skills to a higher level. Big data's expansive applications are helping to solve numerous health and healthcare mysteries that once seemed beyond human capabilities.

For instance, Carrot Health, a rising healthcare start-up based in Minneapolis, Minnesota, can assess and predict the health status of existing populations by analyzing publicly available data from multiple providers. Carrot's analytics engine taps over 70 different sources to gather the consumer data of 250 million identified US adults. It organizes this data with the help of 5,000 different consumer variables such as demographics, purchasing habits, and lifestyles.

Combined with clinical data, Carrot develops very precise health profiles for specific individuals, including the propensity to develop diabetes and to follow prescribed treatment plans. Carrot's predictions assist integrated health companies that are managing the care of large populations. Better data and better data analytics lead to earlier and more effective interventions, preventing acute episodes, enhancing medication adherence, addressing social determinants, and improving health.

This is an era of unprecedented data capture. The world creates 2.5 quintillion bytes of data daily. I have no idea how much this is, but it's enormous and growing exponentially. Google's search engine processes 40,000 searches every second.[2] Finding "signals" within the noise is daunting. Information at such scale is not comprehensible without sophisticated technology.

Healthcare generates more data than any other industry. Only by leveraging artificial intelligence (AI), machine learning (ML), and natural language processing (NLP) tools can healthcare collect, curate, and analyze massive data sets. That data and its analysis can improve care delivery, streamline administrative tasks, and deliver insights that lead to new and better medicines, diagnostics, treatments, and interventions.

Unfortunately, this vision of data-enhanced delivery and discovery remains aspirational. As an industry, healthcare lags behind other industries in understanding and applying big data's performance and insight-generating capabilities. This is partly a function of the industry's scale and complexity. More concerning, however, is healthcare's historic tendency to silo data within closed systems that prevent effective access and sharing. Such hoarding stifles knowledge flows, blocks care coordination, and impedes innovation. Data must flow freely to generate breakthrough insights.

Not surprisingly, the System's data architects build data systems and infrastructure that enhance billing and maximize revenue collection. Serving consumers, optimizing care outcome, and managing expenses are secondary considerations. Most health companies employ "moated" data architecture because it tightens their grip on patients, clinicians, and revenue capture. The System, as always, looks after itself.

James Hereford, CEO of Fairview Health System in Minnesota (a large system with 12 hospitals and medical centers, and nine emergency departments), understands the value of liberated data and the downsides of keeping it fragmented and inaccessible inside data silos. He emphasized this point in a January 2018 speech where he described relatively closed-system EHRs as "one of the biggest impediments to innovation in healthcare." He then called on health company executives to "March on Madison" (Wisconsin), the home of the leading EHR company in the United States, Epic Systems Corp.[3]

Health systems operate like medieval data monasteries, their libraries filled with inaccessible tomes of knowledge. Visionaries like Hereford are storming the castle walls armed with the keys to unlock the imprisoned data. Like Gutenberg's invention of the printing press in 1440, analytic innovation is liberating data and advancing knowledge. This movement is at the leading edge of a healthcare renaissance and essential to Revolutionary Healthcare.

Today, those monastery walls are splintering as liberated data breaks free. The sweet combination of apps, services, tools, and digital mobility that has transformed every other consumer industry is turning its attention to healthcare.

Healthcare is complex. Big data and digital technologies are not magic. They cannot automatically transform care delivery. Big data works best when combined with human judgment and understanding.

The best organizations develop IT systems and workflows that combine high-touch attention with analytic power to improve protocols, enhance insights, and boost performance.

Feisty start-ups like Carrot Health and large innovators like Optum Health are demonstrating big data's potential in healthcare. New industry entrants like Amazon, Apple, and Google are bringing their data muscle and minds to healthcare. They see opportunity in data liberation. Patients, increasingly frustrated by healthcare's digital density, want efficient, personalized, and accessible apps and services to manage their health and healthcare jobs-to-be-done. The customer revolution in healthcare runs on liberated big data.

DATA WOES: WHY EVERYONE HATES ELECTRONIC HEALTH RECORDS (EHRS)

Waiting for What Exactly?

A few years ago, Kathy began to experience sharp abdominal pains. Kathy is not a "complainer," so everyone at home took this pain very seriously. Her husband Chris accompanied her to the emergency department (ED) at the local trauma center known for its exceptional healthcare. Later, Chris wrote to tell me about their experience.

The ED was three blocks from their house. The health system was part of the network offered by Kathy's health plan. In other words, she was a regular or, at least, a known "consumer" in its system of clinics, hospitals, and trauma centers. Upon arrival, Kathy and Chris went through a typical gauntlet of healthcare data collection. ED personnel carefully recorded her personal and health information into their centralized EHR system, capturing all necessary information for subsequent billing and clinical treatment.

This was an exceptionally time-consuming and frustrating experience. Kathy gave her name, address, gender, contact person, insurance coverage, current medications, general practitioner, description of pain, current diet, smoking or drinking habits, weight (and so on and so on) multiple times to different individuals.

Most of Kathy's information was already in the system. Noting Kathy's discomfort, Chris tried to speed up the intake process, but to no avail. They continued to follow the ED's painstaking digital input procedures.

Sitting in the ED waiting room for the next hour, Chris noticed the diversity of the patients and families also waiting. At least half were Somali/Ethiopian or Hmong, two major immigrant groups in their region. Most of the rest appeared to be poor. Even as a theologian, minister, and former college president, Chris found the intake procedure confusing, frustrating, and stressful, as did Kathy, the patient in pain, who has a PhD in marketing. They both have a significant amount of experience dealing with the healthcare system supporting one of their son's chronic illness. How could these other patients and families possibly manage, especially if English wasn't their first language? There were few real "emergencies" among the patients gathered in the ED. Instead, poverty, language barriers, and cultural norms had driven these people to seek expensive, depersonalized emergency care. They had no reasonable alternatives.

After an hour, an RN, a PA, and then a doctor visited Kathy in succession. Each clinician asked many of the same questions and reentered the same information into the EHR. When a doctor finally arrived, he took Kathy's blood pressure, probed her abdomen, and ordered a CT scan. It took time to arrange the CT scan and even more time for another doctor to interpret the test results. The doctors had no answers. Their examinations and Kathy's tests showed nothing abnormal. They suggested that she should rest and follow up with her primary care physician to discuss getting a colonoscopy.

Kathy's abdominal pain persisted, so she followed up with her primary care physician (PCP), who asked if the ED physician had mentioned the 16-millimeter cyst on her liver. No. The PCP referred Kathy to a radiologist, who recommended draining the cyst. Having researched that type of cyst, Kathy asked if draining was the right approach because there's a high probability of them reoccurring after draining. The radiologist said not to worry.

Five months later, the pain reoccurred. Kathy went to her primary care physician, who thought Kathy was having a heart attack. But her ECG and stress test results were normal. The physician suggested panic attack, prescribed anxiety medication, and sent Kathy for a third heart test—a CT angiogram. Kathy asked the cardiologist to check to see if the liver cyst had returned, and it had. Kathy had herself suggested the correct diagnosis—the liver cyst—after thousands of dollars of tests. The physicians trying to diagnose and treat Kathy never had the needed information.

Kathy spent three more months fighting with her "gold" insurance plan to get the recommended surgery from the right specialty surgeon since there wasn't one in-network. She even had to talk to the chief medical officer at her insurance company. Nine months after the first visit to the emergency department, Kathy had the procedure, with the hepatobiliary surgeon, and her insurance paid.

"Technology is great!" Chris wrote to me. "But does data make a difference? Is it readily available? Do practitioners make good use of the information already in their system? Do they have the time, expertise, and willingness to evaluate data in the light of the real-life situation of the person sitting in front of them?"

Chris went on to ask other questions. He wondered how technology benefited the culturally, economically, and linguistically diverse individuals waiting in the ED. Would it make their experience of care better or worse? What good is digital health data, let alone artificial intelligence or machine learning, if they fail to support patients and clinicians or, even worse, build barriers between them?

Chris's conclusion was this:

> My experience with Kathy . . . . tells me that we have a long way, a very long way to go before data-driven medical technology is actually workable, no less effective for the average poor soul in the average ED waiting room.

Even as digital IT and AI marvel the medical world with their potential, Chris's words and Kathy's experiences are sobering reminders of how repetitive, limiting, and unresponsive healthcare data collection and application are to meeting consumers' in-the-moment needs.

Clinicians—the World's Highest-Paid Data Entry Clerks

On the other side of that digital divide, clinicians, especially doctors, suffer as much or even more frustration and stress with EHRs. Dr. Atul Gawande chronicled this experience in a November 2018 *New Yorker* article titled "Why Doctors Hate Their Computers."[4] Gawande works as a surgeon in the Partners HealthCare system in Boston and is a prolific writer and the new CEO of the Amazon–Berkshire Hathaway–JP Morgan health company. When he speaks, healthcare listens.

In his article, Gawande described a 16-hour mandatory training program to prepare physicians for Partner's adoption of the Epic Electronic Medical Record system. According to Gawande, installing the Epic EHR systemwide will cost Partners $1.6 billion, most of which is lost productivity while Partners' 70,000 employees learn how to use the software.

Gawande was among the first people through the training. The training was boring, arduous, frustrating, and often confusing, but Gawande expected it would at least lead to higher productivity, timely access to patient information, and better overall care.

Three years later, he felt the new system had failed to deliver on any of these promises. Worse, it had turned him and his colleagues into data entry clerks. Instead of engaging patients, doctors toiled away on their computers. This diminished patient connection, compromised clinician effectiveness, and intensified stress.

American academic John Culkin observed, "We shape our tools, and thereafter our tools shape us." For Gawande and his colleagues data compilation and exchange became a grinding chore, often one with indecipherable logic to its operation. Gawande observed that clinicians became more disconnected from one other because of these individualized and time-consuming tasks. While patients may ultimately benefit from easier access to records and information, clinicians operate and suffer like workers assembling Model T Fords in the early 1900s. No wonder clinicians are burning out in record numbers.

Data Shackles

In many industries, new technologies automate and improve workflows. In healthcare, new technologies make care delivery more expensive. According to The Hastings Center, new medical technologies and intensified use of existing technologies are responsible for 40 to 50 percent of the annual increase in care costs.[5]

The first rule of performance improvement is to fix systems before automating them. Healthcare organizations ignored this wisdom. Instead, the industry spent tens of billions, most of it government funded, automating a broken, fragmented system. EHR companies profited enormously but failed to transform healthcare delivery. Rather than streamlining and improving information access, EHRs frustrate patients (like Kathy and Chris) and providers (like Gawande), even after full implementation.

In many respects, the nation's investment in EHRs has backfired. A 2019 investigative report, "Death by a Thousand Clicks: Where Electronic Medical Records Went Wrong," by Kaiser Health News and *Fortune* magazine chronicles a litany of unintended consequences related to EHR adoption.[6] These include upcoding, a flood of false alarms, physician burnout, medical errors, blocked data access, gag clauses, and patient harm. Some of the report's findings are truly alarming:

- Based on extensive interviews, KHN/*Fortune* conclude that EHR implementation has been "a tragic missed opportunity. Rather than an electronic ecosystem of information, the nation's thousands of EHRs largely remain a sprawling, disconnected patchwork . . . that has handcuffed health providers to technology they mostly can't stand."

- Twenty-one percent of people surveyed by the Kaiser Family Foundation found mistakes in their EHR.

- Safety-related incidents related to EHRs and other IT systems are skyrocketing.

- An ED doctor makes roughly 4,000 computer clicks over the course of a single shift. This labor-intensive data-entry process invites error and causes physician burnout.

- Alarms, including voluminous false alarms, account for 85 to 99 percent of EHR and medical device alerts.

Despite the nation's investment in EHRs, healthcare data has become even more siloed, stifled, retrospective, and confined to checkboxes and dropdowns. These limitations contribute to suboptimal care, burdensome workarounds, and enormous financial waste.

Patients suffer. A Johns Hopkins study in 2016 calculated that from 250,000 to 400,000 deaths annually result from medical errors.[7] Data systems play a role in many of those deaths. Patient adverse events (PAEs) result from errors in communications and diagnoses orchestrated within EHRs.

Medication errors are commonplace, caused by computerized physician order entry (CPOE) mistakes and flawed EHR documentation. Almost 70 percent of data-related mistakes influence patient care.

Clinicians suffer. On average, physicians spend half of their workday entering data into EHRs and conducting clerical work and spend just 27 percent of their workday with patients.[8] Frontline caregivers operate within a data fog. There's plenty of good data, but it's not curated, accessible, or prescriptive. Caregivers suffer from alert fatigue caused by cognitive overload and the high number of false alarms. To clear the fog, clinicians default to time-consuming workarounds that are ad hoc, haphazard, and error prone.

Closed data systems have hijacked clinician workflow, pulled them away from bedsides, and contributed to burnout. A 2017 Medscape survey stated that 51 percent of physicians report experiencing frequent or constant feelings of burnout in 2017, up from 40 percent in 2013. Fifty-six percent of physicians blame documentation for that burnout, and 24 percent blame it on increased computerization working with EHRs.[9]

With limited options, health systems contract with powerful electronic health record providers at enormous cost and underwhelming results. However both health systems and EHR companies benefit from reduced interoperability. Controlling patient data creates market power. A 2014 RAND study suggests that EHR companies and large health systems find solace and profits in interoperability:

> The shift [to interoperability] will be less welcome to large legacy vendors because it will blur the competitive edge they currently enjoy. Health care systems may be less-than-enthusiastic adopters because functional health information exchanges will make it easier for patients to see non-affiliated healthcare providers or switch to a competing health care system.

Data oligarchs not only restrict data flow, they stifle rather than cultivate innovative technology companies. They insist on incremental improvement to archaic platforms rather than creation of new, more powerful and user-friendly platform technologies.

For example, many EHR vendors use their licensing agreements to solidify their control of source code and data. They consider their source data proprietary and will not allow third parties to access it without their permission. Carefully worded legal agreements prevent health companies from commercializing innovative applications. Data sharing, to the extent it occurs, is one way (into, not out of, the EHR). Efforts to stimulate app development are equally one-sided.

Accessing source data is an epic challenge for third-party app developers. Pun intended. No EHR vendor facilitates seamless access, but Epic is the most zealous in controlling and blocking its source data. In many interviews, Epic founder and CEO Judy Falkner described the company's mission as "Do good, have fun and make money."[10] It's certainly worked for Faulkner. With a net worth of $3.5 billion, she is America's third richest self-made woman.[11] This is the oligarchs' prerogative. They control the factors of production and generate enormous profits. They will continue until forced to stop.

KNOWLEDGE STOCKS AND FLOWS

In a high-functioning, integrated healthcare ecosystem, big data will flow into knowledge networks that standardize, monitor, and enhance care protocols. Clinicians will navigate voluminous data flows in an intuitive way, like we all experience as consumers. Clinicians and consumers will have sufficient time together to make better medical decisions. Consumers and clinicians will engage. Outcomes will improve. Costs will drop. Achieving this desired level of knowledge exchange and shared decision making requires new ways of thinking about data and knowledge flows in the healthcare ecosystem.

Historically, professionals gained market power by stockpiling knowledge, protecting it, and renting it to others (think doctors, lawyers, accountants, and consultants). That approach to professional services is no longer sustainable. Knowledge creation is occurring at an accelerating rate, so existing knowledge depreciates very quickly. For example, medical knowledge will double every 73 days by 2020 (see Figure 6.1).[12] As a consequence, no professional can keep current, and engaging in knowledge exchange is vital to innovation and professional development.[13]

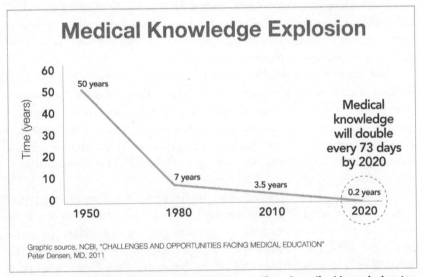

FIGURE 6.1 In 1950, it took 50 years for the totality of medical knowledge to double. In 2020, it will double every 73 days.

Likewise, professional expertise is fast becoming an artifact of another era. It is easy to find and inexpensive to access. Application of expertise within a specific context is valuable in today's increasingly interconnected, dynamic, nonstop, and inherently collaborative working environments. Product life cycles are short. New demands for value-driven services are frequent, and customers are impatient for results. In this brave new information age, data must be free and available for knowledge workers to inform, discover, and create. Those who excel in this environment let go of data control and embrace knowledge flow.

Today's healthcare consumers already participate in knowledge flows. They want more "data liquidity" in their lives, not less. The Healthcare Information and Management Systems Society (HIMSS) holds an annual conference, and in 2018 Accenture released its annual consumer survey on digital health trends.[14] Consumer acceptance of digital technologies is broad based and accelerating as these findings illustrate:

- Use of wearable devices quadrupled between 2014 and 2018 (from 9 percent to 33 percent).

- Use of digital health apps tripled during the same time (from 16 percent to 48 percent).

- Consumers increasingly access their digital health records when their providers give them access, particularly to review lab test results and physician notes.

- Consumers show almost universal willingness (88–90 percent) to share personal data with their healthcare professionals.

- Consumers show more willingness to share personal data with insurance companies (72 percent) and online communities (47 percent) than with government agencies (41 percent) and employers (38 percent).

- Consumers have high satisfaction (74 percent) with virtual care.

- Nearly half of consumers (47 percent) prefer immediate virtual care to delayed in-person care, expressing appreciation for virtual care's convenience and low costs.

- Consumers are accepting of and willing to receive artificial intelligence–related healthcare services.

If the survey swapped the word "consumer" with the word "clinician," I suspect these poll numbers would be similar or higher. Consumers and doctors are human beings, working with great data capabilities in most of their lives. However, they're lost within a healthcare data machine. As scientists, doctors know that current technologies are inadequate. It's time to "think different" and build better ways to collect, curate, and analyze data so Revolutionary Healthcare can achieve its potential.

DATA IS AS DATA DOES

Data does not exist in isolation. It is the middle layer of a three-part integrated hierarchy. Healthcare data flows to and from this middle tier to inform value-based operations (the bottom tier) and fully engaged customers (the top tier). Figure 6.2 captures these flows.

FIGURE 6.2 **Free-flowing big data is essential for customer engagement and value-based care delivery.**

Revolutionary healthcare organizations use data to generate consistent high-quality outcomes, reduce performance variation, and improve operational efficiency. Data inputs flow to and from operations to improve care design and empower care delivery.

At the individual patient level, all relevant data from all sources flows into algorithms that will enable caregivers to optimize diagnosis and treatment. As data proliferates and analytics advance, individual genetic and environmental characteristics will lead to more personalized and less population-based therapies, more precision and less trial-and-error care. Moreover, pricing and outcomes data will be transparent and available to clinicians and consumers.

At the individual disease level, all relevant information from all sources will flow into data systems for analysis that can advance medical research and protocol development.

Unfortunately, getting the medical treatments "right" will not be sufficient to "win." Health companies also must engage consumers to gain their trust, confidence, and loyalty. Fully engaging consumers requires a deep understanding of their needs. Revolutionary Healthcare companies listen and respond to customer preferences. They deliver appropriate, user-friendly healthcare services with transparent prices that are unique, personalized, and seamless. They create value, not friction. None of this should surprise. Consumer purchases drive 70 percent of the US economy. Companies succeed and fail based on their ability to read and respond to consumer sentiments.

Consumer-oriented companies spend billions of dollars on polling, focus groups, test marketing, and behavioral and purchase analysis to enhance their product offerings. Companies can't tell consumers what to do, companies must persuade. However, leading through persuasion is antithetical to most healthcare company cultures, where clinicians have unequal relationships with consumers and dominate medical decision making.

Big data analytics are essential for understanding consumer preferences. Collecting, measuring, and evaluating consumer data drives strategic growth and customer acquisition. Companies use big data to design appealing products and services.

Data wants to be free and flow to where it provides the most value. Healthcare has to overcome legacy IT systems to unlock data's transformative power. This will require the replacement of billing-centric EHRs run by data oligarchs. They impede progress to maintain their market control and generate outsized profits.

TURBOCHARGED TECHNOLOGIES

Kaveh Safavi, MD, manages Accenture's global healthcare practice. During dinner several years ago, Kaveh remarked that he was going to use LinkedIn for managing his contact information. Great idea. That way individuals keeping their own information current in LinkedIn would flow to Kaveh. Trouble is not everyone keeps their LinkedIn contact information current and accessible—but imagine if they did. The time-consuming task of managing contacts would disappear. Welcome to the cloud-based world of prepopulated data sets with real-time updates and no duplications or errors!

That world is at our fingertips and already operating at the Joint Commission (JC). Accreditation is necessary for hospitals and other care facilities to receive payment from Medicare and Medicaid. The Joint Commission is an independent, nonprofit organization that accredits and certifies nearly 21,000 US-based healthcare organizations. It also accredits international healthcare organizations. In 2017, the Joint Commission selected Apervita, a Chicago-based healthcare technology company, to automate and streamline its accreditation process for the nation's hospitals.[15]

Formerly, hospital accreditation was a costly, manual, labor-intensive, many-months-long process for hospitals. Internally, the Joint Commission needed dozens of consultants to manage its review and approval processes. The Joint Commission now uses Apervita's cloud platform to manage the accreditation process, with hospitals submitting their quality data with the click of a button, optimizing time savings and removing cost in the process.[16] With an automated process and without intermediaries, the Joint Commission is more connected to its hospitals, hospitals can get insights into quality performance while care is happening, and both hospitals and the Joint Commission save money and resources. In the course of one year, the Joint Commission onboarded thousands of hospitals and completely transformed the process.

The Platform-as-a-Service (PaaS) technology makes it easy for hospitals to populate necessary data from multiple sources into accreditation reports for submission. Importantly, hospitals can better triage and diagnose data and quality challenges in real time, allowing them to continuously improve performance prior to submission. After 30 years of a paper-based submission process, the shift to PaaS has been transformational for the Joint Commission and its accredited hospitals.

Apervita's cloud platform incorporates the scale, efficiencies, and security of Amazon Web Services (AWS) technology, Amazon's wildly successful cloud-computing service. Healthcare's near-term data future is in the cloud. Software systems designed for cloud-based applications are faster, more elegant, more secure, can be updated more rapidly, and are more powerful than software solutions that run through data warehouses, which are harder to scale up and down with demand. With enhanced computational power, cloud-based solutions accommodate artificial intelligence (AI) capabilities and machine learning (ML) advances and natural language processing (NLP), which turbocharge data curation and analytics for rapid insights.

It was cloud-based analytics that generated the genetic matching data that led to the Golden State Killer's capture and arrest.

For Whom Bell's Law Now Tolls

Technology solutions should make organizational management easier, cheaper, and better like Apervita's technology is doing for the Joint Commission. In this way, cloud-based technologies are a "force multiplier" for Revolutionary Healthcare. They help health companies get the right data to the right people in real time with useful guidance that improves outcomes. Hallelujah. Healthcare desperately needs this boost, so Chris and Kathy no longer linger in ED waiting rooms with other unfortunate souls waiting for the System to get its act together.

- **Moore's law** is the theory made by Intel cofounder Gordon Moore that the number of transistors on a chip doubles every 18 months while the costs are halved.[17] Moore's law predicts that this trend of growth in computer capabilities will continue into the foreseeable future.
- **Nielsen's law** is the theory by Jakob Nielsen that posits high-end users' bandwidth grows by 50 percent per year, which fits data from 1983 to 2018.[18]
- **Bell's law** is the theory formulated by Gordon Bell in 1972 that describes how types of computing systems form, evolve, and often die out. Bell considered the law a partial corollary to Moore's law.[19]

Moore's law, the doubling of computer power every 18 months or 60 percent annually, powers technological innovation. Nielsen's law finds that bandwidth (i.e., connection speed) doubles every two years. Together, they govern the speed and power of software-based technology solutions.

Fewer people are familiar with Bell's law, the most interesting Internet theory of the three. Formulated in 1972, Bell's law holds that data ecosystems require an entirely new architecture roughly every 10 years to accommodate new programming environments and applications that exploit increasing computational power and speed.

In the 1960s, mainframe computing dominated. In the 1970s, minicomputers emerged. In the 1980s, the personal computer and local-area networks proliferated. In the 1990s, Internet-driven browsers on wide-area networks (WANs) with centralized data warehouses (CDWs) came to the fore. In the 2000s, smartphones emerged along with cloud computing. Businesses shifted from data warehouses to centralized servers ("the cloud") hosted by technology companies, including Amazon, Microsoft, and Google. Today, the consumer and general business world is on the brink of another shift in the data architecture paradigm with the emergence of blockchain.

Healthcare is playing catch-up. The industry still operates largely via 1990s-era data warehouses that silo information, communicate poorly, and are susceptible to data breaches. Electronic health record (EHR) and enterprise resource planning (ERP) systems and even revenue cycle platforms rely on data warehouses to collect, curate, and analyze data. An entire sector of the healthcare economy devotes itself to physically scanning and digitizing paper health records and images. As recently as 2016, analysts estimated that 85 percent of hospitals still used pagers. Drug dealers don't even use beepers anymore. Healthcare is keeping the beeper/pager industry alive almost single-handedly.

Riding the Cloud

As the Joint Commission case study illustrated, healthcare is finally migrating into cloud-based technology solutions. Cloud computing places data, software, and applications in secure files within massive "farms" of interconnected computers. All computational activity occurs through the Internet.

Moving into the cloud frees health companies from owning and managing the physical hardware and networking components necessary to run data warehouses. With cloud-based platforms, access to data is faster, easier, more convenient, and secure. Data is always up to date, and software upgrades automatically. Platform capacity scales up or back depending on need. Data is more secure because host companies, like Amazon Web Services (AWS), employ industry best practices to protect it.

Beyond the Cloud to Blockchain

Still several years away from widespread adoption, blockchain will be the next computing system to emerge according to Bell's law. Cloud-based architecture is highly centralized, requires enormous energy to process data, and at some point will reach capacity growth.

Blockchain technology creates virtual ledgers that record transactions in a transparent, decentralized, and public way. Essentially, blockchain enables parties to execute transactions without intermediaries. Cryptocurrencies, like Bitcoin, were the first applications of blockchain technology, but the technology has almost unlimited application for secure monetary and nonmonetary transactions. Unlike cloud-based technologies that store data centrally, blockchain distributes data throughout any and all connected devices.

Blockchain's decentralized and distributed operating technology creates a permanent transaction documentation that is tamper-proof, verifiable, and accessible. This preserves historical truth, reduces fraud, and eliminates middlemen. Bitcoin was once considered a shady tool of the dark web, suitable only for criminal transactions. Today, Bitcoin and hundreds of other cryptocurrencies have gone mainstream and now trade openly. The market capitalization for the top 100 cryptocurrencies on December 18, 2018, was $114,976,009,856 as tracked by coinmarketcap.com.[20]

Beyond cryptocurrencies, individuals and companies are finding multiple uses for blockchain technologies. Pharmaceutical companies are using blockchain technologies to secure their manufacture and distribution of drugs, preventing stolen or counterfeit drugs from entering the supply chain.[21] Webjet uses blockchain to arrange and coordinate travel plans for customers, eliminating the need for manual intervention.[22] Walmart uses blockchain to identify where products break within its supply chain and to guarantee food safety.[23] From these examples, it's easy to see how blockchain technologies will solve healthcare problems related to patient privacy, care documentation, supply chain integrity, and data exchange.

Humana, Optum, Quest Diagnostics, and others are teaming up in a pilot project to use blockchain to share data. The blockchain pilot enables participants to share the same, completed data records in real time.[24] As Lorraine Frias and Mike Jacobs from Optum explain in a *Modern Healthcare* commentary:

> Blockchain can potentially assemble every detail related to healthcare for a consumer. We'll know if a customer had a tetanus shot at a retail health clinic and the serial number of his knee replacement prosthesis.[25]

With permission on the blockchain, clinicians will have access to consumers' complete medical records from all locations. Those records will be secure, accurate, historical, and up-to-date. Blockchain can and will incorporate data from non–health system sources such as wearables. Every piece of data will be time-stamped and unalterable, preventing fraud. As Jill Frew of Cain Brothers writes,

> While we are just beginning to understand blockchain's impact on the healthcare industry, its potential should not be underestimated. In the next five-to-10 years, patient consent and data exchange backed by blockchain could fundamentally alter the way healthcare services are provided by making patient longitudinal data readily available and opening the door to new treatments, new care delivery models and better coordination of care.[26]

This is the holy grail for liberating and securing health data. Revolutionary Healthcare companies will break down the silos shackling data and use liberated data to break down the System's competitive barriers to deliver the right care at the right time in the right place at the right price.

Healthcare operating environments are dynamic and complex. Technologies in isolation cannot solve organizational challenges. Blockchain is largely in the future. Back in present time, healthcare needs organizational systems that enable frontline professionals to make the right decisions and take the right actions in real time. Technology and people together drive innovation and progress. For insights on enhancing human performance, we go back to 2004. The second war in Iraq was raging, and a new general arrived to take command and introduced the "team of teams" operating paradigm to manage war in the digital age.

LESSONS FROM IRAQ TO HEALTHCARE'S FRONTLINES[27]

The teams were operating independently—like workers in an efficient factory—while trying to keep pace with an interdependent environment. We all knew intuitively that intelligence gathered on AQI's [Al Qaeda in Iraq] communications and operations would almost certainly impact what our operators saw on the battlefield, and that battlefield details would almost certainly represent valuable context for intel analysis, but those elements of our organization were not communicating with each other.
—General Stanley McChrystal from *Team of Teams*

By 2004, Al Qaeda in Iraq (AQI) was routinely defeating US forces on the battlefield by employing asymmetric hit-and-run tactics that distributed command control and placed a premium on speed. Networked and nonhierarchical, AQI was a new, formidable type of enemy. Recently appointed commander General Stanley McChrystal knew doubling down on current strategies would not reverse the tide. It was time to think differently.

McChrystal discovered the hard way that central command leaders consistently made the wrong tactical decisions because they lacked real-time information and situational context. Data about AQI moved through military intelligence more slowly than the enemy moved in the field. Traditional command-centric management models focus on planning and prediction. Using this reductionist management model, the military was unable to respond effectively within an increasingly complex and unpredictable environment.

McChrystal realized that he needed a new command structure to respond effectively to the AQI threat. US forces needed to organize and act with adaptability and resilience to succeed on the field of battle. His success in creating a flat, adaptable, resilient command structure turned the tide in Iraq.

The same combinations of complex and dynamic operating conditions hamper the effectiveness of frontline caregivers in US health systems (Figure 6.3). They lack real-time data and authority to optimize care decision making and outcomes. The military's lessons learned in Iraq have direct applications to US hospitals.

US healthcare has the best-trained clinicians, the best equipment, and the best facilities in the world, but it operates inefficiently, makes

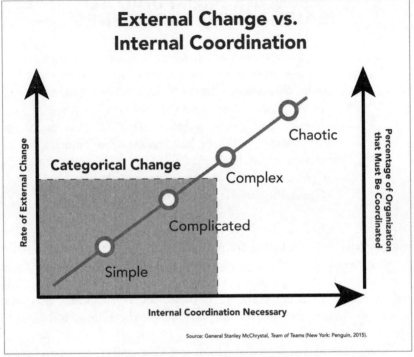

FIGURE 6.3 As situations become more complex and dynamic, organizations require new architecture to coordinate and act in real time.

too many mistakes, frustrates patients, and exhausts frontline personnel. This underperformance occurs despite hospitals having the necessary components of highly efficient and reliable organizations. These include digitized medical records, gigantic data warehouses, elaborate protocols, and centralized performance monitoring.

Like the US military in Iraq circa 2004, the US healthcare system is failing, and it is failing for the same reasons. Outdated management theory is responsible. The industrial age's primary managerial goal was achieving efficiency at scale. Management systems built to optimize efficiency systematically plan for predictable actions and processes. While hospital operating dynamics have become more complex, healthcare's managerial models have not adapted to the increased operating complexity.

Health systems and their leaders require new organizational architecture to manage complex hospital operations. Fortunately, the military has developed high-performing management models for complex environments and has pressure-tested them on the front lines.

Building Organizational Adaptability and Resilience Amid Chaos

In *Team of Teams*, McChrystal identifies three core lessons required for achieving success in dynamic environments.

Lesson #1: Shift from a "Command of Teams" to a "Team of Teams" Model

McChrystal realized AQI's command structure was not hierarchical. It consisted of a dispersed network of connected groups that shared a common purpose and exchanged extensive information. In contrast, US forces used a central command center to control operations. The high quantity and velocity of information overwhelmed central command and limited its ability to guide frontline personnel.

McChrystal's solution was to create a "Team of Teams," an organizing model where the operating dynamics of effective teams replicate themselves throughout the entire organization. Teams that previously operated in silos came together as one with a single "shared consciousness." In essence, he created a network to defeat a network.

Across health systems today, formal and informal teams must navigate through increasingly complex operating environments to make effective decisions in real time. Current management systems fail to develop the trust and information sharing required for teams to solve dynamic problems. Frontline caregivers undertake heroic actions to overcome legacy systems so patients get the services they require.

Healthcare's team of teams cannot function until organizational architecture equips them with the information they require and the authority to use it in real time.

Lesson #2: Arm Frontline Teams with Decision-Critical, System-Level Information

McChrystal realized that frontline teams needed faster access to information to make the right operational decisions. Task Force members needed to operate within an interconnected and decentralized system, not through a centralized command structure (Figure 6.4). Information had to be transparent and available to all members. McChrystal's team assembled the Situational Awareness Room, a vaulted, heavily fortified chamber with large computer screens.

The Situational Awareness room supported information-sharing techniques proven to drive collaboration and performance. These

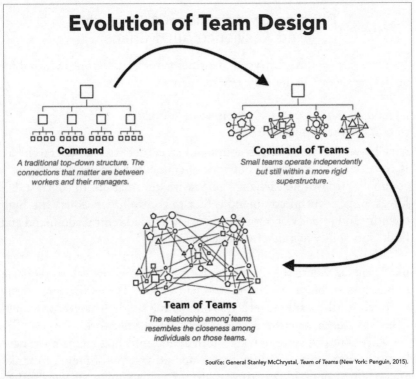

Evolution of Team Design

Command
A traditional top-down structure. The connections that matter are between workers and their managers.

Command of Teams
Small teams operate independently but still within a more rigid superstructure.

Team of Teams
The relationship among teams resembles the closeness among individuals on those teams.

Source: General Stanley McChrystal, *Team of Teams* (New York: Penguin, 2015).

FIGURE 6.4 Changing organizational management paradigm from command and control to team of teams

included the following: (1) face-to-face interaction; (2) direct peer-to-peer communication between teams, not channeled through a leader; and (3) opportunities for side conversations.

With this new communications system, McChrystal's teams could share the right amount of data and contextual information with each other to act in real time. McChrystal convened a 90-minute daily video conference at 9 a.m. to share vital information with all task force members, eventually 7,500 people around the globe.

Despite deep investments in technology, training, and improvement initiatives, health systems struggle to get real-time information to the decision makers on the front line when they need it to act. Centralized data systems (such as EHRs) bury decision-critical data. Moreover, the data itself is often raw and not easily understood. Sometimes it's not even collected. Most data is historical, not real time, which leads to retrospective analysis rather than present action.

Additionally, health systems with traditional command centers centralize decision making. These central command structures often fail to respond to real-time events. To be effective at the point of decision making, health systems need to relay real-time information to frontline staff so they can act with maximum effectiveness.

Lesson #3: Build Trust-Based Relationships Among Traditionally Siloed Teams

While shared information forms a common understanding of objectives between teams, McChrystal needed to create strong relationships between teams to improve system-level problem solving. Teams needed to understand one another's decision dynamics. With a shared consciousness and trust, teams could act independently with a sense of the whole mission. Their individual decisions advanced the overall mission, not just their component part.

McChrystal took a low-tech approach to building relationships and trust. He cross-fertilized teams and established liaison programs. Over time, the trust between individuals grew into trust between teams that, when paired with the common purpose, fostered unprecedented levels of cooperation.

For health systems desiring adaptive managerial architecture, real-time information and technology are not enough. Relationships matter, and trust binds teams together. For frontline staff to take system-level actions in real time, they need to trust that other teams are acting in concert to optimize systemwide performance, not individual-unit performance.

It Takes Teams of Teams to Deliver Great Healthcare

Just as the team-of-teams management model and infrastructure helped US forces in Iraq outmaneuver AQI, health systems can use this model to help frontline teams assess and solve problems in real time on their own authority.

Advanced, cloud-based technology and the team-of-teams organizational architecture give frontline teams the data, tools, trust, and authority to act constructively for patients. Managers and charge nurses get patients into the right beds with less friction. Discharges occur seamlessly. Emergency department diversions (when an ambulance has to take a patient to another ED because the intended ED is too busy) disappear.

Healthcare teams must do a thousand things right to prevent medical errors and deliver appropriate treatments (right care, right time, right place, right price). Coherent protocols, effective communications, real-time data, and understanding patient preferences are essential for success.

It's always hard to prove a negative. It took centuries to learn that handwashing prevents more deaths than brilliant surgical procedures. Defensive proficiency becomes evident by measuring relative team performance over time. This is true for avoided infections, prevented surgical procedures, and unnecessary diagnostic procedures.

Defensive success rests on constant, high-performing collective action. Enterprise participants coordinate, collaborate, and communicate to make correct decisions in real time. This is difficult but necessary in dynamic environments like operating rooms, trauma centers, intensive care units, ambulances, clinics, and patient bedsides.

These team-of-teams systems proactively identify bottlenecks where patients and providers wait for direction. They minimize error. They empower frontline staff. They optimize operational flow by balancing people, equipment, and facilities at capacity. They save lives.

KNOWLEDGE EXCHANGE
AND VALUE CREATION

On October 8, 2018, Paul Romer, an economist at New York University, received two phone calls at home. He didn't answer either because he thought they were spam calls. Turns out it was the Swedish Academy calling to inform Romer that he had just won the 2018 Nobel Prize in Economics.

During the 1990s, Romer published several pathbreaking papers that established how voluntary knowledge exchange expands human capital and societal productivity. Unlike products and services, knowledge flows do not have diminishing returns. Instead, ideas are "nonrival." Many people can use them.

As such, free knowledge exchange generates the ideas and innovation that foster growth. Scale and clusters are also important. Knowledge flows are more vigorous where talented people with similar interests concentrate. Think of the great hubs of innovation like Silicon Valley today and Detroit in the early 1900s.

Knowledge exchange is the elixir of the digital age. Ideas, information, and opinion spread like wildfire. Web-enabled education, connection, and communication amplify and compound the impact of knowledge exchange with good and bad effect. Blockchain enables students to transfer money out of repressive countries to fund their education. Terrorists in Iraq used technology to outfox elite US forces until McChrystal found a new way to combat them.

Healthcare's data silos impede participants from exchanging knowledge and advancing care, but here's the good news. The silos are cracking, and data is breaking free. Given its historic suppression, liberating healthcare data will have a disproportionate positive impact on service delivery, outcomes, and customer experience. Healthcare can replicate what other industries have already successfully implemented. Healthcare can avoid mistakes other industries have made.

Righteous exchange of liberated data is a force multiplier of awesome proportions. It is the tornado blowing Revolutionary Healthcare into every town, hamlet, and city in America.

CHAPTER 7

Pro-Market Regulation

Balanced and enlightened regulation are essential to the orderly function of societies. Without proper rules and enforcement, regular citizens are at the mercy of plutocrats, thieves, and scoundrels. But too much bureaucratic red tape creates overly zealous public control that suffocates ambition and innovation. Achieving the right balance takes time and requires wisdom. America has learned this lesson through hard experience. Today we take safe food for granted, but that hasn't always been the case.

After the Civil War, America became a modernizing industrial nation. Relentless innovation, surging immigration, restless urban migration, and fast-changing social mores transformed American society and its economy. Thomas Jefferson's pastoral vision of a nation of small farmers faded away. America was the world's fastest-growing, most dynamic nation, with brave new opportunities and grave new challenges.

Feeding the growing nation required a vast distribution network. Family farms became factory farms. Meat, dairy, and grain processing plants adopted industrial manufacturing processes. The Chicago stockyards introduced the assembly line to process beef. Relationships between sellers and buyers lost familiarity. Crooked producers and suppliers sold altered, fraudulent, and even toxic food at industrial scale.

The litany of abuses is horrifying to read today. Milk cut with formaldehyde. Lead used to color candy and cheese. Rancid beef tallow sold as butter. There was little regulatory infrastructure to oversee food production and distribution. Fortunately, Harvey Washington Wiley arrived at the recently created Department of Agriculture.

A country boy who served in the Civil War, Wiley became the first professor of chemistry at Purdue University in 1874. On behalf of the state of Indiana, Wiley tested commercial honey and maple syrup to determine its authenticity. Most of it was fake. His acumen as a food tester gained notice, and in 1882, the Department of Agriculture appointed Wiley to become its chief chemist. Wiley spent the next 30 years crusading for food safety and proper labeling. Though largely forgotten since, he is the hero of Deborah Blum's new book *The Poison Squad*.

The "Poison Squad" was a group of young men Wiley recruited to sample questionable food under scientific observation. Their motto: "Only the Brave Dare Eat the Fare." That fare often included common food additives like borax and formaldehyde.

Wiley knew his battle against harmful food handling and labeling practices was political as well as scientific. To counter the powerful, vindictive food industry, Wiley needed to shape public opinion. He turned the members of his Poison Squad into celebrities and heralded their courage in the press and in speeches, even as he attacked companies that poisoned Americans for profit.

Wiley's work contributed to the broader progressive movement led by President Theodore Roosevelt. Investigative journalists helped popularize the cause. Upton Sinclair's *The Jungle* riveted the nation's attention on food safety abuse. Sinclair had meant to shine a light on labor abuses at meatpacking plants, but it was the handling of food that roused a clamorous response. As Sinclair put it, "I aimed at the public's heart and by accident I hit it in the stomach."[1]

That public demanded action. This led to the Federal Meat Inspection and Pure Food and Drug (known as the Wiley Act) Acts in 1906. These new laws required accurate labeling of any addictive substances, including those in patent medicines, and established purity standards. Two decades later, the US government consolidated food and drug oversight under the Food and Drug Administration. The FDA's connection to Wiley's Poison Squad remains strong. Revelations in the fall of 2018 that J&J's famed Johnson's Baby Powder contains traces of asbestos is a case in point.[2]

Consumer advocates are suspicious of industry. Industry resists regulatory interference. The two sides' passions lead them to extreme positions: eliminate all regulation and let the market work its magic versus publicly funded and publicly administered healthcare for all. Appropriate balance between public and corporate interests is essential for healthy, competitive markets in which businesses and consumers thrive.

Human nature has not altered. Achieving regulatory balance is an age-old problem and remains an ongoing public policy challenge. As President Teddy Roosevelt observed at the turn of the twentieth century,

If a corporation is doing square work, I will help it so far as I can. But at the same time, if it oppresses anybody; if it is acting dishonestly towards its stockholders or the public, or towards its laborers, or towards small competitors—why, when I have power I shall try to cinch it.[3]

Appropriate regulatory balance is difficult to achieve and requires ongoing tinkering to ensure both level-field competition and consumer safety. America's ongoing prosperity is testimony to the benefits that competitive markets create. As discussed in Chapter 2, excessive government interference in marketplace interactions leads to suboptimal resource allocation and performance. Does anyone believe the US Postal Service outperforms either UPS or FedEx?

In America today, healthcare regulation and competitive markets are severely out of balance. Unnecessary and burdensome rules squelch innovation and waste resources, while lax enforcement and crony capitalism limit competition and distort prices. Bureaucratic overreach and Iron Triangle behaviors benefit the System's entrenched interests. Healthcare customers and consumers suffer while the System enriches itself at their expense.

Establishing, maintaining, and enforcing an effective regulatory structure for healthcare begins with understanding the fundamental differences between being pro-market (always good) and being pro-business (not so much).

PRO-MARKET VS. PRO-BUSINESS

Every day American newspapers publish scandalous and depressing stories about the healthcare system. Pharmaceutical companies charge exorbitant prices. Nursing homes neglect residents. Veterans Affairs hospitals let veterans slip through the cracks. Insurers shed high-cost patients or refuse high-cost treatments. Depending on your political view, these types of stories illustrate one of two conflicting truths:

1. A decentralized, for-profit healthcare system sacrifices patients for profits. When the government is not in control, costs balloon and patients suffer; or
2. A government-controlled healthcare system stands in the way of patients getting better care. Inefficiency and skyrocketing deficits result.

I'd like to propose a third alternative.

3. For-profit companies and government programs can be either villains or heroes. The challenge is to keep both sides in check so healthy competition can flourish.

When health companies gain enough pricing power to inflate their profits through market manipulation rather than value creation, consumers suffer and society picks up the economic cost. When health companies deliver value to customers, consumers get the care they need, become more productive, and society benefits.

A core thesis in my first book, *Market vs. Medicine* (2016), is that US healthcare operates within an artificial fee-for-service (FFS) economic model where supply drives demand. For example, the best predictor of cardiac procedures in any given market is the number of cardiologists. They and other providers literally create their own demand.

My fundamental belief is that bottom-up, market-driven innovation will transform US healthcare in the same way it has transformed other industries: by giving customers the services they want, need, and desire at competitive prices.

Unfortunately, "market" and "medicine" are often in conflict with one another. Pro-market forces seek to overturn entrenched and wasteful pro-business practices through level-field competition. Pro-market regulatory policies enable buyers of healthcare services to determine "market fitness" through their purchasing decisions. Demand-driven change generates superhero results when buyers, not suppliers, drive value creation.

University of Chicago economist Luigi Zingales makes the nuanced and powerful observation that being pro-business is not the same as being pro-market or pro-customer. His timely book, *A Capitalism for the People: Recapturing the Lost Genius of American Prosperity* (2012), is a master class in understanding the essential characteristics of healthy, competitive markets.

Zingales summarized his perspective during a 2012 interview with *The Economist* in the following way:

> There is not a well-understood distinction between being pro-business and pro-market. Business people like free markets until they get into a market; once they are in, they want to block entry to others.
>
> Pro-marketeers want free markets at all times. The more conservative pro-marketeers are fearful of criticizing business, because they assume they will be seen as criticizing the free market. But we

need to stand up and criticize business when business is not helping the cause of the free market.[4]

Zingales cites rampant cronyism, as I've illustrated in Chapter 4's case study on the opioid crisis, as characteristic of markets that are pro-business, not pro-market and pro-customer. Powerful vested interests (e.g., industry trade groups) influence the creation of business regulations and encourage lax enforcement efforts to optimize revenues, reduce tax liabilities, limit competition, and minimize oversight. It's easier than creating value in competitive markets.

Healthcare is big business, and big business fights for its prerogatives. Tax status has little or no relevance in the societal battle to allocate resources efficiently and fairly. In fact, many of the largest and most profitable health systems in America are "not-for-profit" entities. For the most part, nonprofit health systems exhibit the same self-sustaining behaviors and sins as their for-profit cousins.

In contrast, pro-market activities support competition, transparency, and accountability. They sustain efficient markets and deliver value to consumers. Industry "capture" of the government's policy-making apparatus is dangerous to democracy. Frequent calls to "drain the swamp" reflect the American people's collective frustration. Only 19 percent of Americans say they can trust the government in Washington to do what is right "just about always" (3 percent) or "most of the time" (16 percent).[5]

Unfortunately, the "swamp" is thriving, bipartisan, and aggressively pursuing its interests. Metropolitan Washington, D.C., includes the nation's top four highest-income counties.[6] This translates into legions of highly trained professionals working to nudge government policies and regulations in ways that favor vested interests. But what's good for Washington, D.C., harms the rest of the country. Monopoly and monopsony pricing power deprive communities, employers, and individuals of vitally needed resources.

We the people have to fight back by demanding greater transparency and accountability. The Honorable Louis Brandeis, a future Supreme Court Justice, rightly observed,

> Publicity is justly commended as a remedy for social and industrial diseases. Sunlight is said to be the best of disinfectants; electric light the most efficient policeman.[7]

Toward that end, Professor Zingales believes that an independent press, class-action lawsuits, and whistleblowers are necessary counterweights to powerful vested interests. Properly exercised, they give voice to societal concerns and expose corporate overreach.

Here's a timely and relevant example. On December 16, 2018, *60 Minutes* interviewed Mike Moore, former attorney general from Mississippi.[8] As attorney general in the 1990s, Moore led the settlement negotiations with tobacco companies that paid billions in compensation to victims, funded smoking cessation/prevention programs, and dramatically restricted the ability of tobacco companies to market their products in the United States. This settlement has been a critical feature of the nation's very successful public health campaign to reduce smoking and related diseases. That campaign required an active press, whistleblowers, and class-action lawsuits to achieve its hard-won victories.

Moore is now spearheading the class-action lawsuits against opioid manufacturers, distributors, and pharmacies. He believes the settlements could be in the hundreds of billions of dollars. The state of Oklahoma drew first blood. It settled out of court in March 2019 for $270 million with Purdue Pharma, the maker of OxyContin.[9]

Opioid overdoses killed almost 50,000 people in 2017 alone.[10] Settlement monies could fund rehabilitation for over 2.5 million opioid-dependent individuals and repay state and local governments for the enormous costs they've incurred in related healthcare, social services, legal proceedings, public safety, and policing. As with Big Tobacco, the penalties and publicity that will accompany the opioid lawsuits may be the only forces powerful enough to bring Big Pharma to the settlement table. Without class-action lawsuits, the American people would have little recourse against the corporations responsible for creating and perpetuating enormous social, human, and financial harm.

In contrast to a pro-business regulatory environment, pro-market regulations facilitate competition, transparency, and accountability. They stand up to vested interests and insist on level-field competition. Companies win when they deliver better outcomes, lower costs, and/or superior service to customers. In other words, they create value that helps individuals and communities thrive.

BALANCED REGULATION

Like all organizations, governmental bureaucracies' first principle is to sustain their existence. Unlike corporations that sustain themselves through value creation and profitability, bureaucracies sustain themselves by expanding their regulatory control through reporting requirements, program oversight, and enforcement. Regulation is a necessary evil, a cost of maintaining market integrity and competitiveness in an imperfect world. Unfortunately, bureaucracies often overstep their boundaries. When they do, burdensome rules and overzealous enforcement constrict proper marketplace functioning.

Consequently, there is an art to balanced regulation: enough to restrain anti-competitive behaviors without adding unnecessary burden. Among the many attributes of President Eisenhower's farewell address was his emphasis on balance. Eisenhower's lifetime of leadership experience gave him a hard-learned appreciation for the role balance plays in managing human affairs. He identified these six specific areas of competing interests that require ongoing attention and balancing.

1. Balance in and among national programs.
2. Balance between the private and the public economy.
3. Balance between cost and hoped-for advantage.
4. Balance between the clearly necessary and the comfortably desirable.
5. Balance between our essential requirements as a nation and the duties imposed by the nation upon the individual.
6. Balance between action of the moment and the national welfare of the future.

Eisenhower ended this segment of his speech with this powerful observation:

> Good judgment seeks balance and progress; lack of it eventually finds imbalance and frustration.[11]

Constructive regulation seeks balance and progress. It does this by balancing opposing forces to maintain competition and fairness.

However, the regulatory process is vulnerable to manipulation and often creates imbalance between competing interests. It tilts the marketplace to favor companies with insider influence. Those on the outside conclude that the process is rigged and act accordingly. They either play the influence game themselves or exit the marketplace. Trust diminishes. Performance fades. America's social fabric weakens.

In addition to being balanced, ideal regulatory structures are holistic, with straightforward rules that are easy to understand. For example, it was better to simply separate banks from investment banks as the Glass-Steagall Act did than to create the complicated, reporting-heavy, rule-laden mechanisms embedded within the Dodd-Frank Act to regulate the financial industry. The Dodd-Frank Act was over 2,300 pages long and imposed more than 400 new rules and mandates. By contrast, the Glass-Steagall Act was clear, easy-to-understand, and only 53 pages long. Complexity creates opportunities for manipulation. Lobbyists often insert exactly the provisions they want into new laws and regulations.

Markets require constant tinkering and refinement to guarantee their efficient functioning. In this sense, economists are like mechanics. Given healthcare's fragmentation and dysfunction, it's essential to experiment with regulatory reforms to create mechanisms to make sure they support high-performing healthcare delivery.

Pro-Market Healthcare Regulations

The government should create regulations to accomplish three primary goals: enhance competition, reward innovation, and streamline regulation. If I were healthcare czar, I would undertake the following 10 measures to create a pro-market regulatory environment. All would encounter stringent opposition because they eliminate mechanisms that currently support the System's entrenched enablers.

Enhancing Competition

1. Phase out the Centers for Medicare and Medicaid's responsibility for establishing reimbursement formularies and risk scoring. Transfer care management risk to third parties through full-risk contracting.
2. Insist on pricing transparency; eliminate hidden payment transfers (e.g., rebates between PBMs and drug manufacturers).
3. Reinstate the Individual Mandate: health insurance is a shared civic responsibility—everyone needs to participate to optimize system performance.
4. Eliminate the corporate tax deductibility of health insurance. It should not be more advantageous for companies to grant increases in health benefits than wages.
5. Establish strict pricing guidelines whenever granting monopoly pricing power (e.g., with drug patents). These guidelines must balance fair pricing for essential products/services with reasonable investment returns for those companies providing them.

Rewarding Innovation and Aligned Incentives

6. Pay for high-quality outcomes, not treatment activity. Encourage meaningful and understandable public quality ratings for healthcare providers that are relevant to consumers.
7. Redirect a larger portion of federal research grants toward broad-based societal health goals (e.g., new antibiotics, population health, social determinants).

Streamlining Regulation

8. Establish an independent regulatory body (like the Federal Reserve) to determine treatment efficacy and cost-effectiveness.
9. Eliminate the ability of private vendors to compensate physicians that use their products—no pay-to-play in any form.
10. Establish mechanisms for discovering and addressing market failure. Take steps, wherever possible, to establish and maintain level-field competition.

Implicit in any and all regulatory reform is reducing the level of government capture now influencing healthcare policy and payment. Too many health companies generate higher returns walking the halls of Congress than by creating value in the marketplace.

Balanced regulation is always pro-market, but not always pro-business. As companies gain scale and influence, their natural inclination is to limit competition by influencing the legislative and regulatory processes. The proper role of government is to resist such influence and establish level-field competition that rewards value creation.

Once unleashed, the American innovation machine will transform healthcare by delivering great outcomes at competitive prices with incredible customer service. Pro-market regulation will accelerate positive transformation.

What Is Government / Regulatory Capture?

Regulatory capture occurs when industries and their associations exercise inappropriate influence on the regulatory agencies charged with monitoring and policing their activities. The result is that agencies act in ways that benefit the industry's interests, not the people's interests.

A PRO-MARKET SHERIFF AT US HEALTH AND HUMAN SERVICES

Since taking over for Tom Price on January 29, 2018, as the secretary of Health and Human Services (HHS), Alex Azar has pursued pro-market regulatory reforms with single-minded determination. Under his leadership, HHS and the Centers for Medicare and Medicaid (CMS) are pursuing policies that promote level-field competition.

Azar signaled his pro-market and pro-consumer agenda five weeks into his term, during his first major policy address. He identified the following four "areas of emphasis" to guide CMS's reform efforts:

1. "Giving consumers greater control over health information through interoperable and accessible health information technology"
2. "Encouraging transparency from payers and providers"
3. "Using experimental models in Medicare and Medicaid to drive value and quality throughout the entire system"
4. "Removing government burdens that impede this transformation"[12]

Secretary Azar is using multiple tools to advance these four objectives. While not radical, his areas of emphasis confront a healthcare ecosystem that is opaque, activity based (as opposed to outcomes based), fragmented, overpriced, and in need of transformation. Azar was blunt in assessing the System's dysfunction, in expressing his commitment to consumers, and in demanding more value from its principals.

> Putting healthcare consumers in charge, letting them determine value, is a radical reorientation from the way that American healthcare has worked for the past century. . . .
>
> [The] status quo is far from a competitive free market in the economic sense of the term, and healthcare is such a complex system, that facilitating a competitive, value-based marketplace is going to be disruptive to existing actors.
>
> Simply put, our current system may be working for many. But it's not working for patients, and it's not working for the taxpayer.[13]

Azar acknowledges this transformation will not be easy or painless but maintains it is long overdue. To emphasize this point, HHS issued a 119-page strategic plan in December 2018 with the unambiguous title *Reforming America's Healthcare System Through Choice and Competition.*[14]

The report is in response to President Trump's October 12, 2017, executive order to come up with a plan "to facilitate the development and operation of a healthcare system that provides high-quality care at affordable prices for the American people by promoting choice and competition."

The report makes a compelling case that market-based reforms and deregulation are the keys to unlocking a patient-centered, outcomes-focused, and value-driven healthcare delivery system. In many ways, the HHS report articulates the Republican arguments for market-based reform (bottom-up and decentralized). Given the strong Democratic push for a single-payer "Medicare for all" program (top-down and centralized), it's worthwhile analyzing the logic underlying Azar's positions. Once again, healthcare will be a defining issue in the next presidential election. With that in mind, let's examine the HHS report's policy contours, as summarized by David Burda in an article for *4sight Health*:

Here's what HHS thinks about COMPETITION

"Economists generally accept that free-market competition produces the most efficient production and distribution of goods and services," and that competition can do the same in healthcare. Free-market competition should "encourage providers to charge lower prices and provide higher-quality services."

Here's what HHS thinks about REGULATION

"Many government laws, regulations, guidance, requirements and policies, at both the federal and state level, have reduced incentives for price and non-price competition, increased barriers to entry, promoted and allowed excessive consolidation, and resulted in healthcare markets that lack the benefits of vigorous competition."

Here's what HHS thinks is the CONSEQUENCE

"When government policies and regulations suppress competition, producers may use their market power to raise prices, produce lower-quality goods and services, or become complacent in innovation. In other words, without competitive pressure the incentive to lower prices, improve quality, and innovate diminishes."

Here are HHS's examples of COMPETITION-KILLING REGS

- State licensing and scope-of-practice (SOP) laws and regulations that "may impose unnecessary restrictions on provider supply and, therefore, competition. SOP restrictions limit provider entry and ability to practice in ways that do not address demonstrable or substantial risks to consumer health and safety."

- State licensing and SOP laws and regulations that make it "more difficult for qualified healthcare professionals licensed in one state to work in another state, even though most healthcare providers complete nationally certified education and training programs and sit for national qualifying exams."

- State licensing and SOP laws and regulations that restrict the provision of telehealth services across state lines.

- State licensing and SOP laws and regulations that block "an expedited pathway for highly qualified, foreign-trained doctors seeking licensure who have completed a residency program equivalent to an American GME (graduate medical education) program."

- State certificate-of-need (CON) laws that "restrict investments that would benefit consumers and lower costs in the long term and are likely to increase, rather than constrain, healthcare costs." Further, there is "no compelling evidence suggesting that CON laws improve quality or access, inefficiently or otherwise."

- State certificate-of-public-advantage (COPA) agreements that "displace competition in favor of state regulatory oversight and may, under the state action doctrine, immunize provider activity for conduct that might otherwise violate federal antitrust laws." Further, "These types of regulatory conditions are often difficult to implement and monitor and may not accomplish intended goals."

- State laws that enforce provider non-compete agreements that are "overly burdensome and restrictive on providers. Further scrutiny of these and other restrictive covenants is warranted, particularly where they impede patient access to care and limit the supply of providers. By suppressing competition, these clauses may inflate healthcare prices, elevating patient and federal spending on healthcare goods and services."

- State "any-willing-provider" laws that "make it more difficult for health insurers, health plans, or pharmacy benefit managers to negotiate discounts from providers and tend to result in higher costs."

- Federal regulations that restrict physician ownership of acute-care hospitals when "many studies suggest physician-owned hospitals provide higher-quality care and that patients benefit when traditional hospitals have greater competition."

Here's what HHS recommends . . .
- More vigorous antitrust oversight of healthcare mergers and acquisitions.
- Extend the FTC's jurisdiction to include not-for-profit healthcare entities.
- Revise SOP (scope-of-practice) laws to allow all providers to practice at the top of their license.
- Repeal or scale back CON (certificate-of-need) laws to remove unnecessary barriers to entry.
- Discontinue the use of COPA (certificate-of-public-advantage) agreements to promote market-based competition.
- Rethink the use of noncompete clauses and state any-willing-provider laws.
- Repeal federal restrictions on physician ownership of hospitals.

Secretary Azar's vigor in advocating market-based regulatory reform is bracing. While it is unclear how much of this ambitious agenda Azar can accomplish, his intentions are perfectly clear. CMS will pursue policies and regulations that improve competition, increase transparency, and reduce administrative friction. As a consequence, CMS is undertaking the following initiatives (as of December 2018) to improve healthcare's competitive dynamics, including site neutrality, charge master transparency, increased interoperability, and reduced regulation.

It's about time HHS tackles the System's stranglehold on the healthcare marketplace. These are commonsense reforms, but they face opposition. Health companies welcome the regulatory relief but generally oppose measures that improve pricing parity and transparency. They are on the wrong side of history. Left alone, incumbents tend to hold on to wasteful and self-serving business practices, despite the need for change. Fortunately, HHS is nudging the industry toward greater accountability, consumerism, and value creation.

For example, site neutrality requires Medicare to pay the same price for identical services irrespective of delivery site. When hospitals acquire physician practices, they usually apply hospital-based prices for services provided in physician offices. Overnight, the cost for the same procedure by the same doctor in the same office skyrockets, often doubling or tripling. This is a good deal for providers, but a terrible deal for consumers, Medicare, and self-insured employers.

The lack of EHR interoperability is equally maddening. With today's advanced technologies, it strains credulity that health companies cannot share digitized patient information effectively with one another and with patients. In February 2017, HHS proposed well-crafted rules to address interoperability, patient access to their health data, and data blocking (preventing access to patient data by independent third parties developing apps). If promulgated as proposed, these new rules would dramatically improve data access and spur development of innovative clinical and operational apps.[15]

It's also maddening that patients have little to no information about care costs and their payment responsibilities. There are far too many payment surprises. For example, out-of-network providers working within in-network hospitals have too much power to charge outrageous prices for routine services.

In 2017, the Price Transparency & Physician Quality Report Card gave failing grades for transparency to 43 states and for quality to 42 states.[16] Meanwhile, healthcare costs continue to rise, and healthcare companies remain largely unaccountable for performance.

Though they applaud the regulatory streamlining, hospital representatives have decried the advent of site-neutral payments. The following statement by Tom Nickels, an executive vice president at the American Hospital Association, offers a typical reaction:

> CMS has resurrected a proposal, which it had previously deemed unwise, that would penalize hospital outpatient departments that expand the types of critical services they offer to their communities—preventing them from caring for the changing needs of their patients.[17]

Nothing in CMS's site neutrality rules prevents hospitals from offering critical services. They just cannot charge higher prices for them when performed inside a hospital. Mr. Nickels similarly framed the new chargemaster transparency requirements with the following statement:

> We do not want patients to forgo needed care, especially if the quoted price is for the total cost of the service and not what the patient will be expected to pay out-of-pocket.[18]

While the CMS transparency rules require that hospitals publish their chargemaster rates, hospitals can also provide clarifying information for patients. After all, 43 states received failing transparency grades in 2017. There's significant room for improvement.

Given its high cost, pervasive fragmentation, and imbedded inefficiencies, US healthcare must become more pro-market (value-enhancing) and less pro-business (status-quo preserving). Optimal healthcare practices must displace suboptimal practices.

RANKINGS AND REACTIONS

In the first act of Shakespeare's history play *Julius Caesar*, Cassius entices Brutus to join a conspiracy against Caesar. In making his case, Cassius utters these immortal words, "The fault, dear Brutus, is not in our stars, but in ourselves."[19] This Shakespearean wisdom has direct applicability to emerging STAR rating systems for healthcare payers and providers.

Level-field competition requires pricing, quality, and outcomes transparency. To advance this goal, CMS released its first-ever quality ratings for hospitals on July 27, 2016. Within the week, *U.S. News and World Report* released its twenty-seventh annual "Best Hospitals" report.[20] The *U.S. News* rankings are exceptionally popular with consumers. Hospitals work ferociously to achieve "Best Hospital" recognition. The results of the two reports could not have differed more. Figure 7.1 lists the 2016 *U.S. News* "Honor Roll" hospitals in rank order with their 2016 CMS star ratings.

Of the 20 *U.S. News* "Honor Roll" hospitals in the 2016 report, only the Mayo Clinic received five stars from CMS. Four of their "Honor Roll" hospitals received only two stars. These ranking results reflect differing rating methodologies and illustrate the challenge consumers face when trying to find actionable quality data for decisions.

Healthcare providers have long fought against external performance assessments. It's a losing battle. Amid much teeth-gnashing, hospitals are adapting to market demands for transparency. Expect the CMS hospital ratings to gain currency and shape future demand for hospital services.

Giving Consumers the Hospital Ratings They Want

Desperate for guidance, consumers increasingly rely on third-party provider ratings and report cards to select hospitals and doctors. "About three-quarters of Americans with Internet access have searched for health or medical information online."[21]

2016 *U.S. News* Honor Roll Hospitals with CMS Star Ratings

U.S. News Honor Roll Ranking	U.S. News Honor Roll Points	Hospital Name	CMS Star Rating
1	418 points	Mayo Clinic	5 Star
2	378 points	Cleveland Clinic	4 Star
3	371 points	Massachusetts General Hospital	4 Star
4	349 points	Johns Hopkins Hospital	N/A
5	331 points	UCLA Medical Center	3 Star
6	296 points	New York-Presbyterian Hospital	3 Star
7	273 points	UCSF Medical Center	3 Star
8	266 points	Northwestern Memorial Hospital	4 Star
9	252 points	Pennsylvania-Penn Presbyterian	4 Star
10	247 points	NYU Langone Hospitals, New York	4 Star
11	241 points	Barnes-Jewish Hospital	2 Star
12	236 points	UPMC Presbyterian Shadyside	2 Star
13	235 points	Brigham and Women's Hospital	3 Star
14	227 points	Stanford Health Care-Stanford Hospital	4 Star
15	226 points	Mount Sinai Hospital	3 Star
16	222 points	Duke University Hospital	4 Star
17	220 points	Cedars-Sinai Medical Center	3 Star
18	195 points	Univ. of Michigan Hospitals-Michigan Medicine	3 Star
19	191 points	Houston Methodist Hospital	3 Star
20	190 points	University of Colorado Hospital	2 Star

Sources: U.S. News and World Report; CMS.gov

FIGURE 7.1   **Not all *U.S. News* Honor Roll Hospitals shine brightly.**

Despite strong public support for more accessible quality data, the hospital industry fought the release of the consumer-friendly CMS star ratings in 2016. In response to industry concerns, CMS delayed their release by three months and conducted significant stakeholder outreach. This did little to dampen industry ire.

In the aftermath of their release, industry representatives lampooned the government ratings, particularly noting the poor performance of teaching and safety-net hospitals. In an announcement accompanying the release of the new ratings, CMS Quality Director Kate Goodrich acknowledged industry concerns while heralding the benefits of transparency to American healthcare consumers:

> [CMS star ratings] help millions of patients and their families learn about the quality of hospitals, compare facilities in their area

side-by-side, and ask important questions about care quality when visiting a hospital or other health care provider.[22]

Given the wide variation in hospital quality, outcomes, and costs, external report cards can help consumers make better choices. Highlighting this point, Dr. Goodrich notes, "researchers found that hospitals with more stars on the agency's *Hospital Compare* website have tended to have lower death and readmission rates."

Likewise, a National Bureau of Economic Research study found that hospitals with higher quality ratings for specific medical conditions, including heart attacks, pneumonia, and congestive heart failure, disproportionately gain market share.[23] Market forces work. When given choices, consumers select higher-performing hospitals.

Public demand for better hospital ratings is accelerating. Multiple independent sources have emerged to meet this need. However, these third-party hospital ratings generate as much confusion as clarity.

The Confusing World of Hospital Ratings

All hospital ratings systems contain inherent biases. A widely read *Health Affairs* study analyzed the overlaps between "high" and "low" performers in the following four national hospital ratings: *U.S. News*, HealthGrades, The Leapfrog Group, and *Consumer Reports*. The authors describe the stunning inconsistency of their findings as follows:

> No hospital was rated as a high performer by all four national rating systems. Only 10 percent of the 844 hospitals rated as a high performer by one rating system were rated as a high performer by any of the other rating systems.[24]

The authors attributed the lack of overlap to different rating methodologies, different areas of focus, and different criteria weighting. Their unsurprising conclusions are that few hospitals excel across all service dimensions and that a lack of performance standardization retards hospital performance improvement.

CMS is addressing the lack of hospital quality, cost, and performance transparency through more intense data collection and distribution. Issuing star ratings based on newly collected data is a logical next step.

CMS star ratings for individual hospitals emerge from a statistical analysis of 64 metrics across the following seven categories: mortality, safety, readmissions, patient experience, effectiveness, timeliness, and imaging. The first four categories carry 22 percent weights and the last three carry 4 percent weights. CMS will update and publish its quality ratings quarterly. Individual hospital performance summaries are clear, detailed, and easily comparable.[25]

While controversial and data-dense, CMS star ratings are entirely data driven. CMS took over two years to develop its rating methodology. It leaned heavily on a prestigious technical expert panel and invited widespread public input. Its analytics are statistically rigorous in selecting and assigning weights to metrics and performance categories. Its methodology employed clustering techniques to establish a bell-curve distribution among the almost 4,000 rated hospitals.

By contrast, *U.S. News* targets specialty care measures and relies heavily (27.5 percent weighting) on reputational surveys by board-certified specialists. *U.S. News* also weights 30-day Medicare survival rates (37.5 percent), patient safety (5 percent), and other care-related factors such as nurse-staffing ratios (30 percent). All 20 of *U.S. News*'s "Honor Roll" hospitals are academic medical centers. The *U.S. News* methodology does not incorporate patient experience.

The disparity of star ratings among these Honor Roll hospitals is striking. While CMS's rating methodology may not be perfect, it is data driven and consistent. The inability of the nation's most recognized hospitals to all excel on CMS quality metrics testifies to unacceptable performance variation throughout American hospitals in outcomes, quality, costs, and customer experience.

Industry Reaction

Blustering is a professional sport in Washington. Too many healthcare leaders scorn the CMS methodology because they don't like its results. Dr. Darrell Kirch is the president and CEO of the Association of American Medical Colleges. In a 2016 *Modern Healthcare* commentary titled "CMS New Star Ratings Are Unfair to Teaching and Safety-Net Hospitals," Dr. Kirch castigates CMS ratings in hypercharged language.

> Instead of providing useful information, the new ratings paint a confusing and conflicting picture of the quality of U.S. hospital care because of a deeply flawed methodology that ignores important differences in the patient populations and the complexity of conditions that different types of hospitals treat.[26]

These types of broad-based critiques are disingenuous. It would be equally fair to state that *U.S. News*'s intense focus on specialty care and its dependence on specialist opinion surveys biases its rankings against well-run community hospitals. What else explains that all 20 Honor Roll hospitals are academic medical centers?

It's worth noting that highly rated *U.S. News* hospitals spend gargantuan sums advertising their success. The same is true for CMS five-star hospitals. On a drive from Illinois into Michigan right after the release of the CMS ratings, I saw several billboards where Holland Community Hospital had already proclaimed itself to be the best hospital in Michigan because it received five stars. Holland is a community with 33,000 people.

Back to Dr. Kirch's commentary. In fairness, he makes the following valid points regarding CMS methodology:

* Reporting more metrics lowers some hospitals' scores.

* Socioeconomic status likely influences care outcomes.

* Current ratings may not accurately reflect the benefits of specialization.

To drive his "unfairness" point home, Dr. Kirch notes that "only one major teaching hospital received five stars [and] nearly 90 percent of teaching hospitals rated three stars or below." He then asks, "How is this possible?"

While Dr. Kirsch may have his own biases behind his critique, this is exactly the question lower-rated hospitals should ask themselves. And if they can answer the question honestly, they can find ways to improve.

Despite the challenges Dr. Kirch outlined, Mayo Clinic, Cleveland Clinic, Mass General, New York Presbyterian, and four more Honor Roll hospitals achieved four- and five-star ratings. Rather than complain about the rating process, lower-rated hospitals should investigate what these institutions are doing right and replicate their superior performance.

"Yelping" It: Ratings Speak to Customers

In another intriguing *Health Affairs* study, researchers employed natural-language processing to evaluate Yelp hospital ratings relative to the CMS Hospital Consumer Assessment of Healthcare Providers and Systems quality scores (HCAHPS).[27] They found that hospitals receiving at least three Yelp ratings had almost identical ratings to HCAHPS scores. They also found Yelp's hospital reviews were more expansive than the 32 domains in the HCAHPS scores, covering 12 additional domains (staff compassion, billing experience, nursing quality, amenities, etc.).

Most intriguing, the Health Affairs researchers concluded that Yelp "may provide a more nuanced view [than HCAPHS] of aspects of hospital quality that patients value." Their conclusions illustrate why hospitals must listen to, understand, and respond to their customers' needs. Those that do will prosper in post-transformation healthcare.

Hospital ratings are here to stay. CMS star ratings for nursing homes, Medicare Advantage insurance plans, and dialysis centers are in widespread use. Consumers find these ratings helpful. They influence their healthcare purchasing decisions. CMS plans to develop star ratings for physicians. It's "adapt or die" time for providers.

Health companies that acclimate to consumerism and meet their jobs-to-be-done will earn their trust and win market share. Paraphrasing Shakespeare, "the stars" reward companies that recognize "the faults in themselves" and correct them.

BALANCE, VIGILANCE, AND TRANSPARENCY

Given the opportunity, market-dominant companies tilt the competitive landscape in their favor through manipulation of the regulatory process. It is government's responsibility to maintain competitive markets.

Competition is hard but makes companies better. Free markets depend upon balanced regulation/oversight and effective enforcement to ensure level-field competition. Preserving competitive markets is a delicate exercise that requires constant vigilance and tinkering. Too much regulation and overly vigorous enforcement burden productive companies, stifle innovation, and exert a negative drag on the economy. Too little regulation and feeble enforcement encourage negligent corporate behavior, create moral hazard, and increase societal harm. This also retards innovation and economic growth.

The constant challenge for the American government is to create and sustain a Goldilocks balance (not too hot, not too cold) where regulation and enforcement protect societal interests, encourage innovation, and stimulate economic growth. American consumers need appropriate governmental oversight and regulation with effective enforcement powers to sustain market-driven healthcare transformation.

Given its high cost, pervasive fragmentation, and imbedded inefficiencies, US healthcare must become more pro-market (value enhancing) and less pro-business (status-quo preserving). Pro-market companies will succeed by delivering better, more convenient healthcare services at lower costs. Customers will win when their needs and priorities are met in the market.

For health company executives, the message should be clear. Bob Dylan's "Subterranean Homesick Blues" contains the following couplet that captures the direction pro-market reforms are taking the US healthcare system:

> You don't need a weather man
> To know which way the wind blows

The government is speaking. The American people are speaking. Healthcare's "consumerism" hurricane is forming just over the horizon, and it's headed toward value. As a force multiplier, pro-market regulation balances conflicting interests and creates level-field competition. It speeds innovation, consumerism, and value creation.

Force Multipliers

Revolutions require more than passionate beliefs and stirring speeches to overthrow an entrenched order. The System is a cancerous growth industry that is consuming precious American resources at an alarming rate and harming Americans in the process.

Without concerted and coordinated economic, political, and social effort, the System will raise the cost of universal health and healthcare access to unsustainable levels. It will use its political muscle to frustrate fundamental reforms that make care more affordable and health companies more accountable.

This is our last best chance to slay the System and reinvent healthcare for the betterment of the American people. Fortunately, this customer revolution in healthcare comes with powerful force multipliers that strike at the heart of the System's artificial and perverse economic structure (Figure CII.1). For those ready to jump the barricades and join the revolution, these force multipliers will turbocharge systemwide transformation.

- **Empowered customers (buyers).** Self-insured employers, governments, and individuals who demand and receive more value for their healthcare purchases.

- **Full-risk contracting vehicles.** Public and private insurance plans that align payment for episodic and ongoing care with performance, quality, transparency, service, and value, supported by health systems that pay providers based on those full-risk plans.

- **Liberated Big Data.** Technology platforms that enable data to flow where it provides the most beneficial impact, most importantly to augment human intelligence and actions.

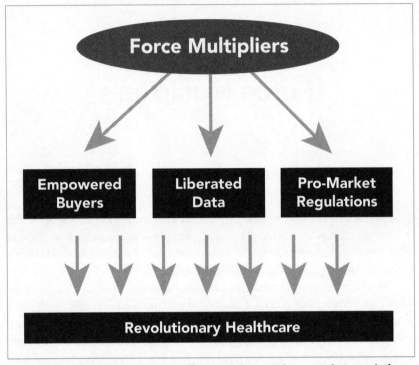

FIGURE CII.1 Empowered buyers, liberated data, and pro-market regulations will turbocharge adoption of Revolutionary Healthcare.

- **New managerial systems.** "Team of teams" organizational architecture that push decision-critical information to situationally aware frontline staff who act in accordance with organization-wide objectives.

- **Pro-market regulations.** Finely balanced regulation, monitoring, and enforcement that support level-field competition without unduly burdening industry participants.

- **Transparent and accessible performance metrics.** Publicly available and understandable price information along with transparent quality, outcomes, and performance metrics that enable consumers to make better health and healthcare choices.

Revolutionary Healthcare

AMERICAN EXCEPTIONALISM

On November 1, 1783, word arrived from John Adams in Paris that the United States and Great Britain had signed a definitive peace treaty. The Revolutionary War was over, and the United States was now an independent nation.

Encamped north of New York City, General George Washington (Figure PIII.1) learned the glorious news, issued a farewell proclamation to his troops, and prepared to march triumphantly back into the city where seven years earlier his badly beaten Continental Army had barely escaped annihilation.

On November 25, Washington, Governor George Clinton of New York, and 800 soldiers marched with the Westchester Light Dragoons through wildly cheering throngs into the liberated city. The British army had vacated their barracks earlier that morning. The contrast between the polished redcoats and the weather-beaten Americans in homespun dress could not have been starker. It had been a long, bloody battle. More than 10 percent of the American army's soldiers had died during the war. They fought under grievous conditions with little pay. Somehow Washington had held the army together and achieved victory. New Yorkers were eager to say thank you to the general and his troops.

FIGURE PIII.1 *Washington Receiving a Salute on the Field of Trenton* by John Faed

A British officer returning to retrieve some personal items witnessed the celebration. He was dumbstruck by the general population's decorum and civility. He made this note for the historical record:

> This is a strange scene indeed! Here in this city, we have had an army for over seven years, and yet could not keep the peace of it. . . . Now [that] we are gone, everything is in quietness and safety. The Americans are a curious, original people. They know how to govern themselves, but nobody else can govern them.[1]

That British officer hit the mark. Americans are a "curious, original people" even 200-plus years later. The United States is a big, pluralistic, loud, opinionated, messy, one-of-a kind, and "exceptional" nation. For this reason, America's approach to reforming its broken healthcare system will be unique and uniquely American.

Today American healthcare is exceptional for all the wrong reasons. Unlike Canada and other nationalized, top-down healthcare systems, Americans prefer decentralized, bottom-up healthcare that caters to individual preference. American healthcare delivers the best advanced medicine money can buy, but it does so in a fragmented manner with a ridiculous amount of waste and without doing basic preventive care well. The United States spends far more per capita on healthcare but achieves worse health status than other advanced economies. This is a national disgrace.

This part of *The Customer Revolution in Healthcare* will explore how American strengths in innovation, entrepreneurialism, consumerism, and marketing are revolutionizing health and healthcare service delivery. With great zeal, revolutionary new entrants (upstarts) and established healthcare companies (incumbents) are experimenting with new business models that get consumers' health and healthcare "Jobs" done with better outcomes, lower costs, and great customer service. The "revolutionary forces" of empowered customers (buyers), liberated data, and pro-market regulation turbocharge their efforts.

The great challenges in healthcare center on creating the right financial incentives within a balanced regulatory framework so that competition rewards value-based health and healthcare services. Such market-based reforms will empower high-performing health companies to deliver appropriate, accessible, and affordable care to all.

Part III describes how Revolutionary Healthcare will become reality through the multiplicity of market-based interactions between buyers and sellers of healthcare services that deliver value to customers.

- **Chapter 8, "Revolutionary Upstarts,"** digs into the differences between sustaining and disruption innovation and the ways in which new market entrants are delivering both types. Focusing on "jobs-to-be-done" within a segmenting marketplace, transformative and disruptive companies are developing innovative business models that are revolutionizing health and healthcare delivery.

- **Chapter 9, "Revolutionary Incumbents,"** describes how established health companies understand that their current business models are not well positioned to compete in a post-reform marketplace characterized by transparency, engaged customers, level-field competition, and value-based service provision.

    Focusing on simultaneously managing transformative and disruptive innovation, revolutionary incumbents are integrating vertically and developing Amazon-like platform capabilities to deliver holistic health and healthcare services to consumers.

- **Chapter 10, "Healthcare for All,"** tackles the moral imperative of creating universal and affordable healthcare coverage. The time to achieve this goal is now. The best way to achieve this goal is by turning American consumers into customers with sufficient purchasing power to stimulate health companies to create products and services tailored to their health and healthcare needs.

CHAPTER 8

Revolutionary Upstarts

When personal computers debuted in the mid-1970s, they carried a hint of rebellion. Until then, computers were *not personal*. Highly trained experts operated giant mainframes at large corporations, industrial research labs, and elite academic institutions. With small, affordable desktop models like the TRS-80 or the Apple II, individuals could use computing power to pursue their ambitions, whims, and dreams. From modest beginnings, these early pioneers of personal computing changed the world.

The makers and users of these early computers were rebels, counterculture warriors from the Vietnam-Watergate era with anti-establishment views. They built their first computers in garages, shared knowledge, and challenged each other's designs through informal social groups. The legendary Homebrew Computer Club held its first meeting in 1975 inside cofounder Gordon French's garage. Members included Apple cofounders Steve Jobs and Steve Wozniak. They saw computer technology as a tool for the masses, expanding human potential and challenging the status quo. They believed in creativity, individualism, and mild anarchy.

Steve Jobs personified this revolutionary spirit. In a world of blue suits, he didn't wear socks and barely showered. Jobs thought everyone should drop acid at least once in their lives to open their minds. He loathed the soul-destroying conformity of giant corporations and their legions of skeptics, critics, and mercenaries who impeded new thinking, progress, and innovation. Ironically, Apple would become the world's first trillion-dollar corporation on August 2, 2018.[1]

Launched in 1977, Apple was the world's most successful personal computer maker by 1982. That year, Apple sold 279,000 Apple IIs while IBM, Apple's giant competitor, sold only 240,000 PCs. The next year was a different story. Recognizing Apple's strategic threat and the PC's market potential, IBM powered its way to becoming the market leader. In 1983, Apple sold 420,000 Apple IIs but IBM sold 1.3 million PCs.

Jobs saw IBM not just as a competitive threat but an existential one. IBM was the establishment, the man, the epitome of big business, an oppressor of freedom and creativity. In Skunk Works fashion, he led a secretive team inside Apple to create the revolutionary Macintosh computer. With its user-friendly technology, mind-blowing applications, and sleek design, Jobs believed the Macintosh would reestablish Apple's innovative edge and industry dominance.

A showman, Jobs wanted a launch campaign for Macintosh that would be as astonishing as the computer itself. He hired Lee Chow at Chiat/Day to create an eyepopping ad for the Super Bowl in January 1984. The year 1984 has mythic properties. George Orwell's classic 1949 novel *Nineteen Eighty-Four* describes a dark, totalitarian society set in the 1980s with mind control, perpetual war, "doublethink," and "Newspeak." Playing off the novel's anti-establishment spirit, Chow envisioned linking IBM's monolithic culture and market dominance with Orwell's Big Brother.[2]

For the 60-second commercial, Jobs approved a budget worthy of a blockbuster movie. Chow hired Ridley Scott, director of the dystopian classic *Blade Runner*, to direct the spot. The ad displays Big Brother on a flickering gray screen speaking to an auditorium of anonymous bald workers, watching in numb obedience. Then an athletic woman carrying a sledgehammer sprints into the auditorium chased by the Thought Police. She races toward the screen and hurls the sledgehammer into it, smashing Big Brother's image just as he says, "We shall prevail." As chaos ensues, a calm voice announces, "On January 24th, Apple Computer will introduce Macintosh. And you'll see why 1984 won't be like '1984.'"[3]

Everyone loved the ad, except the Apple board of directors. They ordered the company to deep-six the commercial and resell the advertising time. With some clever subterfuge and help from Chait/Day, Jobs prevailed, and 96 million viewers watched Big Brother vaporize and learned about Macintosh. An instant classic, *TV Guide* and *Advertising Age* both proclaimed it the greatest commercial of all time. For Jobs, the ad spotlighted Macintosh, propelled its initial sales, and branded IBM as an icon of corporate dullness and the enemy of freethinkers everywhere. By contrast, Apple embodied personal expression and empowerment. Users of its products could "dent the universe."

America's Healthcare Industrial Complex (the System) is the Big Brother of our day. With its rigid rules, its restrictions on choice, and its indifference to individual needs, the System epitomizes bureaucratic authoritarianism. Fortunately, modern-day revolutionaries bearing sledgehammers are on their way. They're planning to smash the System to smithereens.

These rebels are leading upstart companies. Their companies are challenging the System's ponderous incumbents with innovative product offerings that deliver healthcare services customers want. Instead of depersonalized, one-size-fits-all business models, they're offering targeted solutions to distinct customer segments. Instead of scrambling to optimize fee-for-service payment, they're delivering better outcomes, lower costs, and superior customer experience. They're not trying to win the old game; they're playing a different game altogether.

THE DISRUPTIVE PROFESSOR

Harvard Business School professor Clay Christensen has influenced a generation of business leaders. He believes market transformation starts when companies develop a better, deeper understanding of how customers make purchasing decisions. Industries grow stale when innovation slows and/or companies fail to solve customers' "jobs-to-be-done" ("Jobs"). Industry disruption occurs when a smaller company introduces a new product for unserved or underserved market segments. Christensen's theories explain why US healthcare is ripe for disruption today and detail the tactics that upstart companies are using to free healthcare consumers from the shackles of "old economy" business models.

Christensen published his seminal book, *The Innovator's Dilemma*, in 1997. In it, he differentiated between "sustaining" innovation and "disruptive" innovation. Sustaining innovation makes existing products and services better. This is an important priority for successful businesses and their focus on serving their best and most profitable customers.

Disruption happens as an upstart's offering moves from fringe customers to mainstream customers over time because the company's products offer necessary functionality at lower prices. Initially, disruptive products may have lower quality and may not be attractive to an incumbent's customer base. For this reason, market leaders often ignore these disruptive technologies. At best, these products appeal to their lowest-end, least-profitable customers and/or to entirely new customers. Disruptive companies have different business models with different capabilities. Not all disruptive innovations succeed, but some do so spectacularly by replacing incumbent business models.[4]

Netflix is a textbook case study of disruptive innovation. It initially distributed movie DVDs to its customers through the US mail. Customers paid monthly fees in exchange for a predetermined number of ongoing movie rentals (e.g., up to three at any time). Netflix served a fringe market. It took over a decade for the company's streaming technology to attract enough customers to displace Blockbuster's retail store model. By the time Blockbuster recognized the threat to its business model, the company didn't have the time or resources to respond.

Figure 8.1 depicts the process through which disruptive technology displaces existing technology over time.[5]

Incumbent health companies confront a daunting "innovator's dilemma" as they position for post-reform sustainability. Should they maximize profits by giving high-margin customers more features and

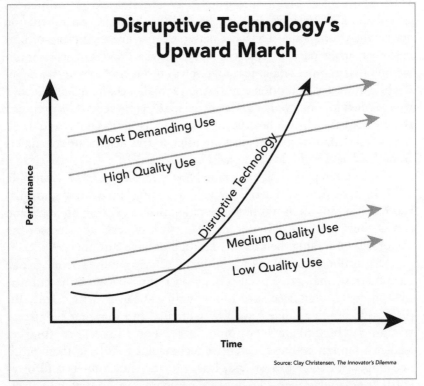

Disruptive Technology's Upward March

Most Demanding Use

High Quality Use

Disruptive Technology

Medium Quality Use

Low Quality Use

Performance

Time

Source: Clay Christensen, *The Innovator's Dilemma*

FIGURE 8.1 Disruptive technologies begin with low-end users and go upmarket as their product offerings gain more functionality.

services, many of which are unneeded? Or should they invest in lower-margin "retail" products/services that have growth potential but cut into profits? The tricky answer may be to do both, but incumbents tend to overserve high-end customers and underserve or even ignore low-end customers. In select industry segments, this exposes incumbents to disruptive competition and market-share losses.

The differences between sustaining and disruptive innovation are nuanced, industry-specific, and often misunderstood. In a December 2015 article titled "What Is Disruptive Innovation?" in *Harvard Business Review*, authors Clayton Christensen, Michael Raynor, and Rory McDonald explain why the rise of Uber and other rideshare companies is a form of sustaining innovation, not disruptive innovation.[6]

Uber did not target low-end users or new market entrants when it launched in San Francisco during the summer of 2010. Uber's sophisticated clientele already knew how "to hire" taxis. Uber's product offering was superior (lower prices, smartphone connectivity, point-to-point services), not inferior, to that offered by taxis. Taxi companies realized the threat posed by rideshare companies immediately and have endeavored to respond.

Ridesharing companies have expanded the marketplace for taxi services. That's not disruption but an organic byproduct of developing a "better, less-expensive solution to a widespread customer need." Bottom line is that rideshare technology is a sustaining innovation that has transformed but not disrupted the taxi industry.

Uber is an anomaly. According to the *HBR* article, only 6 percent of new market entrants pursuing sustaining innovation succeed. Incumbents generally respond well to new business offerings directed at their core customers. Even Tesla, an innovative and well-funded automobile company, is having difficulty establishing a foothold. The authors speculate that the highly regulated character of the taxi industry discouraged innovation, making incumbent business vulnerable to the competitive threat posed by rideshare companies like Uber.

Like the taxi industry, healthcare's highly regulated operating environment and artificial economics make incumbent business models brittle, resistant to change, and poor at solving customers' jobs-to-be-done. As a consequence, healthcare incumbents are exceptionally vulnerable to new market entrants offering sustaining innovation (like Uber in taxi services) and disruptive innovation (like Netflix in movie rentals).

Centralized service delivery, entrenched intermediaries, perverse financial incentives, and administrative complexity drive up costs, alienate customers, frustrate consumers, and stunt innovation. The System overserves and underserves consumers simultaneously, which creates both over- and underconsumption of healthcare services. The System's endemic fragmentation distorts the industry's supply-demand dynamics to the point where doing the right thing for consumers does not optimize profitability.

The normalization of healthcare's supply-demand relationships creates significant opportunities for new entrants with sustaining and disruptive product offerings. They are offering new services to fill unmet customer and/or consumer needs with business models that expand access, offer convenience, and lower costs. They win by fulfilling customers' jobs-to-be-done.

JOBS-TO-BE-DONE

Too many companies forget they exist to solve customer problems. Harvard economist Theodore Levitt termed this syndrome "marketing myopia."[7] Railroad companies, for example, may think they are in the railroad business when customers actually "hire" them to transport people and products. Not understanding the "Jobs" for which customers "hire" and fire them clouds strategy development and resource allocation.

In another *Harvard Business Review* article titled "Know Your Customers 'Jobs to Be Done,'" authors Clayton Christensen, Taddy Hall, Karen Dillon, and David Duncan discuss why companies must develop a deep understanding of their customers and their needs to drive innovation and maintain market competitiveness. From the authors' perspectives, jobs-to-be-done have the four following characteristics:[8]

1. Jobs aren't tasks; they are more holistic and involve experiences.
2. The customer's circumstances are the most important factor to understand.
3. Good innovations solve problems that had either poor or no solutions at all.
4. Jobs have powerful social and emotional dimensions.

A classic Christensen case study illustrates the power of "Jobs." McDonald's wanted to increase milkshake sales. Its attempts to use consumer data and focus groups failed to develop marketing strategies that moved the needle. A deeper inquiry revealed why customers actually "hire" milkshakes. Believe it or not, McDonald's sold half of all its milkshakes before 8:30 in the morning. Turned out that many customers "hire" milkshakes because they are both filling and relieve the tedium of long commutes.

Milkshakes are easier to consume, longer lasting, and less guilt-inducing than cookies, doughnuts, candy, and other products competing for that "Job." With this knowledge, McDonald's realized that the potential milkshake market was seven times larger than it had previously estimated. So it went back to the food laboratory and created a "Morning Milkshake" that was thicker (longer lasting) and contained small chunks of fruit (healthier, enticing) to make long commutes more palatable. Sales skyrocketed.[9]

Companies succeed by deeply understanding the specific reason customers make purchasing decisions. Focusing on "Jobs" creates great customer experiences that are difficult for competitors to replicate. Any store can sell a milkshake. Not every store understands its customers are "hiring" milkshakes. That knowledge makes all the difference.

In their article, the authors suggest five ways that companies can identify their customers' jobs-to-be-done.

1. **Examine existing operations for poorly solved problems.** In healthcare, this could be tedious and duplicative personal data collection at doctors' offices.
2. **Look for nonconsumption,** which is often where the richest opportunities lie. In healthcare, where are the people who choose not to engage with primary care providers?
3. **Take note of workarounds,** where there are only inefficient solutions to pressing problems. In emergency departments, nurses sometimes write patient notes on their hands.
4. **Consider tasks people want to avoid,** the negative jobs, and make them more tolerable. For example, now there are in-home colon cancer screening tests.
5. **Be alert to new uses for established products.** Minoxidil, a drug used to treat high blood pressure that also stimulates hair growth, became Rogaine.

Healthcare is replete with jobs yet to be discovered, let alone done. Innovators find solutions when they focus on customers' unmet needs. One of healthcare's biggest unfolding stories illustrates how employing jobs-to-be-done logic could get a blockbuster company up and running.

AS EASY AS ABJ[10]

In January 2018, Amazon, Berkshire Hathaway, and JPMorgan Chase (ABJ, now Haven) announced their intention to create an independent venture to manage the companies' combined million-plus employees and dependents. In June, after an extended search, ABJ announced that acclaimed author and surgeon Atul Gawande would lead its new health company. Gawande applies a surgeon's care, technocratic expertise, and a storyteller's magic to inform and engage his expansive audience on health policy, economics, and patient experience. Atul Gawande is healthcare's most effective thought leader. He is an inspired choice for an organization that aims to change healthcare.

In the press release announcing the venture, Berkshire Hathaway CEO and legendary investor Warren Buffett made this harrowing comment:

> The ballooning costs of healthcare act as a hungry tapeworm on the American economy. Our group does not come to this problem with answers. But we also do not accept it as inevitable.

In the same press release, Gawande noted that "the [healthcare] system is broken, and better is possible." Being ABJ's CEO requires far more than executive experience. Being credible, trusted, and persuasive are prerequisites for healthcare's most visible CEO role.

Effective communications with internal and external audiences will constitute at least half of Gawande's new job responsibilities. Employees will wonder what's happening to their benefits. Pundits will question how ABJ is "transforming" healthcare.

Gawande's deep industry knowledge and communication skills will be vital in winning the hearts and minds of ABJ's employees. Their collective quest for better health and wellness can provide a blueprint for reorganizing how Americans engage with healthcare providers.

By focusing on the health and healthcare "Jobs" by both consumers and companies, ABJ could organize its resources to achieve both near-term and longer-term success. The functional matrix (Figure 8.2) identifies these "Jobs" and how they intersect with one another.

Essentially, individuals have three "Jobs" with regard to their health and wellness.

1. **Fix me when I'm broken.** Address an acute issue to return consumers back to their previous health status.

	Consumer Jobs-to-Be-Done		
	Fix Me When I'm Broken	Sustain My Health	Enhance My Health
ATTRACT & RETAIN TALENT			
Purchasing Healthcare			
Episodic	X		
Ongoing	X	X	
Wellness		X	X
End-of-Life Care & Planning	X	X	
Advocacy	X	X	X
MAXIMIZE PRODUCTIVITY			
Social Care		X	X
Incentives	X	X	X
Wellness		X	X
Stress		X	X
Smoking		X	X
Exercise		X	X
Diet		X	X

Corporate Jobs-to-Be-Done

FIGURE 8.2 **Healthcare must address all three of consumers' "Jobs."**

2. **Sustain my health.** Support consumers' existing health journeys, enabling them to accomplish what is important and feasible given existing health status.
3. **Enhance my health.** Enable consumers to make the necessary changes to improve their health status.

Employers essentially have two "Jobs" for which healthcare and benefits are potential solutions. They need to attract and retain top talent as well as maximize employee productivity. Offering attractive health benefits and engaging in workplace wellness are proven strategies for getting and keeping productive employees productive.

Consumers' first Job, "fix me when I'm broken," falls squarely within the purview of the healthcare system. Parts of the second and third do as well. To facilitate an employee's ability to "sustain my health" and "enhance my health," employers must acknowledge and address the reality that lifestyle choices have a far greater impact on long-term health than medical treatment.

All three "Jobs" require the active engagement of individual consumers to achieve optimal results. A heart attack patient gets medical care in the hospital, but complying with the new medications and diet after he or she goes home is critical. Moving to Jobs two and three, changing individual behaviors increases in importance.

For the most part, employers have not been effective purchasers of healthcare services, nor have they created wellness-oriented work environments and cultures.

Under Gawande's leadership, ABJ has the ability to do both by helping employees "solve" their health and healthcare "Jobs" more successfully through benefit design, healthcare purchasing, corporate wellness, and end-of-life care/planning.

- **Benefit design.** Promote more holistic care coverage through benefit structures that incorporate both health and social care services. Encourage employees to seek the right care at the right time in the right place at the right price with a creative mix of financial and health-oriented incentives. Capture and measure improvement in biometric health data. Reward those who improve.

- **Healthcare purchasing.** Develop high-performing networks that funnel volume to high-quality, high-value providers. Help employees make the right healthcare decisions consistently with second opinions and care navigation services. Make primary care easily available through on-site clinics. Pioneer technologies that support informed healthcare decision making. Use market leverage where possible to support direct contracting for episodic care and shift care management risk to third parties.

- **Corporate wellness.** Prioritize the health of the many over the healthcare for the few. Be patient, since successful corporate wellness programs require behavioral change, which takes time to engender. Create personalized wellness programs that accommodate each individual's unique circumstances.

After its launch in 2007, the Cleveland Clinic's Wellness Institute lost money for several years before seeing declines in utilization and increases in worker productivity. Today, the Clinic has a more productive workforce (many fewer days lost to illness and injury) and saves $150 million annually in health insurance premiums for its 101,000 covered lives.

- **End-of-life care/planning.** Recognize that the cost and pain associated with ill-advised end-of-life care is astronomical, as is the impact on an individual's health (and productivity).

Good luck Atul and ABJ/Haven. Your country needs you to succeed.

MARKET SEGMENTATION

The US healthcare marketplace is changing rapidly and segmenting into four distinct areas—commodity care, specialty care, complex care, and chronic care—based on care duration and care uncertainty. Each segment requires a different business model to compete effectively (Figure 8.3).

Most medical treatments are routine and subject to commoditization. With outcome certainty, consumers judge quality based on speed, convenience, and service. Commodity care is a high-volume, low-margin business. Specialty care requires focused "factories." Complex care is a "solutions shop" business. Chronic care requires intense, non-acute customer engagement.

As discussed above, new market entrants search for opportunities to address unmet market needs (Netflix) and/or exploit existing inefficiencies (Uber). Upstart companies target their points of market entry based on where they believe they can deliver competitive advantage with either a sustaining or disruptive innovation. The "Commodity" and "Chronic" quadrants are where the majority of healthcare activity and transactions occur. They are also the two quadrants where new market entrants are best positioned to challenge incumbents.

For example, Smart Choice MRI offers $600 (or less) MRIs throughout metropolitan Chicago in convenient centers that operate six days a week. Clinicians from the Cleveland Clinic review each Smart Choice MRI for diagnostic accuracy. Imaging services are "commodity care" and should be priced accordingly. Smart Choice advertises that "MRIs shouldn't cost an arm and a leg" and hails their platform as "the cure for the $2,600 MRI."

Each quadrant has different types of customers and requires a different business model to succeed. This creates significant opportunities for

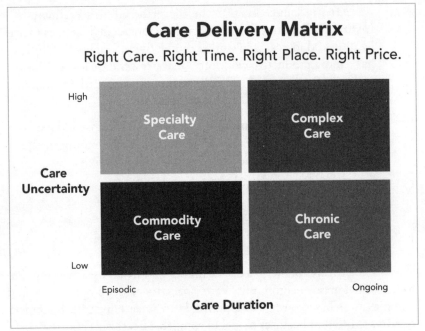

FIGURE 8.3 Consumers need different types of medical care, and care delivery models are adapting to address those needs.

companies with new and innovative business models that solve customer "Jobs" that the System's incumbents aren't addressing. In post-reform healthcare, winning healthcare companies must deliver positive outcomes and great competitive prices.

TRANSFORMERS AND DISRUPTORS

Most new market entrants strive for incremental improvement in products, services, and delivery. The System has plenty of gaps and much need for performance improvement. A host of companies want to fill these gaps. They earn traction with customers by lowering costs, improving convenience, and providing great service. Record numbers of start-up companies are jumping into healthcare, particularly in healthcare technology and services. Established companies also see opportunity in the sector.

"Smart" venture, corporate, and private equity investment is flowing into healthcare in record amounts to fund new entrants. The range of these investments is breathtaking. For example, in 2018 investors poured $662 million into direct-to-consumer companies combining virtual doctor visits and the delivery of prescriptions for everything from birth control pills to contact lenses to Viagra to hair loss medications.[11]

Revolutionary companies have a passion for making healthcare more accessible, affordable, convenient, and humane. They're committed to doing whatever it takes to make healthcare better and more accountable. Revolutionary companies are not only passionate, they're smart. They're applying sustaining and disruptive innovation to challenging "Jobs" and developing new business models that get those "Jobs" done.

At this breakpoint in the industry's history, established healthcare companies ignore revolutionary upstarts at their own peril. Healthcare upstarts, transformers, and disruptors fall into one or more of the following forms of Revolutionary Healthcare:

- Enhanced primary care services

- Focused factories

- Asset-light healthcare delivery

- Retail healthcare services

- Customized health insurance products

Enhanced primary care services are the most transformative and disruptive of these four delivery components. Moreover, many asset-light and retail health businesses incorporate enhanced primary care services into their operations.

Enhanced Primary Care Services

In 1970, "Marcus Welby, MD," became ABC's first show to top network television ratings. Dr. Welby was a cheerful family practice physician with a soothing bedside manner who was on a first-name basis with his patients. In the toughest cases, Welby focused on his patients' clinical, social, and even spiritual needs. In turn, patients trusted Welby, embraced his care, and got better.

The best, most cost-effective health outcomes occur when providers build long-term, trusting relationships with patients and proactively treat disease through real engagement, frequent dialogue, and shared decision making. At its best, primary care helps prevent, mitigate, and manage chronic disease and other serious conditions.

Unfortunately, American healthcare has largely forgotten the wisdom of patient-centered primary care. Specialization, technology, and activity-based billing practices rob consumers of vital time and engagement with their primary care doctors. Personal connection atrophies as patients move through mechanized treatment regimens.

Fortunately, powerful new primary care companies are emerging to fill America's care management void. Although their business models vary, these companies share an unshakable belief that relationship-based healthcare generates better outcomes, happier customers, and lower all-in costs. Somewhere, Marcus Welby is nodding in vigorous agreement.

Capitalism's genius is that it empowers enterprising companies to find and fill market needs. The demand for relationship-based primary care services combined with aligned payment models is catalyzing the growth of care management businesses that offer more coordinated, holistic, and concierge-like services.

The primary care market divides into four quadrants based on care duration and intensity (Figure 8.4).

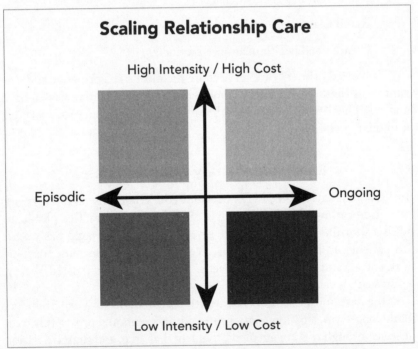

FIGURE 8.4 Different primary care "spokes" for "folks" with different healthcare jobs-to-be-done.

Maintenance and Urgent Care (Episodic)

New primary care businesses models are emerging that provide better, more convenient, and lower-cost care. Telemedicine companies such as Zipnosis or Doctor On Demand and walk-in clinics such as MinuteClinic offer low-cost primary care services that tackle immediate care needs.

Other companies offer economical concierge-like services that enable primary care physicians to practice relationship-based care with an emphasis on prevention and long-term health. These new models extend the capabilities of primary care physicians and delight customers.

Chronic and Complex Care (Ongoing)

Risk-based contracting (e.g., through Medicare Advantage) rewards providers that deliver integrated, relationship-based, holistic, and preventive care. This creates a robust revenue source for enhanced, relationship-based primary care companies. Many are emerging to exploit this business opportunity.

People with multiple comorbidities, behavioral health problems, addiction issues, and significant social deficiencies (isolation, lack of housing, poor nutrition, etc.) require complex care services that address their clinical and social needs. Treating complex patients requires "going the extra mile" to stabilize patients, monitor their progress, and provide necessary services.

High-growth primary-care organizations target different populations (different folks) and orient their delivery (different spokes) to meet client-specific needs. Though approaches vary, they share the following important characteristics:

- Capitated, value-based, or at-risk payment models in distinct market segments that align physicians and care teams with patient needs, better outcomes, and lower costs.

- Team-based care models that engage patients as consumers in convenient settings with comprehensive services.

- Supportive infrastructure that reduces administrative burdens and costs while enabling engagement, experience, and service.

- Coordinated care services that promote early diagnosis, prevention, and appropriate care interventions.

- Robust data sourcing, analytics, and technology to identify risk, improve performance, and enhance growth.

Enhanced primary care services are essential for higher-functioning healthcare. As capitated payment models expand and evolve, new entrants emerge to address that societal need. The battle for better primary care takes place on two fronts. Business model innovation focuses on market share and member satisfaction. Care delivery innovation focuses on clinical precision, optimal outcomes, reduced utilization, and lower costs. The main lesson is that value works. When payment models align with consumer needs, care delivery improves, and care providers rediscover the joys of practicing medicine.

This bottom-up, customer-focused, business-savvy approach to healthcare transforms healthcare services, lives, and even communities. The "Dr. Welby" approach to relationship-based medicine is their formula. Their divergent "spokes" encompass the totality of America's primary care needs and holds great promise for the future of American healthcare.

Focused Factories

"Focused factories" are high-volume, specialized service providers. They position themselves to deliver high-quality care at lower costs with great customer service. With high volumes come superior outcomes, operating efficiency, and customized services. Focused factories specialize in "fix me when I'm broken" solutions.

For example, DaVita Healthcare serves patients with kidney ailments. Their unusual approach to care creates a de facto community center for patients who often spend many hours each day receiving dialysis treatments. Other focused factories address orthopedic, cardiology, cancer, gastrointestinal, and other specialty areas of care.

Asset-Light Health Companies

In an industry burdened by overinvestment in high-cost infrastructure, asset-light health companies are powerful transformers of existing business models. These companies refrain from heavy facility investments and concentrate on effective care management. Many are vertically integrated companies offering health insurance coverage as well as care delivery.

Asset-light companies come in many flavors. They deliver primary and specialty care services, manage care risk for large populations, provide Internet-based home care services, and support shared decision making. Notable examples of asset-light health companies include Group Health in metropolitan Seattle (now part of Kaiser Permanente Washington);

HealthPartners in the Twin Cities; HealthCare Partners in El Segundo, California; Dean Clinic in Madison, Wisconsin; and Kaiser Permanente in California.

While these organizations have existed for decades, they're now poised to exploit marketplace demands for more efficient and cost-effective care delivery through a number of distinct advantages.

- Asset-light health companies are *not burdened by high overhead and facility costs*. They use their facilities intensely and, when necessary, rent capacity at favorable prices to reduce per-unit care costs.

- Asset-light business models *align with patient/customer needs*. They focus on prevention, provide appropriate care in multiple, convenient settings, and avoid unnecessary hospital-based treatments.

- Asset-light health companies are *well positioned for full-risk contracting*. They combine insurance capabilities with targeted treatment expertise. That lends itself to direct contracting with employers, managing capitated population health contracting (e.g., for Medicare Advantage).

- Asset-light health companies threaten centralized, asset-heavy business models. They are *more efficient, customer-friendly, and lower cost* than traditional hospital providers.

Chicago-based DuPage Medical Group (DMG) is the largest multispecialty physician group in Illinois, and it's quickly becoming much more. Beginning in late 2015, when DMG sold a minority stake to private equity firm Summit Partners, the company has expanded rapidly by acquiring physician practices and expanding service offerings. DMG's Management Services Organization (MSO) equips new physician groups to work within the company's vertically integrated platform.

DMG's asset-light business model delivers high-value healthcare services in the following ways:

- **DMG assumes payment risk in all its contracts.** It adjusts transaction structures to meet customer and market needs. DMG welcomes the opportunity to take full capitated risk with Medicare Advantage patients. Many providers aspire to offer superior care management, but few achieve that goal. As DMG CEO Mike Kasper observes, "I've never met a provider who didn't think they can manage risk. Few ultimately can."

- **DMG's BreakThrough Care Centers manage care for fragile Medicare patients.** Coordinated teams consisting of primary care physicians, micro-specialists, extenders, pharmacists, social workers, and health coaches, all working together to tailor care plans to individual needs. The team goal is to improve customer well-being and eliminate unnecessary acute interventions. For example, BreakThrough hospitalists approve and guide emergency care at local hospitals.

- **DMG has engaged with Blue Cross Blue Shield of Illinois to access member cost and quality data.** DMG bolsters its care management capabilities through deeper understanding of patient risk stratification, outcome variation, and facility costs. This helps DMG physicians deliver the right care at the right time in the right place.

Another massive capital infusion in 2017 from Ares Capital fuels DMG's ongoing growth.[12] DMG applies the additional funding to purchase physician practices, expand into new geographies, and enter into complementary service lines such as physical therapy.

In every consumer market, customers care more about outputs (products, services, and customer experience) than the production process. Hospitals were once the primary symbol for healthcare. Increasingly, they are becoming niche components within robust health and wellness networks.

Innovative health companies like DuPage Medical Group eschew facility ownership to focus their investments and resources on delivering what consumers crave—better, more convenient and affordable healthcare services. They beat incumbents by building more efficient, cost-effective, and ever-improving platforms of connected capabilities, suppliers, and data, assembled to identify and fulfill customer needs.

Doctors are flocking to asset-light health companies because they want to practice medicine, not churn patients. Companies like DMG remove barriers, facilitate integration, and engage consumers by making routine care quick, easy, and reliable. Asset-light providers invest in physician groups and low-cost clinics and ambulatory facilities. Consequently they run efficient, high-volume practices with very low per-unit costs. They apply technology (e.g., telemedicine) appropriately to improve care access and efficiency.

Retail Healthcare Services

In 2018, retail went healthcare as a variety of large retail companies (Walmart, Walgreens, CVS) and a mix of promising upstarts (Smart Choice MRI, CityMD, Aligned Modern Health) enlarged their care-delivery footprints. These companies and others like them provide high-volume routine care and diagnostic services. They cover an increasing range of medical services, including urgent care, MRIs, colonoscopies, vision services, and back pain. Their convenient locations, customer-friendly hours, and transparent low prices are at the forefront of healthcare's customer revolution.

As consumers increasingly avail themselves of retail healthcare services and appreciate the quality they receive, they will come to expect such a better, more consumer-friendly experience from all their care providers. Woe to traditional providers that don't accommodate their demands.

Best Buy's August 2018 acquisition of GreatCall is part of the broader retail-driven movement to engage consumers more directly in their healthcare. Best Buy's strategy reflects a nuanced understanding of consumerism, retail market dynamics, and America's need for more connected, holistic care services. Retail giants Amazon, Apple, CVS, Walgreens, and Walmart among others are also targeting healthcare for sales growth. Their collective efforts are reconfiguring healthcare's competitive landscape.

Founded in 2006, GreatCall's initial vision was to connect people through simple, easy-to-navigate phones. The concept caught on with elderly subscribers.[13] GreatCall now operates a broad-based platform that incorporates phones, apps, wearables, urgent care, alert services, health coaching, and more. They strive to improve life quality for the growing population of America's seniors and those who care for them.[14]

With an $800 million purchase price, GreatCall is the largest acquisition in Best Buy's storied history. Having survived the 10-year onslaught of Amazon, Best Buy understands the necessity of meeting customer needs in flexible, tailored ways. In its press release announcing the acquisition, Best Buy precisely describes how it will attack the healthcare marketplace:

> [Best Buy is] specifically focused on addressing the growing needs of the aging population with the help of technology products, services and solutions.

The health space is a large, growing market where technology can help in particular address the needs of aging consumers, their caregivers, payers and providers.

Today, there are approximately 50 million Americans over age 65, a number that is expected to increase by more than 50 percent within the next 20 years.[15]

GreatCall's premier product is the Jitterbug mobile phone service. With big print and easy-to-use navigation, the Jitterbug phone is ideal for seniors. It connects them to the services they need when they need them. My mother had one and loved it. Imagine Best Buy delivering Geek Squad in-home care capabilities to GreatCall's large and growing subscriber base. That's transformational power in action.

Consumerism has the force and precision of heat-seeking missiles. Customers flocked to Walmart because it offered more selection, greater convenience, and lower prices than local "mom-and-pop" retailers. Amazon threatens Walmart because it offers even more selection, even greater convenience, and even lower prices.

Customized Health Insurance Products

A Tree Grows in Minnesota (and Beyond)

In 1998, seven exiles from Deloitte & Touche and Hewitt Associates launched a new healthcare start-up in Minneapolis named Definity Health. The driving idea behind Definity was radical for the time: consumers should have more decision power over how to spend their healthcare dollars. This was the birth of health reimbursement accounts, the predecessor of Health Savings Accounts (HSAs), and the nation's first foray into consumer-driven healthcare.

UnitedHealthGroup acquired Definity Health in 2004. By then, the thriving start-up served nearly 100 employer clients, including 23 Fortune 500s, providing 500,000 consumers with self-funded benefit plan arrangements.

Typically after a successful exit, founders and senior leaders go on to launch new ventures, forming new branches from an entrepreneurial tree. Often, those founders search for new ways to solve similar societal and market needs. So it was with Definity's founders.

Three cofounders, Kyle Rolfing, Abir Sen, and Pat Sukhum, cofounded RedBrick Health, a corporate wellness and employee engagement company. Tony Miller cofounded Carol Corporation, a platform that enables consumers to comparison shop for healthcare services.

After exiting RedBrick and Carol, these entrepreneurs went on to launch other ventures in the health insurance sector. Their current companies are representative of a new breed of payers attacking the Healthcare Industrial Complex with consumerism.

In 2015, Kyle Rolfing cofounded Bright Health with former United-Healthcare CEO Bob Sheehy and former Carol cofounder Tom Valdivia. Backed by $440 million in venture capital, Bright Health provides individual, family, and Medicare Advantage health plans.

Bright Health partners with one health system per market. It then brings deep knowledge of insurance, provider networks, and patient experience to bear on the problem of incentivized alignment. Bright Health's platform combines consumerism, provider network expertise, benefits design, and big data analytics to give health system partners the capabilities of an integrated "payvider" with a sharpened focus on better consumer-clinician relationships.

"We thought if we could align with a leading health system and physician groups, we could work together to improve the value that we bring to the consumer," said Bright Health CEO Bob Sheehy.[16]

Tony Miller launched Bind in 2016 to offer what the company calls "on-demand health insurance." Backed by $70 million in seed funding from UnitedHealthcare, Ascension Ventures, and Lemhi Ventures, Bind's goal is to make coverage more affordable, more transparent, and less confusing.

The premise of on-demand coverage is simple. People access healthcare when they need it for a variety of predictable and unpredictable health conditions. They rely on insurance to help cover those costs.

Bind enrollees get their basic healthcare needs met through a core insurance plan that includes preventive care, primary care, chronic care management, pharmaceuticals, emergency care, and treatment for diseases like cancer. That core plan does not require coinsurance or deductible payments but does require co-pays. For expensive, predictable treatments such as knee or hip surgery, Bind offers condition-specific "add-ins" to an individual's core plans to cover additional costs and co-pays.

For all coverage and care, Bind uses data analytics to determine optimal care paths that reduce waste and improve outcomes. It pushes costs down and quality up by nudging consumer behavior through co-pays that vary depending on condition, provider, and setting.

A patient with the flu who seeks treatment via an e-visit or at an urgent care clinic will likely pay a lower co-pay than one who visits the ED or who has a more serious condition. Likewise, co-pays and premium costs will vary for add-in conditions depending on the treatment path the patient chooses.

Bind provides enrollees transparent information about those costs and quality measures about the outcomes delivered by different care paths and providers. This transparency enables consumers to make the decisions that best meet their financial and health needs. Consumers select the right care at the right time in the right setting at the right cost for themselves and/or family members.

In cofounder Tony Miller's words: "What [Bind] is doing for the first time in health insurance is pairing a coverage decision with clinical choice at the point of need, instead of at the point of enrollment."[17]

Bright and Bind are among a host of other powerful upstarts in the insurance sector. Oscar Health aims to connect insurance payment with patient needs by applying digital tools and transparent claims payments. Lumeris operates as a value-based care managed services company that aligns providers and payers with the deeper needs of patient populations. Devoted Health focuses primarily on Medicare Advantage beneficiaries, supporting them with care guides, a network of trusted providers of healthcare and digital technology.

Such companies are developing value-based insurance coverage products that differentiate price, service, quality, and consumerism. Will these upstarts succeed? As Tony Miller says, "Disruptive startups are like a horde of zombies storming the walls. It only takes a few making it over the wall to take down the system and change everything."

Incumbent organizations are fooling themselves if they believe traditional business models that impede consumerism are safe from these hungry disruptors.

Consumerism is an intricate, never-ending dance between companies and their customers. Businesses exist only to find and keep customers. Success requires constant engagement, constant adjustment, and a consistent ability to give customers what they want at competitive prices. As healthcare becomes more consumer driven and retail oriented, winning health companies will develop deep consumer instincts to connect with customers and enhance strategic effectiveness.

GETTING "HEALTH" JOBS DONE

As evidenced by the Amazon, Berkshire Hathaway, and JPMorgan Chase (ABJ) discussion above, companies must invest in both healthcare and wellness services to address customers' jobs-to-be-done. Health and wellness go together like love and marriage.

The US healthcare industry (the System) focuses disproportionately on offense (treating disease) even though playing better defense (preventing disease) would yield more victories. Not requiring a surgical procedure is always a better outcome than even the most successful procedure by the world's greatest surgeon. Healthy individuals are happier, more productive, and more engaged with their communities. Promoting health and preventing disease generate huge societal dividends.

America needs more balance between preventing and treating disease. By any measure, healthcare is a weak-link enterprise, only as strong as its weakest link. Effective preventive care, health promotion, behavioral health, and chronic disease management dramatically reduce the need for high-cost acute interventions. Addressing harmful social, environmental, and lifestyle factors successfully reduces the need for acute interventions.

In weak-link enterprises, it's tempting to recognize and reward individual success. Real glory, however, belongs to cohesive teams working together within well-crafted operating systems. Reinvigorating primary and preventive care services for individuals will do more to achieve Revolutionary Healthcare in America than any other intervention.

As discussed above, the primary-care marketplace segments into the following four quadrants based on consumers' social and care needs: maintenance care, urgent care, complex care, and chronic care. Fortunately, upstart and established companies by the dozens are charging into primary care and practicing the right kind of defensive medicine—the type that prevents disease and promotes health. Their results are stunning and transformative. As they grow, enhanced primary care companies will break the System's back and deliver for the American people.

The profiles of the four companies below illustrate how enhanced primary care providers tailor their services to sustain and enhance their customers' health. They get consumers' health and healthcare "Jobs" done!

Absolutely Necessary: Complex Care

The most expensive patient in Maryland, let's call him George, was a frequent user of emergency department services, often with multiple same-day visits. George's insurer shifted responsibility for his ongoing care to a company with a different strategy. AbsoluteCARE is a patient-centered ambulatory ICU that utilizes innovative population health management tools to care for individuals with complex chronic disease.

George's care team huddled one morning to discuss strategies to improve George's health. The team's van driver mentioned that George was outgoing and an active churchgoer, so they determined that his social needs were as urgent as his medical needs. Another team member suggested asking George to become a clinic greeter to make sure he'd get his daily medications and more social interaction. Problem solved! George stopped needing ED visits almost immediately. With help from his care team, George managed his chronic disease as he made community connections.

AbsoluteCARE launched in 2000 when it opened its first HIV Center of Excellence in Atlanta. In 2009, the company expanded its scope of services to also offer primary and chronic care services. In 2016, Guardian Life Insurance of America acquired AbsoluteCARE's parent company, Avesis, and AbsoluteCARE became a separate business providing holistic disease management services to individuals with severe chronic disease. Essentially, the company provides ambulatory ICU services to growing numbers of patients in Atlanta, Philadelphia, and Maryland.

AbsoluteCARE treats the "sickest of the sick," specifically the 5 percent of patients with the most challenging social and healthcare needs. These complex patients often live under stressful socioeconomic conditions and suffer from addiction and behavioral health problems. They typically consume 30–40 percent of a health plan's care expenditures.

Operating under full-risk contracts with government and commercial payers, AbsoluteCARE uses claims data and predictive analytics to design social and healthcare programs for its members at attractive medical centers in urban neighborhoods. Team members do "whatever it takes" to address members' needs.

Patients get five-star concierge service and are "treated with love and respect," according to AbsoluteCARE CEO Alan Cohn. Engagement starts with the basics, including food, clothing, shelter, addiction treatment, and behavioral health services. The care teams address longer-term chronic care needs once patients stabilize. Routine services include regular check-ins and checkups, nutrition counseling, diagnostics, pharmacy, medication adherence, lab, infusion, radiology, counseling, community outreach, and education. The centers also have a wing that provides acute care for exacerbations of chronic conditions. Walk-ins are welcome.

"We're changing lives," Cohn notes. "We see a real difference within six to nine months." Cohn says that progress cycles through generations. "If parents do better, children do better. Ideally we can stop intergenerational chronic disease."

AbsoluteCARE's approach to serving this population reduces emergency visits by 43 percent, inpatient admissions by 45 percent, inpatient days by 42 percent, and health plan costs by more than 30 percent annually. Its STAR measures have increased from the twentieth percentile to the ninetieth percentile. The company plans to add 10 more locations over the next several years.

A Tree Grows in Chicago: Chronic and Complex Care

Oak Street Health is on a mission to "rebuild healthcare the way it should be." Oak Street launched in 2012 with the belief that aligning the right people, resources, and payment models would generate better outcomes and healthier consumers at lower costs.

Oak Street's consumers are low-income urban seniors (dual-eligible to receive Medicare and Medicaid services). The company builds clinics that double as community centers in underserved neighborhoods. Oak Street's centers offer a broad range of services related to clinical care, social work, education, and entertainment that encourage frequent visits.

When opening a new neighborhood center, Oak Street's first challenge is to build community awareness. Oak Street staff conducts "boots on the ground" outreach to local churches and social clubs. Their integrated care teams spend extensive time with new members to get to know them and assess social and care needs.

One member, let's call him Tom, learned about Oak Street through a church meeting. With some encouragement, Tom started giving talks on World War II history at his neighborhood Oak Street clinic and then became a member. Tom's care team noticed he missed a few classes, checked in, and learned from Tom that he had a sore foot that kept him from walking. An Oak Street driver brought him to the clinic, where staff diagnosed a serious infection. Untreated, the infection would have cost Tom his foot. Instead, a timely course of IV antibiotics cured the problem, and he was walking again in no time.

Predetermined payments from Medicare Advantage and Medicaid fund Oak Street's business model. As CEO Mike Pykosz says, "We can take care of people knowing we'll be fairly compensated." Oak Street assumes full financial responsibility for its patients and gets a percentage of savings from its health plan partners. This revenue allows Oak Street to devote significantly more resources to members with complex care needs.

Oak Street is currently growing on three fronts: expanding its care model, moving into new geographies, and increasingly treating higher-risk Medicaid-only patients. "If their clinical needs are the same, and we can achieve better outcomes by serving those patients, we'll do it," Pykosz says.

Two outstanding care management companies, Iora and ChenMed, featured prominently in my previous book *Market vs. Medicine*. Like Oak Street, these companies serve Medicare Advantage patients. Their collective ambition is reaching enough scale to meaningfully challenge current primary care practice within individual marketplaces.

Once More with Feeling: Maintenance/Concierge Care

Founded in 2005 by entrepreneur Dr. Tom X. Lee, One Medical offers concierge medicine to on-the-go professionals without high annual fees. Attracting young, healthy patients is essential to the company's business model. For an annual $199 membership fee, patients receive the attention and services they want from trusted care providers. One Medical's clinics resemble boutique hotels. Short waits and last-minute availability are the norm.

Care delivery combines high-touch service with high-tech tools and applications. Members can access care through 24/7 phone support, virtual services, and mobile apps that include health coaching. Patients can e-mail their doctors with follow-up questions. One Medical's agile technology and data platforms keep administrative costs low.

The company increasingly offers direct contracting with enterprise customers, including Google and Uber. One Medical is expanding aggressively into new markets and recruiting more primary care physicians. Its market valuation exceeds $1 billion.

It Takes a Village: Broadband and Primary Care

VillageMD CEO Tim Barry says, "The problem with primary care is that we've taken this profession of people who love caring for a community of patients and forced them to work in ways that lead to suboptimal outcomes." In response, VillageMD returns job satisfaction to the practice of medicine.

The company accomplishes this through expansive provision of primary care services. VillageMD's "platform" incorporates data, technology, incentives, and protocols to support its doctors in delivering superior primary care services. In essence, VillageMD helps physicians serve their patients better.

Their primary care model focuses on total care quality and outcomes. They strive to eliminate unnecessary hospital admissions. As cofounder and CMO Clive Fields notes, "We're concierge medicine without the concierge or the cost."

VillageMD enters new markets, partners with existing primary care physician groups, and converts its physicians to risk-based contracts through management service organizations (MSOs). This aligns payment with desired treatment practices. To achieve optimal performance, the model requires leveraging size and scale across large patient populations.

VillageMD invests in technology, analytics, and management systems that reduce administrative burdens on physicians and drive aligned practices that lead to better outcomes, lower costs, and less utilization. High levels of physician satisfaction drive patient satisfaction.

VillageMD works closely with its health plan partners to deliver 15–20 percent lower cost care with better outcomes and member satisfaction. In 2015, it formed a joint venture with Community Health Network of Indianapolis called Primaria Health. This organization expanded rapidly to cover 130,000 members, becoming the largest primary care provider in central Indiana.

Convergence

The commitment to address individual health and healthcare jobs-to-be-done in holistic ways unites these four revolutionary primary care companies and others. Jesuit theologian Pierre Teilhard de Chardin's essay "Omega Point" was published in 1956, the year after his death. It contained this powerful observation, "Everything that rises must converge."

Convergence is the opposite of fragmentation, healthcare's nemesis. It's not enough to do one thing well. Health companies must do everything well to deliver great outcomes. Convergence occurs when healthcare professionals supported with real-time data and decision tools deliver tailored, compassionate, patient-centered care.

HERE'S TO THE CRAZY ONES

Eleven years after his ouster, Steve Jobs returned to Apple in 1997. The company was a shadow of its former self. Its market share had fallen from 16 percent to 4 percent. Its stock price had fallen from $70 to $13. As Jobs took the helm, Apple posted a $1 billion loss and was 90 days from insolvency. Clearly it was time to "Think different."

Steve Jobs undertook an intense three-week business and product-line review. Apple had become a bloated company with multiple business lines, numerous licensing agreements, and dozens of inferior products tailored to the whims of retailers. Product teams couldn't answer the simple question "Which Apple products should I tell my friends to buy?"

Steve Jobs exited the printer and server businesses, stopped providing software upgrades to Macintosh clones, shed jobs, and partnered with "evil" Microsoft to bring Microsoft products to Apple computers. When the dust settled, he bet the company's future on the Power Mac and PowerBook for the professional market and the iMac and iBook for the consumer market.

Through massive corporate restructuring, Jobs narrowed and sharpened Apple's business focus. Even more important, he reinvigorated the Apple brand by asking and answering these key questions: "Why does Apple exist, and what does it stand for?" To Jobs, the answer was clear: "At its core, Apple believes people with passion can change the world for the better."

To reintroduce the new Apple to the world and reconnect with consumers, Jobs launched the "Think Different" campaign with a commercial called "The Crazy Ones." The intent was to honor historical figures "crazy enough" to believe in their ability to change the world. "The Crazy Ones" linked historical icons as disparate but inspirational as Muhammad Ali, Pablo Picasso, and Bob Dylan with the Apple ethos and mindset.

The campaign won multiple awards and set the stage for Apple's launch of remarkable products that propelled the company to historic

CHAPTER 9

Revolutionary Incumbents

The 1950s was a perilous time for the tradition-bound British monarchy. A young queen's adaptability, resilience, and agility were essential to repositioning the monarchy for long-term sustainability. Facing similar existential challenges, leaders of established health companies can find durable lessons in change management from studying Queen Elizabeth's early reign.

In 1952, at the tender age of 25, Elizabeth Alexandra Mary Windsor became Queen of England upon the death of her father King George V. The first two seasons of the popular Netflix series *The Crown* depict the early years of Queen Elizabeth II's reign as she assumes her new responsibilities and the monarchy adapts to a rapidly changing postwar world where many questioned the monarchy's continued relevance.

This was a period of profound social change for Great Britain. Devastated by German bombing and catastrophic human losses during World War II, the country needed to rebuild. At the same time, the English people began a euphoric rush into a modernizing world characterized by growing prosperity, liberalizing social norms, and powerful new technologies, most notably television.

As Elizabeth assumed the throne, the British monarchy was out of step with the British people. Resolutely tradition-bound, it carried on as though nothing had changed. The monarchy's inability to connect meaningfully with its subjects threatened its relevance. This became apparent in 1957 when a routine speech at a Jaguar factory triggered a constitutional crisis. Performing her ceremonial duties, Queen Elizabeth spoke in a perfunctory and patronizing fashion to the assembled workers:

> We understand that in the turbulence of this anxious and active world, many of you are leading uneventful, lonely lives where dreariness is the enemy. Perhaps you don't understand that on your

steadfastness and ability to withstand the fatigue of dull, repetitive work depend, in great measure, the happiness and prosperity of the community as a whole.

The upward course of a nation's history is due, in the long run, to the soundness of heart of its average men and women. May you be proud to remember how much depends upon you and that even when your life seems most monotonous, what you do is always of real value and importance to your fellow countrymen.

To a people weary of sacrifice, this stiff-upper-lip rhetoric no longer resonated. Lord Altrincham, the same age as the Queen and a staunch monarchist, heard the speech in a dentist's packed waiting room. The other patients' distinct lack of interest in and respect for the Queen's remarks appalled him, but he believed the Queen herself was primarily responsible for the public's declining interest in the monarchy.

Altrincham circulated a harsh and controversial critique of the Queen in the August 1957 *National and English Review*, a publication he edited.[1] In it, he described the Queen's speaking style as a "pain in the neck" and attacked her public persona in unsparing terms:

The personality conveyed by the utterances which are put into her mouth is that of a priggish schoolgirl, captain of the hockey team, a prefect, and a recent candidate for Confirmation.

Altrincham's rebuke created a sensation and resonated with many. In a nationally televised interview with Robin Day, he made a prescient warning that the British monarchy needed to evolve or die. As Altrincham put it,

Until recently, monarchies were the rule and republics the exception, but today, republics are the rule and monarchies very much the exception.

The powerful are often the last to know that their influence has diminished. Loyalists tell them nothing has changed. Conservative instincts persuade them to stay the course. They miss obvious signals that the old rules no longer apply. They're in more trouble than they realize but often fail to take timely action. Only the agile, adaptive, and resilient survive.

To her great credit, Queen Elizabeth listened to the criticisms and initiated sweeping changes to improve her connection with the British people. She replaced debutante balls with garden parties, began televising her annual Christmas Message, and opened Buckingham Palace to the British people.

Unlike most monarchies that have vanished over the past century, the British Crown continues to navigate an ever-changing world. In Prince Harry's larger-than-life royal wedding on May 19, 2018, the Queen warmly welcomed once-divorced American Meghan Markle into the royal family. This was a sharp contrast to the traditional royal practice of forbidding marriage with divorcées. The Queen's uncle Edward VIII abdicated the throne to marry twice-divorced Wallis Simpson, and the Queen herself forbade her sister Margaret from marrying her divorced fiancé Peter Townsend.[2] How times change.

Queen Elizabeth's skill in transforming the Crown's relationship with the British people has kept the monarchy intact and relevant. Her adaptability to changing circumstances has been the hallmark of her remarkable 60-plus-year reign.

Like the postwar British monarchy, established US health companies confront a daunting transformational challenge. Their traditional business models are unsustainable and resistant to change. Customers and consumers want greater price transparency, care coordination, access, convenience, and value. Companies that meet those needs and deepen their customer connections will thrive as Revolutionary Healthcare takes hold.

There's no time to waste. December 2017 illustrated how far some established health companies are willing to go to respond to healthcare's changing market dynamics.

FIVE DAYS IN DECEMBER

When historians chronicle the transformation of the US healthcare system, they will cite the events of December 3–7, 2017, as a major turning point. In that remarkable five-day period, a series of blockbuster announcements rocked the healthcare industry. These transactions signaled that large health companies know status-quo operations are insufficient to meet customer demands for higher-value healthcare services. It's not enough to get bigger—health companies must also become better by reconfiguring their business models to compete more effectively in the post-transformation marketplace.

Starting December 3, 2017, the following four seminal merger/acquisition announcements occurred:

- **December 3: CVS Health announced its intention to acquire Aetna and its 47 million health insurance subscribers for $69 billion.** The CVS release stressed that the "transaction fills an unmet need in the current healthcare system and presents a unique opportunity to redefine access to high-quality care in lower cost, local settings whether in the community, at home, or through digital tools."

- **December 4: Advocate Health Care (Illinois) and Aurora Health Care (Wisconsin) agreed to merge their state-leading health systems.** Advocate CEO Jim Skogsbergh captured the transaction's path-breaking aspirations when observing that "this merger is about transforming care delivery and reimagining the possibilities of health as bigger meets better and size meets value to benefit consumers."

- **December 6: UnitedHealth Group announced the acquisition of the DaVita Medical Group (DMG) for $4.9 billion.** DMG serves 1.7 million patients annually through 30,000 affiliated physicians at roughly 300 medical clinics in six states. United stressed that the DMG acquisition will advance "care quality, cost and patient satisfaction through integrated ambulatory care delivery systems enabled by information technology and supportive clinical services."

- **December 7: Dignity Health and Catholic Health Initiatives (CHI) announced their intention to merge.** The combined organization will be massive, with 700 care sites, 139 hospitals, 159,000 employees, and 25,000 physicians operating in 28 states. CHI's chief executive officer Kevin Lofton emphasized the importance of building healthier communities: "We are joining together to create a new Catholic health system, one that is positioned to accelerate the change from sick-care to well-care across the United States."

More evidence of healthcare's transformational tipping point came on **December 19, 2017, when Humana announced it was acquiring Kindred Healthcare's home health, hospice, and community care businesses** in partnership with private equity companies TPG Capital and Welsh Carson. Kindred operates 609 home health, hospice, and non-medical home-care sites of service throughout the country. "Kindred at Home" will operate as a stand-alone company and enhance Humana's ability to manage chronic disease patients more efficiently and effectively.

Describing the transaction, Humana CEO Bruce Broussard noted its ability to "advance [the company's] vision for integrated care delivery . . . while building a transformative platform for the future." Broussard added that "care in the home is a vital element of improving the health of seniors living with chronic conditions, allowing them to receive services in the comfort of their home, [and spend] less time in [high-cost] institutional settings."[3]

2018 MEGAMERGERS

As 2018 unfolded, the hits just kept on coming: Cigna–Express Scripts; Mercy–Bon Secours; Beth Israel Deaconess Medical Center–Lahey Health; not to mention consistent rumors of a Walmart–Humana combination. Then in March 2019, health insurer Centene announced its intention to acquire fellow insurer WellCare, its biggest competitor offering health insurance products on public exchanges.

In January 2018, Amazon, Berkshire Hathaway, and JPMorgan Chase announced their intention to form a new healthcare company to serve their employees. As the *New York Times* noted:

> The alliance was a sign of just how frustrated American businesses are with the state of the nation's health care system and the rapidly spiraling cost of medical treatment. It also caused further turmoil in an industry reeling from attempts by new players to attack a notoriously inefficient, intractable web of doctors, hospitals, insurers and pharmaceutical companies.[4]

These announcements represent a major market shift. Value follows payment. Payment formularies are increasingly rewarding integrated health companies that provide superior health prevention, health promotion, and care management. To provide Revolutionary Healthcare, companies must reconfigure operations to deliver better care more conveniently at lower prices. They must keep their customers healthy as well as treat them when they're sick or injured. They must consistently deliver great customer experience.

The power of bottom-up, market-driven reform emanates from the multiplicity of business models competing to win market share and generate profits. Many companies fail as markets evolve. Some companies succeed spectacularly by delivering more value to customers. This dynamic process constantly reshapes the marketplace.

AVOIDING INDUMBENCY[5]

Despite the value orientation implied by this torrent of blockbuster M&A transactions, most healthcare companies continue to invest in volume-based business models. This "defensive" strategy will work in traditional fee-for-service markets near term. Longer term, the failure to position an organization to succeed under full-risk contracting carries significant risk.

When incumbents cling to outmoded business practices at the expense of future competitiveness, they become "indumbent." Indumbent business practices are myopic, rigid, and brittle. They double down on revenue-optimizing strategies dependent on negotiating leverage, while leaving themselves vulnerable to competition from value-seeking companies.

Failing to imagine alternative futures is the greatest risk that confronts established health companies during periods of industry transformation. To avoid nasty surprises, organizations must undertake an honest assessment of their internal strengths and weakness. Leaders must answer these types of fundamental questions to gain full awareness of their company's strategic positioning and potential vulnerability:

- What is our mission? How well are we fulfilling it?

- What businesses are we in? Do we do them well?

- Who are our customers? How well are we meeting their needs?

- What are our competitive advantages and disadvantages?

- Which risks should we own? Which can we shift to others?

- Is our leadership and governance up to transformational change?

- Are we too dependent on current revenue models?

- How strong is our brand? What does it say about us?

- Do our operations square with our rhetoric?

An in-depth competitive analysis is the critical next step. Understanding market dynamics and competitors' relative strengths are essential components of any repositioning exercise. Beyond this, health companies must dig into the following aspects of demand-driven change to gain strategic clarity regarding their potential to disrupt current operations:

- Full-risk contracting (episodic bundles and capitated payments)

- Alternative low-cost delivery channels (e.g., telemedicine)

- Price and convenience-driven services and diagnostics

- Consumer-preference healthcare (e.g., alternative medicines)

This type of strategic analysis is essential for all health companies, but particularly for hospital-based companies. Despite their differences in tax status and governance, both not-for-profit and investor-owned health systems have prospered under fee-for-service reimbursement. Healthcare's activity-based payment models have generated significant operating margins to offset losses associated with weak market positioning, subpar governance, and/or poor execution.

In more stringent and value-based payment environments, health companies must reduce operating costs to achieve positive margins. There is less room for error. Marketplace demands for greater pricing and outcomes transparency are forcing industry consolidation, advancing integrated delivery, and exposing underperforming business lines. Incumbent health companies are repositioning. New competitors are emerging. Performance standards are rising.

Markets are agnostic and results driven. Customers care about quality, costs, and outcomes, not organizational mission or tax status. Given declining provider margins, achieving high volume with minimal quality and cost variation is essential to success (see Figure 9.1).

As industry consolidation continues and health companies accept more risk, provider and payer business lines are blurring. To excel in this new environment, health companies will need to make tougher resource allocation decisions, adopt more flexible funding approaches, make smart capital/strategic investments, and leverage strategic partnerships. Performance will drive competitiveness.

In Revolutionary Healthcare, health companies will provide care where, when, and how customers want to receive it. Operating in this retail paradigm will require companies to rethink market positioning, strategic alliances, capital formation, and governance. Sustainability requires making the right strategic and resource allocation decisions. It also requires superior execution.

True measures of success relate to outcomes, quality, costs, and customer experience. Health companies with a clear understanding of their competitive strengths and weaknesses make better strategic positioning

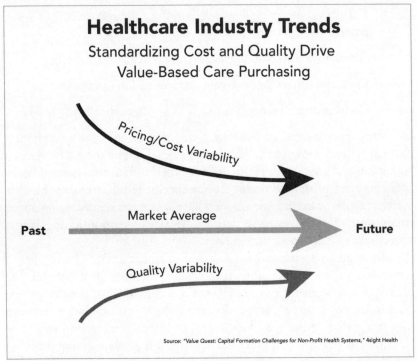

Healthcare Industry Trends

Standardizing Cost and Quality Drive
Value-Based Care Purchasing

Pricing/Cost Variability

Market Average

Past

Future

Quality Variability

Source: "Value Quest: Capital Formation Challenges for Non-Profit Health Systems," 4sight Health

FIGURE 9.1 **Increasing price transparency and new competitors are driving routine healthcare delivery toward commoditization.**

and resource allocation decisions. They determine when, where, and how they should invest and divest. Then they execute fearlessly.

Indumbent health companies that practice business as usual, that rely on robust fee-for-service payments for sustainability, that fail to address competitive weaknesses, are in for a rude awakening. They will lose market relevance. As Charles Darwin famously observed, "It is not the strongest of the species that survives, nor the most intelligent, but the one most adaptable to change." The future belongs to Revolutionary Healthcare companies that can adapt to new market realities.

DUAL TRANSFORMATION[6]

Strong companies in declining markets (see Figure 9.2) need to undertake a form of dual transformation to remain competitive. As industry transformation and disruption unfold, these companies adapt their core

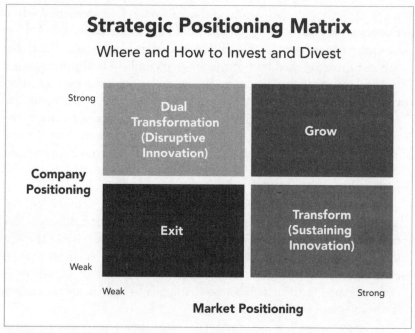

FIGURE 9.2 **Company and industry positioning determine strategic choices.**

business to new market realities while nurturing new business models that position the company for long-term success.

As discussed in Chapter 2, large payers and providers have resisted transitioning to more holistic and value-based business models. They have deeply embedded organizational practices and cultures built for activity-based healthcare delivery and payment. Organizational requirements for assuming care management risk conflict with current business practices and limit strategic flexibility.

Trite but true, change is hard. Many leaders understand that their organizations' long-term sustainability requires more efficient and effective provision of health and healthcare services. Yet they don't know how to make the transition from current "sick care" business models to holistic "health care" business models.

Dual transformation is a methodology for making strategic transitions from old-world to new-world business models. Authors Scott Anthony, Clark Gilbert, and Mark Johnson chronicle dual transformation's architecture and components in their insightful book *Dual Transformation: How to Reposition Today's Business While Creating the*

Future. Building on their work, authors Clayton Christensen, Andrew Waldeck, and Rebecca Fogg published a 2017 white paper titled "How Disruptive Innovation Can Finally Revolutionize Healthcare."[7] In it, they apply the theory of dual transformation to incumbent health companies.

Dual transformation recognizes that major organizational transformations are not monolithic efforts, but two separate and distinct journeys. "Transformation A" repositions core business operations to adapt over time to marketplace changes. This effort is undertaken even if those changes result in lower revenues profitability. The reason is simple: the development of new capabilities creates "new and better ways to solve old problems."

"Transformation B" creates separately governed business ventures that develop disruptive business models. Transformation B "solves new problems in related ways." For example, effective preventive health services reduce acute admissions. This generates superior outcomes that are better for consumers at lower costs. Nevertheless, such desirable outcomes are detrimental to the core business that depends upon acute admissions for revenues and profitability.

A "capabilities link" sits between Transformations A and B. Senior management judiciously allocates capabilities to sustain Transformation A's operations while protecting and promoting Transformation B operations as they develop. Operationally, such an approach helps distribute difficult-to-replace assets and capabilities while keeping the organizations separate. It allows each organization to develop its own brand and partnership relationships while attracting the right talent. Essentially, Organization A does A while B does B.

This solution flips "the innovator's dilemma" discussed in the last chapter. For health companies, it allows the organization to avoid the death spiral created by pursuing only higher-margin activities that benefit higher-profile customers. By design, Transformation A focuses on what's best for core customers. Meanwhile, Transformation B can develop and pursue its disruptive business model. This often requires the development of entirely new capabilities and new revenue sources (see Figure 9.3).

For health systems, Organization A pursues effective and efficient healthcare delivery by "fixing patients when they're broken" while also "sustaining their health" as appropriate in acute settings. In other words, they will satisfy the first two of the three customer jobs-to-be-done described in Chapter 8. Even as they provide these services, they will also strive to reduce unnecessary treatment activities.

Innosight Transformation
Where Today Meets Tomorrow

A C B

Transformation A	Capabilities Link	Transformation B
Strengthen Today	**Flip the Dilemma**	**Create Tomorrow**

Source: Christensen Institute, "*How Disruptive Innovation Can Finally Revolutionize Healthcare,*" Spring 2017

FIGURE 9.3 Dual transformation enables companies to manage the current business (A) while developing the future business (B). Effectively allocating capabilities (C) is essential to organizational success.

In this way, Organization A will provide the right care at the right time in the right place at the right price. To do so, they will need to coordinate care efficiently, avoid overtreatment and undertreatment, utilize technologies such as telemedicine and smartphone apps, and decentralize care delivery to make it more convenient and less costly for customers.

Meanwhile, Organization B pursues the disruptive business of competing on "health," not treatment, by fulfilling the last two of the customer jobs-to-be-done: sustaining and enhancing health. In other words, Organization B emphasizes prevention and wellness, areas that are desperately needed but poorly served with fee-for-service medicine. Organization B accomplishes this by providing enhanced primary care services, addressing social determinants of health, and attacking root causes of disease, which are usually social and environmental. Organization B seeks out new customers and new revenue streams through new channels. For example, such businesses may provide alternative medicine, meditation, fitness, and other health services that advance wellness.

"Liberated" data and analytics support both Transformations A and B. For both transformations, data flows to frontline professionals at the right time in the right formats to optimize decision making, resource allocation, and value creation. By focusing on consumers' health and healthcare needs in this integrated and holistic way, health companies can engage consumers more fully and frequently. This builds brand loyalty and limits customer leakage to competing organizations.

The Fairview Health Services case study presented later in this chapter is a textbook example of dual transformation in action. Whether competing on healthcare or health, such companies optimize performance by delivering superior outputs more efficiently.

PLATFORMING HEALTHCARE[8]

Adapting to transformative and disruptive change is difficult for companies in any industry. It is particularly challenging for health companies because their current business models and practices conform to artificial supply-driven economics.

Traditional healthcare business models have generated profits but also created significant fragmentation in care delivery and coordination. Health companies must master efficient, convenient, and effective care delivery as they adapt to full-risk payment models for episodic and ongoing care. This makes the "Transformation A" process described above essential to long-term success.

The societal need for acute care services is not disappearing; however, the business mechanics of meeting that need are undergoing transformational and disruptive change. Delivering high-quality outcomes and high-value services will differentiate winning companies. This requires an Amazon-like "platforming" approach to business operations.

Relentless customer focus fuels Amazon's business practices. The company's goal is to own customer relationships through low prices, limitless choice, ridiculous convenience, and constant touch points. This strategy reveals a core truth: customers care about outputs (products, services, and customer experience), not the production process.

Platform companies like Amazon, Uber, Airbnb, and Netflix disrupt and reconfigure incumbent business practices. Essentially, they connect suppliers (where costs are) with customers (where the money is) by delivering superior products and services at competitive prices with great customer experience. They prioritize outcomes, not ownership and control.

Despite skewed markets, health companies are not immune from natural laws governing economics, human behavior, and innovation. To thrive in customer-oriented markets, incumbent health companies must redesign operating platforms to deliver better healthcare services at lower prices. They must relentlessly focus on outcomes through business model optimization (see Figure 9.4).

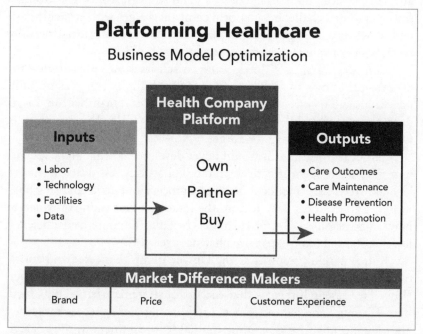

FIGURE 9.4 **Great companies focus on outputs, not ownership and control of production functions.**

All companies have inputs and outputs. The managerial art of great companies is organizing owned, partnered, and contracted activities to create superior products and services that customers want at competitive prices. Getting the formula right is essential to succeeding in competitive markets.

Traditional health companies invest in facilities and want full production control. Insistence on ownership and control makes these companies asset heavy and strategically flat-footed. They insource even when it's more efficient to outsource. They frustrate customers. Platform companies are agnostic about ownership and control. They win market share by building efficient, cost-effective, and ever-improving networks of connected capabilities, suppliers, and data, assembled to identify and fulfill customer needs.

Healthcare delivery is complex. It requires coordinated execution across hundreds of business functions. At the same time, buyers of healthcare services increasingly demand performance consistency and pricing transparency. This market pressure pushes health companies to optimize all their physical, human, intellectual, and strategic assets. Confronting this operational challenge, platform companies align with strategic partners to deliver superior products and services. Great strategic partnerships create superior value for customers and partners alike.

Consider Target's 2015 decision to sell its 1,600 pharmacies and 80 medical clinics to CVS Health for $1.9 billion. This was no ordinary transaction since the pharmacies and clinics remain within Target department stores while operated and branded by CVS. This was great for CVS, but it was also great for Target.

Target realized that it would never develop the scale and expertise necessary to compete effectively in retail pharmacy. Shedding its health business freed Target to focus on its core grocery and merchandising businesses. Target stores benefit from the increased foot traffic provided by new CVS customers. Target customers benefit from improved efficiency, lower costs, and more expansive pharmacy services.[9]

Kate Vitasek, professor at the University of Tennessee and author of the book *Vested Outsourcing*,[10] studies collaborative business partnerships. Her research reveals that successful strategic partnerships focus on achieving targeted outcomes, establishing clear success measures, aligning incentives, and building mutual trust. In this way, the strategic partners operate from "the same side of the table," pursuing agreed-upon objectives on predefined terms. Successful strategic partnerships exhibit the following characteristics:

- A mutual focus on client objectives, not transactions or processes

- Incentive-based compensation tied to clearly defined outcomes (e.g., reduced costs, higher sales, fewer errors)

- A shared commitment to mutual learning and adaptive program evolution

- Honest and regular program assessment (what's working, what's not, how to be better, new win-win opportunities, and whether the engagement should continue)

Given their importance and the resources required to manage them effectively, Vitasek believes companies should have only a handful of strategic partnerships. The best relationships are mutually beneficial and focused on outcomes.

Healthcare transformation and disruption will emerge largely through service innovation, not product innovation. They will occur as payment programs (risk-based, outcome-focused, bundled, transparent) reformulate incentives and retail-oriented competitors deliver routine healthcare services in new ways.

Healthcare's essential participants are providers and consumers. An Amazon-like focus on meeting consumers' jobs-to-be-done will differentiate winning companies. Platform companies will reorganize episodic and ongoing care delivery into discrete service offerings and compete on price and customer experience.

This platforming strategy is already occurring in select markets as evidenced by established and emerging businesses.

- **Direct primary care (DPC) practices** offer comprehensive services through activated care teams under capitated payment models, freeing them up to meet individual customer needs.

- **Laser eye surgery clinics, colonoscopy centers, and freestanding MRI facilities** offer transparently priced, low-cost, highly reliable procedures in convenient centers that are open nights and weekends.

- **High-volume, high-quality, low-cost specialty surgery centers** (i.e., focused factories) like the Hoag Orthopedic Institute are well positioned for profitability under bundled joint replacement payment programs.

- **Online price-shopping apps like Vitals, a provider selection and price-comparison service.** It matches patients with high-quality providers and offers cash incentives to encourage patients to seek lower-cost treatments.

- **Improvements in home infusion services** enable patients to receive care delivery at home. Outcomes are better, costs are lower, and patients are happier.

The list goes on. While the types of companies and services described above do not constitute total care integration, they can become effective component parts of service offerings assembled by health-oriented platform companies.

The movement to value-based care negates activity-based revenue optimization by paying for health outcomes, not specific transactions. In its purest form, value-based payments convert hospitals to cost centers. Established health companies are vulnerable to emerging platform companies precisely because their incumbent business models do not solve customers' healthcare jobs-to-be-done. Pursuing revenue-first business practices as consumerism transforms healthcare is equivalent to fighting gravity. It works for a time but ultimately fails.

By contrast, platform companies are evolving to succeed under healthcare's bundled and capitated payment models. They are powerful exemplars of revolutionary health and healthcare practices.

Revolutionary Healthcare companies strive to become "total integrators of health" by operating high-functioning, holistic business platforms. Buyers flock to companies that assure high-quality services, transparent prices, and great customer service. The AdventHealth case study later in this chapter illustrates how one revolutionary incumbent is changing everything to become the "connective tissue" for all its consumers' health and healthcare needs.

Revolutionary Healthcare companies understand their strengths and the risks they should own. They relinquish control to partners and/or vendors that add value and generate better outcomes. They exert a relentless push to achieve competitive advantage by fulfilling consumers' jobs to be done.

REVOLUTIONARY INCUMBENTS

No incumbent beats disruption and transformation by just doing what it does today better. Disruptive and transformative business models fundamentally challenge current business practices. There is no way to play the old game well enough to win the new game.

Instead, revolutionary incumbents acknowledge and embrace the disruption and transformation roiling the healthcare industry. They adapt operations in ways that improve their long-term strategic positioning and market relevance. Here are several case studies depicting how revolutionary incumbents are changing business models to solve customers' and consumers' health and healthcare jobs-to-be-done.

On a Fairview Day

Fairview Health Services is an integrated health system affiliated with the University of Minnesota and serving the residents of Minnesota through an expansive care continuum. Its portfolio includes 12 hospitals, more than 100 primary and specialty care clinics, more than 70 senior and long-term care facilities, more than 40 retail and specialty pharmacies, pharmacy benefit management services, rehabilitation centers, counseling and home health care services, an integrated provider network, and health insurer PreferredOne.

Under CEO James Hereford's leadership, Fairview is pursuing dual transformation. Fairview's Transformation Center is redesigning the company's healthcare delivery platform (Transformation A) to be leaner, data driven, and customer-centric. At the same time, Fairview's Primary Care Transformation Design Team is redesigning the company's primary care platform to compete on health and wellness (Transformation B). These parallel initiatives operate independently but with the same mission of making Fairview the best place for customers and consumers to address all their health and healthcare needs.

Hereford believes care delivery is rapidly moving from inpatient to ambulatory, retail, and home-based care sites. As care moves to lower-cost, more convenient settings, Fairview must rationalize its facilities and capabilities to serve consumers appropriately. This requires both care redesign and a powerful technology platform to guide information exchange and real-time decision making.

To that end, Fairview's transformation initiatives center on the following three principles:

- **One contact does it all.** As Hereford puts it, "Fairview needs to vastly simplify how consumers receive service. We make it incredibly hard. We need to own the complexity for the patient. It shouldn't matter if a patient is seeking a specialty appointment, an answer to a clinical question or a second opinion. There should be just one point of contact."

- **Precise coordination of care across events, settings, and time.** Hereford emphasizes that coordination must expand beyond specific episodes of care: "Think about individuals undergoing a health journey over time. Fairview must support, monitor, predict, anticipate, check-in, consult and intervene appropriately on consumers' behalf consistently and continually."

- **Solve the left-hand/right-hand problem.** Hereford notes, "We're a big system and we're often not using our capabilities and capacity well. How do we leverage the system most effectively? Fairview must develop the ability to predict demands on resources while enabling staff to anticipate and respond strategically, not reactively. This will improve quality, limit mistakes and reduce costs."

To operate effectively in complex and dynamic environments, Hereford decided that Fairview's centralized data and management model needed a makeover. To implement a new delivery model, Fairview has partnered with Qventus, a company that applies AI-powered solutions to optimize patient flow. The Qventus platform ingests data from Fairview's electronic medical record system and others. It then provides real-time operational and clinical data to frontline personnel who coordinate care within and between Fairview facilities.

With this system, Fairview's frontline teams can see the larger picture, predict events, and make course corrections in real time. This "team of teams" approach pushes informative data to frontline staff to "nudge" optimal actions. Fairview also uses a combination of existing protocols and "intelligent interventions" that identify operational barriers and coordinate cross-functional activities to streamline patient placement, discharge planning, and ED activity flows. Hereford believes intelligent and timely data exchange is essential to solving consumers' jobs-to-be-done. "I see this as one of the critical capabilities necessary to transform the experience of our patients. It is part of a larger strategy to redefine how a care delivery system works."

Moreover, Fairview and the University of Minnesota Medical School are working together to reinvent academic medicine. They are redesigning their combined education, research, and clinical functions to support population health, frontline caregiving (through a master clinician program), social determinants of health, and right-sized tertiary/quaternary care delivery.

With the Minnesota marketplace rapidly migrating toward full-risk payment models, Fairview is pioneering innovative business strategies to deliver superior outcomes and manage associated operational and financial risks.

Guiding Florida Well

GuideWell Mutual Holding Company is a not-for-profit parent company created in 2014 from Florida Blue (the Blue Cross Blue Shield plan in

Florida). Florida Blue's leaders wanted to move beyond insurance provision in Florida to providing holistic, innovative, and transformative services that help "people and communities achieve better health." Its CEO Pat Geraghty says, "We're more than an insurance company, we're a health solutions company." GuideWell reaches more than 15 million people through its insurance products and provider services. Fewer than half of the people GuideWell serves are traditional Florida Blue policy holders.

GuideWell believes it should be an easy and seamless experience for its customers to choose the right coverage, consult with healthcare providers, and learn about healthy activities. GuideWell employs sophisticated data algorithms to segment their population of members and match people with the right insurance products and healthcare providers. Its service platform includes ED doctors, population health expertise, and in-home care delivery. GuideWell wants to give its customers the right information, the right coverage and the right care at the right places.

GuideWell operates state-of-the-art retail centers where individuals can walk in, discuss their care needs with a clinician, buy individualized health insurance coverage, talk to a dietician, participate in a class, and get a checkup. Geraghty says, "On any day you might see 60 seniors doing yoga. It's dramatically different than being an insurance company on the sidelines of healthcare."

GuideWell understands that addressing social determinants of health is essential to individual and community well-being. Seeing the proven links between literacy and lifelong health, GuideWell partnered with Marvel and Disney to create a health-oriented comic book, *Habit Heroes*, where superheroes applied sunscreen, brushed teeth, ate vegetables, etc. It was a huge hit. *Habit Heroes* became Florida's book of the year and was read by teachers to students in all the state's elementary schools.

GuideWell sponsored Habit Hero programs, where costumed heroes would visit its retail centers around the state. Geraghty said, "At the Jacksonville store, we had 1,000 people waiting to meet Iron Man when the doors opened. While at the center those families enjoyed games and educational activities, ate healthy food, and the kids received baseline health screenings. That's not selling insurance."

Beyond the consumer focus, GuideWell works with global leaders in healthcare and start-ups through the GuideWell Innovation Center. The center anchors a health science cluster in Orlando, Florida, where it facilitates collaboration to bring ideas and health solutions to the market quickly.

"We convene around major topics like mental health, cancer, and opioids, facilitating different stakeholders in their innovation round solutions. To address opioids, we had patients, caregivers, providers, law enforcement in to get a 360 view of the issue and outline projects the group can take out and develop," said Geraghty.

The results of the expanded approach? GuideWell took ACA health exchanges into all 67 Florida counties and grew from 4 million to 5 million members in five years. GuideWell also administers traditional Medicare contracting for the federal government in 12 states and Puerto Rico. In 2017, Florida Blue had the highest member-retention rate of all the Blue Cross Blue Shield companies nationwide. "Retail centers are absolutely one of the key factors that drove that growth. People vote with their feet, and they've voted to join and stay," says Geraghty.

Wasting no time, Geraghty is chairing an effort sponsored by the Florida Council of 100 (Florida's 100 largest companies) to make Florida the "world's health capital" and "healthiest place to live in the world." Geraghty and GuideWell are making no small plans. They're getting consumers' health and healthcare "Jobs" done!

The Advent of a New Era

With over 5,000 clinicians and 80,000 employees working in more than 1,000 care sites, AdventHealth (AH; formerly Adventist Health System) operates an integrated care network of hospitals, urgent care centers, home health and hospice agencies, and skilled, compassionate nursing facilities across nine states.

After his wife Paula suffered a serious brain injury in a car accident, AdventHealth CEO Terry Shaw had difficulty finding her appropriate neurological care and strained to navigate through his own health system. They left the hospital with a stack of discharge papers and a good luck wish. Terry felt he and Paula were on their own to manage her care. That experience changed everything at AdventHealth. Shaw is repositioning the company to manage their customers' entire care journeys wherever it may take them. Here's how he explains AH's new operating paradigm:

> I never want to not care-manage you, not know where you are. I want to provide health for you where you are on continuum. We're trying to put connective tissue back into a very disjointed system in a way that lets people understand that someone's actually here and cares for you.

To bring this paradigm to life, Shaw simplified AdventHealth's vision statement to five powerful words: Wholistic, Exceptional, Connected, Affordable, and Viable. AH applies these values to four understandable and relatable service standards: Keep Me Safe; Love Me; Make It Easy; and Own It. "Engaging the Consumer" is the first and most important of six new core work imperatives. AH is applying multiple strategies to engage customers. Check them out.

- A sophisticated **"Hello Well App"** places a powerful new care navigation and education tool in consumers' hands.

- Partnering with Simplee, AH offers **patient-friendly billing** with multiple payment options.

- Spending $5 million per year to **advance spiritual care**.

- The ambitious **"Project Fulcrum"** aids middle-aged people with chronic disease to reduce stress and lead healthier lives.

- An even more ambitious project is **the new AH network card** that works like a wallet app through which customers can get lab results, schedule appointments, arrange consults, touch base with spiritual counselors, engage with lifestyle coaches, and more.

Shaw says, "Our goal is to get where our network card is more important to you than your insurance card. . . . I want customers and even their insurance companies to contact AdventHealth first because we take such good care of you." The other five core work imperatives improve people and products, expand the network, lower the cost, and improve risk management.

With the strategic blueprint finalized, Shaw has gone door-to-door to communicate this new vision to managers and frontline professionals. All 80,000 AH staff, including physicians, are attending multiple "whole care experience" sessions. Terry Shaw says he is "not going anywhere" and is determined that AH will achieve the goal of offering consumers "a continuum of connected care to address every stage of life and state of health." The Customer Revolution is alive and well at AdventHealth!

Revolutionizing Oral Health

DentaQuest is the nation's largest Medicaid dental provider serving 27 million Americans across 30 states. It's working to provide efficient, quality dental care services while also positioning itself as the nation's leading prevention-based oral health company.

Historically, American medicine has segregated "oral" health from "physical" health in terms of access, coverage, and service delivery. This occurs despite the fact that prevalent chronic conditions, like diabetes, often first present in the mouth and require dental care as part of an ongoing care management program. This fragmentation is costly and wasteful. Lost productivity due to dental conditions costs employers over $6 billion each year. Over 2 million consumers visited emergency departments (ED) in 2012 for preventable dental conditions.

ED visits are the proverbial tip of the iceberg with dental care. Overall, 74 million Americans don't have access to dental care services. These individuals are 29 percent more likely to have diabetes, 50 percent more likely to have osteoporosis, and an alarming 67 percent more likely to have heart disease.

DentaQuest president and CEO Steve Pollock says, "The current oral health system is broken. Too many people lack access to quality care or cannot afford the care they do get, and the industry overall is in dire need of innovative solutions."

DentaQuest designed its ambitious "Preventistry" platform to fundamentally change the delivery of and payment for better oral health. The company has invested over $200 million to transform the oral health care system of delivery. Pollock gleams with optimism when discussing Preventistry:

> Everyone can get a fair shot at oral health if we focus on prevention. The idea that we will prevent the problem before it occurs will lead to better outcomes for millions of people.

The company's strategic emphasis is on implementing value-based oral healthcare as a component of holistic, systematic care. It's pioneering this approach through Medicaid programs throughout the country. For example, DentaQuest has partnered with Advantage Dental in Oregon and the state's Medicaid program to create patient-centered health homes and accountable care organizations (ACOs) that integrate physical, oral, and behavioral health.

The results speak for themselves. In 2016, over 11,000 children in Oregon received dental care in the community from DentaQuest, which is 10 times more than in 2012. Further, the Medicaid dental costs for children served by DentaQuest *decreased* by 10 percent compared to a national *increase* of 41 percent over this time period. Its Westborough, Massachusetts, center serves all types of patients. In that center, DentaQuest has reduced the percentage of patients requiring oral surgery from 22 percent to 9 percent.

DentaQuest has revolutionary spirit and intentions. Its Preventistry campaign features a clear call to action, "Revolutionizing Oral Health for Everyone." Sound familiar? The Health Revolution will continue until all Americans receive whole-person care that encompasses physical, mental, spiritual, and oral care.

A Better Healthcare Steward[11]

In April 2008, CEO Ralph de la Torre took the helm of Caritas Christi Health Care, New England's second-largest health system. At that time, Caritas Christi Health Care was among the United States' worst-performing health systems. As a surgeon, engineer, and self-described "evangelist for integrated delivery," de la Torre knew continuing the current approach would not solve Caritas Christi's strategic and operating dilemmas. To add complication, the Catholic, not-for-profit system needed papal dispensation before selling its assets. With its sale to Cerberus Capital Management in 2010, the Caritas Christi converted to for-profit status and changed its name to Steward Health Care.

Changing ownership changed everything. As de la Torre observes, "Steward was founded as a business plan for a vertically integrated healthcare delivery, and Caritas Christi became its first acquisition." De la Torre and his team set to the task of reinventing Steward as a competitively priced "integrated, community-based Accountable Care Organization (ACO)."

What a difference a decade makes. Now, de la Torre describes Steward as "a glorified managed care" company. It strives for global, capitated payments with financial rewards for achieving high-quality outcomes. Empowered primary care physicians "own their patients" and quarterback care.

In a landmark 2016 transaction, Steward sold its 9 hospital facilities and a small equity stake to the Birmingham, Alabama, REIT Medical Properties Trust (MPT) for $1.2 billion. Subsequently, MPT served as Steward's capital partner in acquiring 8 CHS hospitals and all of Iasis, which included 18 hospitals and an insurance company. Today, Steward is an $8 billion health company operating in 10 states with a new corporate headquarters in Dallas.

Steward's operating-company business model focuses on aggregating consumers into its care networks by being customer-centric. It affords greater flexibility without the heavy burden of facility ownership. It facilitates consumer connection.

Consumers want easy, mobile-friendly solutions for making appointments, getting directions, and finding physicians. Steward listened and delivered. Steward has revamped its digital and mobile platforms to ease, customize, and personalize patient/customer communication. The new platform mimics digital media for major online retailers like Amazon and Airbnb. Mobile traffic is skyrocketing.

Once an underperforming hospital-centric health system with limited capital access, Steward has become a dynamic for-profit health company with a national footprint, high-performing ACO, and expansive capital access. With its care management expertise and efficient operating platform, Steward is moving aggressively into Medicaid managed care programs.

Giving customers the services they want is a recipe for success in any business. As healthcare shifts toward value-based payments and consumerism, de la Torre believes health companies must engage and align with their patients/consumers. In a September 2016 interview with the *Boston Globe*, de la Torre stressed that Steward "will seek partners with a focus on wellness and prevention services."[12] In this way, Steward's integrated and accountable care model provides solutions for all three of consumers' health and healthcare jobs-to-be-done.

Having risen from the ashes of Caritas Christi by embracing customer-centric delivery, Steward sees abundant opportunity to bring accountable care into other US markets. Revolutions disrupt the status quo and create winners and losers. Like American patriots in 1776, Steward has marched outward from Boston with a revolutionary agenda. It's bringing Revolutionary Healthcare to towns, hamlets, and cities throughout the land!

Selecting Care That Matters[13]

In 2014, Utah-based Intermountain Healthcare changed its mission statement to "Helping people live the healthiest lives possible." A commentary accompanying the announcement demonstrates the power of organizational purpose:

> We are now focusing even more strongly on prevention and wellness, on shared-decision making with our patients, and on using our resources and technology to help patients enjoy their lives without needing our hospitals and clinics, if possible. Our new Mission reflects that expanded role—it describes "why we exist."[14]

Wow! Who wouldn't want to receive healthcare services from a company that lives this mission?

Of course, rhetoric is cheap. Intermountain Healthcare put its lofty brand ambitions into practice when it launched a "shared accountability" insurance product for 2016. SelectHealth Share operates on the premise that providers, insurers, employers, and employees must collaborate to create affordable healthcare that delivers necessary medical services, promotes well-being, and engages all participants.

To participate, employers, employees, providers, and SelectHealth agree in writing to comply with provisions that support "predictable premiums, greater affordability and healthier lives." SelectHealth Share excludes no one, but participation requires commitment and accountability. This can be particularly difficult for physicians and subscribers who cherish independence. The offsetting benefits, however, are wonderful—healthier workplaces, communities, and individuals.

People are flocking to SelectHealth Share not for what it does, but for why it does it. Customers connect with Intermountain Healthcare's values because they make them feel better about themselves. These values burnish the image customers wish to project to others. Shared values create powerful company-consumer connection. It's brand love in the making.

Bert Zimmerli, Intermountain Healthcare's chief financial officer, repeatedly makes the statement, "Healthcare is personal. It touches our teams, family and friends." Intermountain Healthcare lives its values. It truly cares about its community and its customers. Nothing is more important in winning customers' trust and loyalty.

Not only does SelectHealth Share practice Revolutionary Healthcare, the company has embraced the terminology. Their website asks the question, "Ready to experience revolutionary healthcare?" How great is that! We couldn't have said it better ourselves.

CONCLUSION:
PUTTING MISSION FIRST[15]

During the 1992 vice presidential debate, Admiral James Stockdale, Ross Perot's running mate, opened with these two questions: "Who am I? Why am I here?" That line generated a huge laugh, but its purpose was deadly serious—to establish rapport with the audience, share the Perot-Stockdale vision for the country's future, and earn trust for a shared journey toward a better America. Health companies can benefit from similar introspection and connection. In Asheville, North Carolina, Mission Health did exactly that.

Mission is a highly regarded health company with six hospitals and $2 billion in annual revenues. At its biannual strategic retreat, Mission's CEO Ron Paulus always asks his board a version of Admiral Stockdale's existential questions: "Are we still best positioned as an independent not-for-profit (NFP) company to fulfill our organizational mission?" In 2017, the answer came back "No." Paulus and the board concluded that Mission needed to be part of a larger health system to best serve its community.

Paulus then led a process to evaluate potential strategic partners. In March 2018, Mission announced its intention to sell to HCA Health-care, the nation's largest for-profit healthcare system. This was a landmark transaction. For the first time in recent history, a strong not-for-profit health system chose to sell to an for-profit system to achieve scale, rather than acquire or merge with another NFP health system.

In the wake of the announcement, many questioned the proper role of the profit motive in healthcare delivery. Yet, focusing primarily on profits and ownership transfer obscures whether NFP health system conversions advance community health and wellness.

In Mission's case, there is more to the transaction than the HCA sale. Residual proceeds from the transaction will flow into an independent nonprofit foundation, the Dogwood Foundation. This new foundation will be among North Carolina's largest, with assets higher than $5 billion. It will invest between $50 million and $75 million annually to improve health in Western North Carolina. Mission Health describes this new foundation as "transformational."

As a for-profit company, HCA also must pay sales, property, income, excise, and other applicable state and local taxes. Early estimates suggest new property taxes will add roughly $15 million to the city of Asheville's coffers. This represents a substantial increase, the equivalent of adding 8,000 new homes valued at $200,000 each. Mission's board weighed all these factors before unanimously approving the sale to HCA.

The Mission-HCA transaction is part of a broader, disruptive trend confronting established health companies as they position to compete in a revolutionizing marketplace that emphasizes transparency, outcomes, efficiency, consumerism, and growth.

HCA is highly proficient at back-office operations. Its investment in artificial intelligence (AI) and the sophistication of its supply chain oper-ations particularly impressed the Mission team. According to Paulus,

HCA's scale and operating efficiency make it "one of the lowest, if not the lowest-cost operators in the country." For example, HCA makes a small margin on Medicare patients, while Mission loses 4–5 percent. While there is naturally grieving for lost independence, Paulus and the Mission board believed that their circumstances required a radical rather than an incremental solution.

Market dynamics are forcing many health companies to consider relinquishing local ownership and operating control. Ultimately, ownership and tax status are tactical decisions that do not define, in and of themselves, organizational mission. True measures of health system performance and community benefit relate to care access, care quality, operational efficiency, customer experience, and health status.

On these measures, a reconstituted Mission Health delivers. Selling to HCA enables Mission Health to contribute millions in local tax revenues, invest more in community health, operate nimbly, and innovate strategically. This means Mission Health is truly putting its community health mission first and sustaining it for the future.

Mission Health's board chair, Dr. John R. Ball, made this point persuasively in describing the board's decision-making process during an interview with the *Citizen Times*' editorial board after the sale announcement:

> The basic measure was what our mission is, which is to improve the health of people in Western North Carolina and the surrounding regions. That was the measure. Does any deal do that and do it better than we could independently down the line?

This is the type of game-changing strategic move that is transforming US healthcare for the better. Health companies across America would do well to heed Mission's example of asking the tough existential questions honestly and evaluating the benefits and drawbacks of potential strategic transactions.

Revolutionary clarity and resolve are evident in Mission's strategic repositioning. Paraphrasing SelectHealth Share's provocative question, "Was Mission ready for Revolutionary Healthcare?" The answer is a resounding *yes*!

CHAPTER 10

Healthcare for All

Throughout the fall of 2004, CBC (Canadian Broadcasting Company) launched a six-week television series to identify the greatest Canadian in history. The campaign riveted the country's attention. From 50 initial nominees, CBC narrowed the field to 10 based on widespread polling. It then broadcast individual documentaries on the finalists, hosted by Canadian celebrities. Over a million Canadians voted in the competition. On November 29, CBC broadcast the series finale and revealed the winner.

The 10 finalists included Alexander Graham Bell (inventor of the telephone), Pierre Trudeau (statesman who formalized Canadian sovereignty), Wayne Gretzky (greatest hockey player of all time), Sir Frederick Banting (discoverer of insulin), and Terry Fox (the one-legged athlete who ran across Canada to raise money for cancer research). From this legendary group, voters selected Tommy Douglas as the greatest Canadian in history. Little known in the United States, Tommy Douglas was the former premier of Saskatchewan who became the father of Canada's universal healthcare program. The selection of Tommy Douglas speaks to the enormous pride Canadians feel for their national healthcare system.

Canadian Medicare is not perfect. There are long treatment wait times[1] and high levels of unnecessary care.[2] Still, Canadian public opinion strongly favors Medicare with approval ratings approaching 90 percent.[3]

Contrast that with healthcare's dismal approval ratings in the United States. Seventy-one percent of Americans believe the US healthcare system either is "in crisis" or has "major problems."[4] As mentioned in Chapter 3, healthcare's availability and affordability have become the number one concern for Americans.[5] It's not a stretch to believe Americans would support universal and affordable healthcare coverage with the same enthusiasm as their Canadian cousins. Universal healthcare coverage and accessible, affordable care should become US national policy objectives.

Much of this book's narrative concentrates on the System's structural flaws and strategies for overcoming them. I've taken great pains to distinguish customers (the buyers of healthcare services) from consumers (the users of healthcare services).

In many industries, consumers are also customers, but not in US healthcare. For more than 90 percent of the US population, institutions (companies and governments) fund healthcare insurance that pays for the services consumed by individuals. Following the money, the healthcare industry focuses on delivering treatments for which it can receive payment. Consequently, and despite rhetoric to the contrary, health companies largely disregard consumer preferences when making strategic positioning and resource allocation decisions.

Lost amid healthcare's vicious politics and artificial economics are millions of vulnerable Americans without the means and resources to navigate a complex and extremely expensive healthcare delivery system. The customer revolution in healthcare is their story, too. Revolutionary Healthcare can declare victory only after it provides affordable healthcare insurance coverage and appropriate, high-quality care to all Americans.

It's time for consumers to receive their due attention. This chapter will explore the System from the consumer's perspective and present strategies for turning more consumers into customers (buyers). The more consumer-oriented healthcare becomes, the more value it will create by meeting consumers' health and healthcare jobs-to-be-done.

Before tackling consumerism, let's go back up north and learn how Canada built a universal healthcare system that its people revere. Turns out it was quite a battle against many of the same institutional interests that stymie healthcare transformation in the United States.

O CANADA

Any discussion of Canadian healthcare has to begin with the fighting Scotsman from Saskatchewan. Tommy Douglas was born in Scotland in 1904 and moved to Manitoba, Canada, in 1910 with his family. He became an accomplished boxer and won the Manitoba Lightweight Championship twice in the early 1920s despite breaking his nose and losing some teeth during those bouts. On the academic front, Douglas studied theology and sociology before becoming an ordained minister.

Douglas's beliefs about healthcare were formed at an early age. When he was seven, young Tommy developed osteomyelitis, a bone infection, in his right leg. He was hospitalized for 18 months. Since his parents couldn't afford a surgeon, his doctors recommended amputating his leg. A noted orthopedic surgeon agreed to treat young Tommy for free if his medical students could observe the case. Several operations later, Tommy not only regained full use of his leg, he also became convinced that healthcare should be free for all. Douglas later observed,

> I felt that no boy should have to depend either for his leg or his life upon the ability of his parents to raise enough money to bring a first-class surgeon to his bedside.[6]

At age 25, Douglas and his wife Irma moved to Weyburn, Saskatchewan, where Douglas became a practicing minister at the Calvary Baptist Church before entering politics. In 1935, he was elected to the Canadian House of Commons. Douglas became Saskatchewan's premier in 1944 in a landslide election. He became the first democratic socialist to lead a government in North America.

Like the individual states in the United States, Canada's 13 provinces and territories exercise substantial control over their own governance. As premier of Saskatchewan, Douglas created programs and passed legislation that provided universal healthcare coverage for Saskatchewan's residents.

In 1947 the Saskatchewan Hospitalization Act provided universal coverage for hospital care. This was the first program of its kind in North America. It spread to other Canadian provinces and became national law in 1957 with the passage of the Hospital Insurance and Diagnostic Services Act.

In the 1960 provincial election, Douglas fought to expand universal healthcare coverage to include physician services with payment rates that would be acceptable to both doctors and patients. Doctors in Saskatchewan campaigned vigorously against the measure, but Douglas prevailed. In 1962, the Saskatchewan Medical Care Insurance Act established universal publicly funded medical insurance. This was the first program of its type in North America.

Despite Douglas's legislative victory, his fight for universal coverage in Saskatchewan was far from over. The new law precipitated a nasty, well-funded strike by doctors across Saskatchewan who resented government involvement in medical decision making and feared loss of income.[7] The strike began on July 1, 1962, and lasted three weeks. Doctors whipped up support among local citizen groups. The government recruited doctors from other provinces and countries, including Great

Britain and the United States, to fill the coverage void. It was a harrowing time.

The strike ended after the government agreed to opt-out provisions and protections for the fee-for-service private practice model. Four years later, the popular Saskatchewan medical insurance program became nationalized with the passage of the federal Medical Care Act of 1966. It established shared federal-province/territory financing responsibility for universal coverage of hospitalization and physician services. By 1972, every Canadian province and territory had passed legislation to participate in the program.[8]

Tommy Douglas became the face of Canada's healthcare reform movement and the father of its Medicare program. He worked tirelessly for universal healthcare coverage. Douglas characterized his logic as follows:

> I came to believe that health services ought not to have a price tag on them, and that people should be able to get whatever health services they required irrespective of their individual capacity to pay.

Lionized in death as the people's relentless, happy warrior, Douglas never lost sight that government exists to make people's lives better. He famously observed, "Courage, my friends; 'tis not too late to build a better world."

The Canadian Health Act unanimously passed the Canadian Parliament in 1984. It codified the funding mechanisms between the federal and provincial/territorial governments for universal healthcare coverage. Canadian governments fund 70 percent of healthcare expenditures, which is below international averages for advanced economies, but above the US level of 50 percent.[9] The program covers physician services and hospitalization costs but excludes dental care, home care, prescription drugs, and long-term care. Roughly 75 percent of Canadians have supplemental insurance to cover healthcare costs not funded by the government.

Canada spends roughly 11 percent of its GDP on healthcare vs. the 18 percent the United States spends but has equivalent health status.[10] Canada has an egalitarian culture that prioritizes fairness and common good over individual need. Canada's single-payer healthcare system reflects these national values. Two-thirds of Canadians live within an hour of the US border. America's excess supply of acute-care capacity provides a safety valve to accommodate incremental treatment needs. Many Canadians also choose to pay independently for healthcare services in the United States.

Universal healthcare coverage in Canada did not happen by accident. Led by Tommy Douglas, the Canadian government overcame virulent opposition from the medical establishment to gain legislative passage and enactment. America's neighbor to the south, Mexico, implemented universal healthcare coverage in December 2013 (Seguro Popular), making the United States the only country in North America that doesn't provide health insurance for all its citizens.

CONSUMERS BEWARE

The United States is a much larger, more complex and diverse country than Canada. By 2050, the United States will become the first pluralistic democracy in the history of the world. It is among the few nations that place individual benefit over group benefit. Home to 4.5 percent of the world's people, the United States is the global leader in innovation and has the world's largest economy constituting roughly a quarter of global GDP. On balance, the American people distrust centralized government programs and embrace market-oriented policy solutions.

> **Pluralistic democracy.** A model of democracy in which no one group dominates politics and organized groups compete with each other to influence policy.

Like Canadian healthcare reform, US healthcare reform must align with the nation's priorities. By definition, any US healthcare system must be uniquely American. It will reflect the nation's culture, values, and experience. That's why a Canadian-style national healthcare system has not gained traction. President Obama's signature legislative accomplishment was the 2010 passage of the Patient Protection and Affordable Care Act that created marketplace mechanisms to increase healthcare coverage.

It is ironic that a Democratic president and Congress passed Obamacare with no Republican support because the law's core provisions (public exchanges, mandates, and risk corridors for health insurance) originated in conservative think tanks. Even more ironic, the model for Obamacare was Romneycare in Massachusetts led by then Republican governor Mitt Romney, who ran against Obama for the US presidency in

2012. As the 2020 presidential elections approach, liberal Democrats are now advocating for a Canadian-style Medicare-for-all single-payer system. Healthcare's politics in America are never dull.

Americans have strong opinions regarding the nation's healthcare, and they are increasingly dissatisfied with its cost. Even after passage of Obamacare, which includes Medicaid expansion and massive subsidies for lower-income individuals, four in five Americans are dissatisfied with "the total cost of healthcare," and two-thirds believe healthcare coverage is "only fair or poor." Moreover, only 55 percent believe the quality of healthcare is excellent or good.[11]

From the Americans people's perspective, healthcare receives failing grades in cost, coverage, and quality. It's no surprise that the healthcare (–14 percent) and the pharmaceutical (–23 percent) industries are at the bottom of Gallup's 2018 survey of 25 business/industry sectors. Only the federal government is worse with a –27 net score (see Figure 10.1).[12]

These negative opinions emanate from real-world experience. In January 2016, the Kaiser Family Foundation and the *New York Times* released an extensive survey titled "The Burden of Medical Debt."[13] The survey's results depict the financial stress the System causes for high percentages of Americans, particularly lower-income individuals and families. Among the survey's findings are the following:

- Twenty-six percent of US adults say they or someone in their household had medical debt problems in the last 12 months.

- Sixty-two percent of US adults with medical bill problems had health insurance.

- Twice as often, payment problems stem from one-time events (66 percent) than from ongoing treatments for chronic disease (33 percent).

- Twenty-nine percent of US adults either lost a job or experienced a pay cut due to illness.

Moreover, those with medical bill problems made significant sacrifices to pay their bills. For example, 70 percent cut back their spending on food, clothing, or basic household items. They also were more likely to skip or delay needed care. Finally, they have little understanding of actual treatment costs or knowledge of payment assistance programs.

A March 2018 survey by the West Health Institute and NORC at the University of Chicago examined "Americans' Views of healthcare costs,

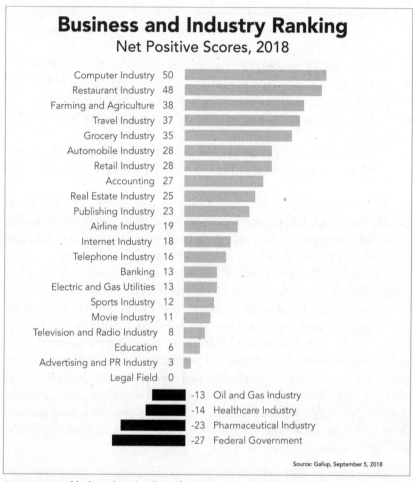

Business and Industry Ranking
Net Positive Scores, 2018

Industry	Score
Computer Industry	50
Restaurant Industry	48
Farming and Agriculture	38
Travel Industry	37
Grocery Industry	35
Automobile Industry	28
Retail Industry	28
Accounting	27
Real Estate Industry	25
Publishing Industry	23
Airline Industry	19
Internet Industry	18
Telephone Industry	16
Banking	13
Electric and Gas Utilities	13
Sports Industry	12
Movie Industry	11
Television and Radio Industry	8
Education	6
Advertising and PR Industry	3
Legal Field	0
Oil and Gas Industry	-13
Healthcare Industry	-14
Pharmaceutical Industry	-23
Federal Government	-27

Source: Gallup, September 5, 2018

FIGURE 10.1 **No love lost by Americans for the healthcare and pharmaceutical industries**

coverage, and policy."[14] If anything, this survey's findings were even more discouraging than the KFF/NYT's survey. Here are its five key findings.

1. Three-quarters of respondents say that our country doesn't get good value for what we spend on healthcare.
2. Forty percent of respondents skipped a recommended medical test or treatment in the last 12 months due to cost, and 32 percent were unable to fill a prescription or took less of it because of its cost.

3. Four in ten respondents say they fear the costs associated with a serious illness, which is more than the number who say they fear the illness itself.
4. Over half of respondents say they received a medical bill they thought was covered by insurance, or where the amount they owed was higher than expected, and more than a quarter say they had a medical bill sent to a collection agency in the past 12 months.
5. About half of respondents disapprove of the way their representative in Congress is handling the cost of healthcare.

In October 2018, the *New York Times,* the Commonwealth Fund, and the Harvard T.H. Chan School of Public Health surveyed 1,500 people, adults with serious illnesses and their caregivers, to provide insights on how best to navigate America's scary and confusing care delivery system (the "System"). Margot Sanger-Katz described the survey's results in an aptly titled article, "Advice from Health Care's Power Users."[15]

Their advice to consumers, patients, and caregivers was straightforward: keep records and bring them to medical appointments; find an advocate to be a second set of eyes and ears; and ask questions and listen well to the answers. Despite their experience, many survey respondents described the System as "perplexing and overwhelming." Sixty-two percent said their interactions with the System had made them feel "anxious, confused or overwhelmed." Sanger-Katz described the survey respondents and their world-weary and wary approach to navigating the System with compassion and insight:

> The people in our survey tended to have very serious health problems, sometimes several at once. They counted on the system to help them, but also recognized that it often let them down.

What's a person to do? It seems that average healthcare consumers should receive a "buyer beware" notice upon entering medical facilities. Accessing appropriate healthcare shouldn't be a game of chance, with extra credit going to the well-prepared, but that is what healthcare in America has become.

There is a clear and present danger confronting ordinary Americans who engage with the System. Spotty coverage, inconsistent quality, inadequate consumer education, and undue financial harm are the System's hallmarks. And it appears to be getting worse rather than better.

The real policy question for the United States is whether our legislators can design an affordable healthcare system with universal coverage that employs market mechanisms to align the purchase of health insurance with individual preference. Before we tackle that thorny question, let's see how truly scary the System can be for people confronting serious illness and needing its help to treat their illness.

Don't Hate the Player; Hate the Game

In 2005 Hedda Martin, a 47-year-old animal lover and gardener living in Grand Rapids, Michigan, learned that she had an aggressive form of breast cancer. Doctors treated Martin's cancer with a powerful drug called doxorubicin and saved her life.

Unfortunately, Martin's aggressive chemotherapy regimen triggered a form of congestive heart failure (CHF) called doxorubicin cardiomyopathy. After a dozen productive years, Martin's cardiomyopathy forced her to stop working and rely on disability payments to cover her living expenses.

By the fall of 2018, Martin's heart disease had become lethal. Doctors from Spectrum Health's Heart & Lung Specialized Care Clinics treated Martin. Her best option for long-term survival was a heart transplant. While waiting for a new heart, Martin's doctors recommended surgery to implant a ventricular assist pump. The pump gives congestive heart failure patients like Martin an extra eight years of life expectancy on average. She gave her assent and prepared for the surgery.

Then the shock came. Martin received a letter dated November 20, 2018, informing her that the Clinic's transplant committee had decided not to place her on the national registry for a heart transplant (Figure 10.2). They made this decision because they did not believe she had the financial means to cover the co-pays for the immunosuppressive drugs required to keep her body from rejecting the transplanted heart. They recommended a fund-raising campaign to get the $10,000 to cover her payment responsibilities.

This story has a happy ending. Martin's son Alex launched a GoFundMe campaign that posted a photo of the Clinic's letter. The campaign went viral and raised over $30,000 with help from a hard-hitting tweet by incoming New York Congresswoman Alexandria Ocasio-Cortez. Ocasio-Cortez's tweet misidentified the Clinic as an insurance company, but her message hit home with tens of thousands of people:

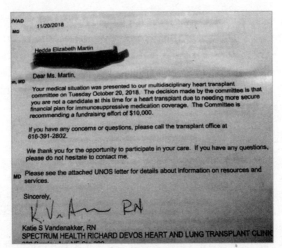

FIGURE 10.2 **Letter from Spectrum Health to Hedda Martin, denying heart transplant and recommending a personal fund-raising effort.**

Insurance groups are recommending GoFundMe as official policy—where customers can die if they can't raise the goal in time—but sure, single payer healthcare is unreasonable.

With financial support secured, the Clinic's transplant committee agreed to make Martin a heart transplant candidate and placed her on the national organ transplant registry. Martin's implant surgery went well, and she's now waiting to see if she'll get a new heart.[16]

It's easy to paint the Clinic as the villain in this story. After all, it initially denied Martin a chance for lifesaving surgery because she couldn't afford her share of their cost. Only after securing the necessary funds did the Clinic put Martin on the transplant list. Spectrum Health issued a statement explaining its transplant policies while noting the generosity of the online community that supports patients in need.

At the same time, the Clinic operates a business that requires revenues and profits to sustain itself. While empathizing with Martin in her dire circumstances comes naturally, it's unrealistic to expect organizations to grant unlimited philanthropy. The System itself must be called to account.

Nearly half of the $2 billion generated between 2010 and 2016 on GoFundMe supported health campaigns like Hedda Martin's.[17] It turns out the success of Martin's GoFundMe campaign was an anomaly.

A 2017 study in *Social Science and Medicine* found that 90 percent of crowdsourced health expense campaigns reach 40 percent or less of their targeted amounts. In assessing their research results, the study's authors made the following insightful observations regarding crowdfunding's inequity and capriciousness as well as its ability to mask the System's structural flaws that necessitate crowdfunding in the first place:

> Successful crowdfunding requires that campaigners master medical and media literacies; as such, we argue that crowdfunding has the potential to deepen social and health inequities in the U.S. by promoting forms of individualized charity that rely on unequally-distributed literacies to demonstrate deservingness and worth.
>
> Crowdfunding narratives also distract from crises of healthcare funding and gaping holes in the social safety net by encouraging hyper-individualized accounts of suffering on media platforms where precariousness is portrayed as the result of inadequate self-marketing, rather than the inevitable consequences of structural conditions of austerity.[18]

The real villain in Hedda Martin's story is the System and the increasing pressure it places on consumers to finance their vital care needs, often at exorbitant costs. The phrase "Don't hate the player; hate the game," gained traction in the 1990s. There are many incredible people in healthcare; most hate "the game" they have to play. Denying anyone proven lifesaving treatments because of an inability to pay is cruel, particularly in a rich country like the United States. Philanthropy saved Tommy Douglas's leg, but he recognized the fundamental unfairness of a healthcare system that chooses who does and doesn't receive treatment based on their financial circumstances.

The verdict is in: the System is guilty of malfeasance. It exacts an enormous emotional, economic, and human toll on the nation. Too often, consumers encountering the System experience confusion, fear, frustration, a loss of control, financial impairment, and physical harm.

Fueled by perverse economic incentives, the cumulative harm caused by the System's uncaring institutional practices is almost beyond comprehension. Canadian healthcare seems like a dream compared to the American experience.

Without question, America needs leaders like Tommy Douglas to stand up and fight for kinder, smarter affordable care for all Americans. There is a better way. Revolutionary Healthcare is coming to the rescue.

A REVOLUTIONARY MANIFESTO

When speaking on healthcare reform, I often ask attendees the following yes-or-no questions and receive predictable responses:

- "The US spends 18 percent of its economy on healthcare. The developed country with the next highest percentage is France at 12 percent. How many believe that the US must spend more than 18 percent of its economy to provide superior healthcare to everyone in the country?"

  No one raises a hand.

- "Seventy-five percent of total healthcare spending and 95 percent of Medicare and Medicaid spending goes to treat chronic disease.[19] How many believe we're winning the war against chronic disease?"

  No one raises a hand.

- "On a relative basis, how many believe the healthcare system should shift resources from acute and specialty care into primary care, health promotion, behavioral health, and chronic disease management?"

  Everyone raises a hand.

- "Finally, how many have a family member, including themselves, who have had a bad experience with the healthcare system?"

  Everyone raises a hand.

This short exercise clarifies the System's dysfunction. Even though there is sufficient money to fund needed healthcare services for all Americans, healthcare has terrible customer service and doesn't meet consumer needs.

Healthcare has a distribution challenge, not a funding challenge. Healthcare is not attacking its most pressing challenge, chronic disease. Healthcare ignores consumers. Healthcare requires major restructuring.

The real question isn't what to do. It's how to overcome the obstacles, most notably the Healthcare Industrial Complex, that prevent all Americans from receiving the healthcare they need, want, and desire.

The ultimate challenge is doing the right thing for American consumers and rewarding companies that do this consistently. This cannot happen until the American people retake control of American healthcare.

The Time Is Now

On April 12, 1963, the police arrested the Reverend Martin Luther King Jr. for violating a court injunction by leading a nonviolent protest against Birmingham's segregationist practices. *Time* magazine, among others, including a group of clergymen, criticized King for the timing and aggressiveness of the nonviolent protest.[20] In response, King penned his now famous "Letter from the Birmingham Jail" in which he responded to those criticisms with compelling logic:

> My friends, I must say to you that we have not made a single gain in civil rights without determined legal and nonviolent pressure. Lamentably, it is an historical fact that privileged groups seldom give up their privileges voluntarily. Individuals may see the moral light and voluntarily give up their unjust posture; but, as Reinhold Niebuhr has reminded us, groups tend to be more immoral than individuals.
>
> We know through painful experience that freedom is never voluntarily given by the oppressor; it must be demanded by the oppressed. Frankly, I have yet to engage in a direct-action campaign that was "well timed" in the view of those who have not suffered unduly from the disease of segregation. For years now, I have heard the word "Wait!" It rings in the ear of every Negro with piercing familiarity. This "Wait" has almost always meant "Never." We must come to see, with one of our distinguished jurists, that "justice too long delayed is justice denied."[21]

In my office, there is a small eighteenth-century needlework. It reads, "Hypocrisy is the homage that vice pays to virtue." That insight into human nature is certainly as true today as it was in the 1700s. Too many healthcare leaders speak the language of reform but do the System's bidding. They sustain status quo business practices. They tolerate unnecessary harm. They caution against moving too fast. They believe in their own virtue.

The time is now for the American people to revolt against the System. On March 25, 1966, at the second convention of the Medical Committee for Human Rights in Chicago, Dr. King made the following statement, "Of all the forms of inequality, injustice in healthcare is the most shocking and inhumane."[22] Fifty-plus years later, American healthcare is still unjust and inhumane.

A Dozen Declarations

Out of deference to America's Founding Fathers, Dr. Martin Luther King Jr., and the millions fighting for better, more equitable, and affordable healthcare, I offer the following 12 opinions about the System and the path to Revolutionary Healthcare:

1. It is beyond time for universal healthcare coverage in the United States; however, universal coverage does not require a single government payer. It does require programs and subsidies that enable all Americans to have access to health insurance. Multiple sources of healthcare insurance, done properly, stimulate innovation and create value by more effectively meeting customer needs.

2. There is a fundamental disconnect between the System and the people. The System will transform by resolutely focusing on three jobs-to-be-done: (1) fix me when I'm broken; (2) sustain my health; and (3) enhance my health.

3. Value in healthcare comes from receiving the right care, at the right time, in the right place, at the right price. This simple formula leads to the best care outcomes for consumers at the lowest prices.

4. The System will not change the way it practices healthcare until America changes the way it pays for healthcare. Rewarding health companies that deliver great outcomes, treat the whole person, address social determinants, and promote health will reconfigure healthcare's dysfunctional supply-demand relationships.

5. Payment reform is necessary but insufficient to transform the System. Revolutionary Healthcare also requires balanced regulation and the elimination of government "capture" by industry groups.

6. The disruptive catalyst for payment reform is full-risk contracting. When markets tip (as some are now doing) toward full-risk contracting, payers and providers reorganize to deliver transparently priced value-based services. These include bundled/fixed payments for episodic care and capitated (per member per month) payments for population health.

7. Bottom-up, market-driven, customer-centric business models deliver greater value than centralized, top-down

payment formularies. No matter how well-intentioned government policy may be, the marketplace is always more adaptable, flexible, and ultimately smarter than central planners in meeting dynamic needs. Health companies will always manipulate centralized payment formularies for their benefit. Conversely, a level competitive field and a pro-market regulatory environment stimulate innovation, value creation, and customer delight. Unleashing the American innovation machine with proper incentives and fair competition will transform healthcare.

8. Market-based regulations require constant tinkering to sustain level-field competition.

9. Technology that makes healthcare better for consumers and caregivers by improving decision making, communication, and resource allocation will enable to Revolutionary Healthcare to achieve its potential.

10. Shared healthcare decision making between clinicians and consumers is universally better. Informed consumers generally make more conservative treatment decisions that lead to better health outcomes, greater consumer satisfaction, and lower costs. This is particularly true in end-of-life-care decision making.

11. Revolutionary Healthcare balances expenditure, expected outcomes, fairness, and customer experience when determining appropriate healthcare treatment protocols. Knowing when and how to say no to unnecessary and inappropriate care is essential to long-term community health and wellness.

12. Market power flows from the people. Always doing the right thing for consumers is essential for Revolutionary Healthcare to thrive. Giving consumers power over their own data and turning them into informed customers who make health and healthcare purchasing decisions will turbocharge Revolutionary Healthcare's success.

Revolutionary Healthcare will unfold minute by minute in millions of healthcare encounters between customers and service providers. With skin in the game, and guided by transparent pricing and outcome information, American consumers will purchase the personalized, value-based healthcare that they need, want, and desire.

ACHIEVING UNIVERSAL COVERAGE

The fundamental problem in healthcare is that the System does not solve consumers' health and healthcare jobs-to-be-done. It does other things for other reasons at enormous cost to American society. In the process, it causes needless harm to American consumers.

The right way to fix the problem is to shift healthcare decision making to consumers. Give consumers the responsibility and tools for managing their healthcare, and they will make informed, value-based decisions. Giving consumers purchasing responsibility without knowledge and evaluation tools is an exercise in futility. GuideWell retail insurance stores demonstrate how engaging and educating consumers lead to both better healthcare coverage decisions and increased brand loyalty. Consumers will reward companies that help them solve their health and healthcare jobs-to-be-done.

Let me be clear. This does not mean granting consumers full access to any care they want at any time. It does mean, however, granting consumers access to appropriate care at all times.

The best way to achieve universal health coverage is to give individual consumers the power to purchase the health insurance coverage that best meets their individual needs, irrespective of the funding source. It's the American way. Let's see what engaged health insurance purchasing looks like.

A Revolutionary Couple's Quest for Great Health Insurance

George and Martha are discriminating shoppers who want great health insurance.[23] When it came time to enroll in Medicare, Martha stressed, "We knew we had to take ownership. No one else would look out for our best interests." They dug in and did the research.

The couple reviewed Medicare plans, benefits, and costs. Martha stresses, "Before we ever purchase anything, we research everything about it. Knowledge equals power." The knowledge-powered couple quickly realized the need to compare the costs and benefits of traditional Medicare with Medicare Advantage plans but found it hard to get "really true answers because there are a lot of rumors going around."

They decided their ideal plan would be "cost-effective, comprehensive and coordinated, emphasize preventive care, include high-quality physicians, offer a good drug plan, and have affordable out-of-pocket costs," says Martha.

Like most of their friends, George and Martha's inclination was to enroll in traditional Medicare and purchase a supplemental plan. Since traditional Medicare doesn't cover co-payments, coinsurance, and deductibles, they assumed a supplemental plan would defray those costs. They also wanted to make sure they'd have coverage when traveling, even if it's just across the Delaware River.

To their surprise, they learned that Medicare Advantage plans cover urgent and emergency care outside local networks. That encouraged them to look at Medicare Advantage plans more closely. George explains that "it just took a while to get comfortable with the information we were receiving."

With an understanding of their criteria and information from the plans, George and Martha created a battle-plan-like spreadsheet to compare traditional Medicare and Medicare Advantage plans. The spreadsheet answered the following questions:

- Are our current primary care doctors and specialists in the plan?

- What hospitals are in the plan? What are the ratings for those hospitals?

- What are the costs?
  ○ Premium
  ○ Co-pays
  ○ Coinsurance
  ○ Deductibles
  ○ Maximum out-of-pocket expenses

- What health improvement and prevention services did the plan include?
  ○ Vision care
  ○ Dental care
  ○ Prescriptions
  ○ Wellness care
  ○ Gym memberships

- What was the level of out-of-network coverage?

- What are the star quality ratings for prospective Medicare Advantage plans?

When they tallied the results, the choice was a "no brainer." The Medicare Advantage plan that they chose was cheaper and more comprehensive than traditional Medicare and their other Medicare Advantage options: no monthly premiums; competitive/lower out-of-pocket costs; and included dental, vision, prescriptions, and a great gym membership near their home.

George and Martha love their Medicare Advantage plan. "We would give our first year a nine out of ten!" Keeping their primary care provider and lowering costs made the shift to Medicare Advantage the logical choice. The plan they chose was more affordable than traditional Medicare, and its out-of-pocket costs were predictable. Martha notes, "We definitely saved money on health insurance this past year. That's giving us more disposable income."

George and Martha love to share their victory with their friends who are also eligible for Medicare but afraid to take sides. They've found many are either afraid to plunge into something new—Medicare Advantage—or they're indifferent about doing the research. George says, "People are afraid to change. They're comfortable with lousy service just because they're not comfortable changing."

Given what they've learned, George and Martha are eager to spread the positive news about Medicare Advantage. They now encourage their friends to compare all health insurance options, and more than a few have followed them into Medicare Advantage plans. It's beginning to feel like a movement.

In 2000 Malcolm Gladwell published his mega-bestseller *The Tipping Point*.[24] The book details how products, ideas, behaviors, entertainment, and all manner of things explode into the public consciousness. Gladwell's terminology helped explain the emerging digital age. "Going viral," "being sticky," "social contagion/epidemic," "weak ties," and "tipping point" spread into the American lexicon.

According to Gladwell, social epidemics engage the following three unique types of individuals to gain traction: *Connectors* (individuals with huge networks who bring diverse people together), *Mavens* (information specialists who spread knowledge), and *Salesmen* (charismatic persuaders who engage the masses).

George and Martha are quintessential "mavens," expertly informed individuals who first help themselves and then help others. As Gladwell details, mavens start social epidemics because of their in-depth knowledge, fluency, and communication skills. People trust them and follow their advice. Momentum builds.

By the thousands, mavens like George and Martha are sweating the details and persuading their friends by the millions that Medicare Advantage is the best alternative for health insurance. As Martha says, "I think anybody can do the research. We did it together. You just have to be interested and inquisitive. And ask questions, especially with something so important as your healthcare."

This is what consumerism looks like in Revolutionary Healthcare. When they become customers, George-and-Martha-style consumers will change everything.

Consumers as Customers (Buyers)

Legendary clothing retailer Sy Syms coined the phrase "An educated consumer is our best customer" and repeated it endlessly in radio and television commercials. Syms sold brand-name clothing at steep discounts, and cost-conscious customers flocked to his value-driven stores.

Like Syms's "educated consumers," George and Martha have discovered real value in their Medicare Advantage plan. They believe it's critical to stay educated and informed about their benefits "and keep healthy." Martha adds, "People need to understand they have to advocate for their own healthcare and focus on preventive care, rather than waiting for something bad to happen."

Medicare Advantage is a powerful change agent precisely because it turns consumers into customers. It shifts care-management risk to private plans that must attract consumers directly and keep them enrolled by providing good service. Medicare Advantage is among the most successful public-private partnerships in American history. Fixing the program's structural flaws (as discussed in Chapter 5) will make Medicare Advantage an even more powerful catalyst for Revolutionary Healthcare.

In addition to Medicare Advantage, consumers become buyers when they purchase insurance on the public health exchanges. Unfortunately, performance on the public exchanges has been inconsistent. Some state exchanges, most notably California and Florida, are working very well (ample plan choices, moderate premium increases, expanding enrollment) and can become models for other states. Some states have enacted measures to strengthen their exchange and seen beneficial results. Minnesota has introduced reinsurance for health plans participating on its exchange and seen premiums decline. New Jersey has implemented an individual mandate and seen premiums decline.

In an intriguing opinion article in the *New York Times* titled "How Healthcare Hurts Your Paycheck," authors Regina Herzlinger, Barak Richman, and Richard Boxer suggest employer-administered health plans may be nearing the end of their useful lives.[25] Approximately 150 million Americans receive subsidized health benefits through their employers. In its place, the authors recommend tweaking tax law to allow employers to pass the tax-advantage subsidies directly to their employees, who could then purchase approved plans directly through public exchanges.

This proposal would turn subsidized consumers (those with employer-sponsored health funds) into customers who could buy health plans that directly meet their families' needs. Employees could keep any unspent monies as taxable income.

As the authors emphasize, competition would incent both payers and providers to offer more value to these customers:

> Freeing workers' choices for insurance would also bring pressures on insurers to create new products that control costs, such as bundling of homeowners, auto and health insurances, or enabling people between 55 and 64 years old to access Medicare. State legislatures would feel similar pressures to adjust regulations to support competitive insurance marketplaces.
>
> Stiffer competition and cost pressures on insurers, in turn, would force providers to offer more efficient care, such as by replacing outpatient and emergency room visits with telemedicine technology.

Greater transparency, more product selection, and more innovative service delivery would loosen the grip of local-market monopoly producers and monopsonist purchasers to manipulate prices. That's great for customers and for health companies that deliver value to customers.

Even without an adjustment to tax law, intermediaries can deliver value directly to consumers by letting them participate in selecting their care providers while generating significant savings for their self-insured employers. The story of a retired Santa Barbara deputy sheriff illustrates the point.[26]

Self-insured Santa Barbara County in California encouraged Leslie Robinson-Stone, a former deputy sheriff and bike enthusiast, to undergo knee replacement surgery at a Scripps hospital in La Jolla (250 miles away) rather than have the procedure at a higher-priced local hospital.

Working with San Francisco–based Carrum Health, the county saved over $30,000. Living its "Bringing common sense to healthcare" mantra, Carrum arranged a bundled payment that covered Robinson-Jones's surgery costs, travel costs, and out-of-pocket costs, as well as giving her over a thousand dollars in spending money.

Robinson-Stone chose her surgeon, worked with a personal concierge who oversaw every aspect of her treatment, and received physical therapy at her hotel, the Estancia La Jolla Hotel and Spa. She loved the experience, was able to return to biking two months after the surgery, and lost 20 pounds. She is still a very satisfied customer, "I just celebrated one year from surgery, and I'm a happy camper." As Carrum Health promises on its website, this was "no trade-offs" healthcare.

Educated consumers really are healthcare's best customers.

HEALTHCARE'S "REAL DADDY"

As discussed earlier in this chapter, Saskatchewan adopted universal coverage of physician services in 1962 in spite of a tumultuous doctors' strike. In 1964, the Royal Commission on Health Services recommended establishing a national plan for funding healthcare services. The Canadian Parliament then passed the Medical Act of 1966, which took six years to ratify across all 10 provinces and territories. Throughout the prolonged political debate, the dogged and charismatic Tommy Douglas was the guiding spirit behind Canada's passage of universal healthcare coverage for its people.[27]

During this same period, US President Lyndon Johnson parlayed his detailed knowledge of legislative protocols and legendary deal-making skills to promote his "Great Society" program. This included passage in 1965 of an amendment to the Social Security Act that created Medicare for seniors and Medicaid for low-income people (Figure 10.3).[28] The legislation provided federal funding for Medicare and shared federal-state funding for Medicaid. Seventeen years later in October 1982, Arizona became the last of the 50 states to join the Medicaid program.

As in Canada, the political opposition to national healthcare programs was fierce. For example, the American Medical Association hired future president Ronald Reagan to make the case against Medicare. In a 1961 radio address, Reagan described national health insurance as a stepping stone to socialism:

> One of the traditional methods of imposing statism or socialism is by way of medicine. It is very easy to disguise a medical program as

FIGURE 10.3 Lyndon B. Johnson signing the Medicare Act on July 30, 1965.

Photo credit: LBJ Library. Photo by Unknown.

a humanitarian project. Most people are a little reluctant to oppose anything that suggests medical care for people who possibly can't afford it.[29]

Johnson was unable to find enough support for universal coverage, so he focused his legislative efforts on covering older and poorer Americans. Even that required significant compromises (discussed in Chapter 1) to placate America's doctors and other opposition groups. Ultimately Johnson prevailed and expanded government's role in funding, administering, and policing the delivery of healthcare services in the United States.

With Harry Truman by his side, President Johnson brought Medicare and Medicaid to life on July 30, 1965. Recognizing Truman's advocacy for national healthcare, LBJ staged the signing ceremony in Truman's hometown of Independence, Missouri. Leaning over Truman (as only he could do), LBJ proclaimed,

We want the entire world to know that we haven't forgotten who is the real Daddy of Medicare.

Under Medicare, health coverage for America's seniors has grown from under 50 percent to 96 percent. Medicare also provides health insurance to people with permanent disabilities. Medicare and Medicaid cover 130 million Americans[30] and are fundamental components of the country's social safety net.

Unfortunately, Medicare has woven a fee-for-service transaction and payment structure in the fabric of American healthcare delivery. These fee-for-service payment models have generated disastrous economic, social, and human consequences.

At Medicare's inception, prominent UCLA professor Milton Roemer saw the future. He observed, "Supply may induce its own demand in the presence of third-party payment."[31] In other words, doctors and hospitals would create their own demand for treatments. Fifty years later, the United States can no longer tolerate supply-driven demand for healthcare services. It's too expensive, too inefficient, and too error prone.

Demanding customers, service-oriented providers, user-friendly technologies, and retail health companies have enough market power to normalize healthcare's distorted supply-demand relationships. The revolution will continue until all Americans have access to affordable and appropriate healthcare services.

Who is healthcare's real "Daddy"? It is and must be empowered consumers and customers in the healthcare marketplace.

Long live the customer revolution in healthcare!

E Pluribus Unum

In his farewell address to his troops in November 1783, General George Washington marveled at how soldiers from different states, backgrounds, and cultures had developed into a unified and cohesive Continental Army:

> Who that was not a witness could imagine that the most violent and local prejudices would cease so soon and that men who came from different parts of the continent . . . would instantly become but one patriotic band of brothers.[1]

Washington hoped that the Continental Army could become a model for unifying the new nation. That is what happened. For all its glaring flaws, the United States is a single nation that binds together a heterogeneous, multicultural, ethnically diverse "band of peoples." Healthcare, which touches every American, is the living embodiment of this reality.

The front of the Great Seal of the United States (Figure CIII.1) depicts an eagle with the phrase "E Pluribus Unum," Latin for "Out of Many, One." That phrase encapsulates the genius and challenge of America. In healthcare, America needs to create a system that works for the many, not just the few. It must accommodate regional, cultural, and individual differences while guaranteeing access to appropriate and affordable care for all.

On the back of the Great Seal is a pyramid with the Latin words "Novus Ordo Seclorum". This translates into "A New Order for the Ages." These words have relevance for healthcare as well. Out of the System's ashes, a new American healthcare must rise that serves all Americans with personalized, value-based health and healthcare services.

It's appropriate that both sides of the Great Seal appear on the back of the US one-dollar bill. Money and medicine go together like America

FIGURE CIII.1 Great Seal of the United States, front and back

and apple pie. Perverse financial incentives combined with insider wheeling and dealing have created a healthcare monstrosity that is suffocating American productivity and human potential. Aligning financial incentives with desired outcomes, leveling the competitive playing field, turning consumers into customers, and unleashing the American innovation machine on the System will turn it to dust, replacing it with a new, uniquely American healthcare that dazzles rather than disappoints.

Revolutionary Healthcare will encompass the following:

- **New innovators.** Large numbers of nimble, innovative, and well-funded new market entrants that will selectively attack imbedded system inefficiency where they can deliver value-creating solutions.

- **More precise markets.** Segmentation of the healthcare marketplace addressing varying degrees of care duration and care uncertainty. The resulting four quadrants are commodity, specialty, complex, and chronic care. They have different customers, competitors, supply chains and price points.

- **New business models.** Disruptive and transformative business models advance systemwide outcomes. The most promising new business models are enhanced primary care services, focused factories, asset-light care provision, and retail health services.

- **Enhanced understanding of patient needs.** More emphasis on solving customer and consumer "jobs-to-be-done" (Jobs) in health and healthcare. Consumers' three Jobs are (1) fix me when I'm broken, (2) sustain my health, and (3) enhance my health.

- **Repositioning of incumbents.** Massive repositioning by established health companies to accommodate market demands for full-risk contracting, outcome accountability, and holistic health and healthcare services.

- **Decentralized service delivery.** Transformation of healthcare services to accommodate greater price transparency, decentralized service delivery, new technologies, and greater consumerism.

- **New levels of engagement.** More engagement of consumers in health and healthcare delivery and purchasing. Turning more consumers into customers (buyers) is a necessary component of universal access to appropriate and affordable healthcare services.

- **Emphasis on health.** Emergence of health and employer companies that choose to "compete on health" with emphasis on prevention, early diagnosis, health promotion, disease management, and behavioral health services.

- **A dynamic marketplace.** An unleashed American innovation engine that will revolutionize American healthcare.

Healthcare's Moral Imperative

The year 1863 was transcendent for President Abraham Lincoln (Figure C.1). After shaking hands at a White House reception much of New Year's Day, Lincoln retreated to his study to sign the Emancipation Proclamation. The president's signing hand trembled with fatigue, so he waited several minutes for it to strengthen. With resolve, Lincoln then signed what he considered his most important document.

At the moment Lincoln signed the Emancipation Proclamation, all slaves in the rebellious southern states became "then, thenceforward and forever free." Later that day, the president put his action in perspective:

FIGURE C.1 Abraham Lincoln

I never in my life felt more certain that I was doing right than I do in signing this paper. If my name goes into history, it will be for this act, and my whole soul is in it.[1]

Eleven months later on November 19, Lincoln delivered his renowned Gettysburg Address at the dedication for the Soldiers National Cemetery. With the ravages of the ferocious July battle still evident, President Lincoln's two-minute address redefined American democracy and its "Union" of states within the context of the nation's bloody sectarian battle over slavery and states' rights.

Lincoln's signing of the Emancipation Proclamation and his Gettysburg Address redefined the context and purpose of the US Civil War from the North's perspective. Prior to signing the Emancipation Proclamation, Lincoln's sole goal was keeping the Union together. Ending slavery added a powerful moral dimension to the war's purpose. At Gettysburg, Lincoln spoke of "a new birth of freedom" for the nation.

Since its founding, America had struggled to harmonize an egalitarian vision of humanity within a governing structure that legalized slavery, the nation's original sin. The inability of America's North and South regions to accommodate their differing worldviews led to a brutal civil war.

A civil war of a different sort is underway within US healthcare. The gleaming vision of proficient modern medicine duels with an unrestrained Healthcare Industrial Complex that ravages societal resources and mis-serves the American people. Like the Civil War, the origins of healthcare's conflict lie in the gap between lofty ambitions and unfulfilled promise.

In 1965, at Medicare's creation, President Lyndon Johnson agreed to debilitating structural flaws in Medicare's payment mechanisms to ensure legislative passage. These provisions, including activity-based payment and precluding governmental participation in medical decision making, fragment and depersonalize care delivery.

Since the mid-1960s, US healthcare has struggled to harmonize an ideal of effective healthcare with an inefficient, fragmented, and profligate operating reality. These inherent contradictions are made worse by the efforts of Congress, industry, and government agencies to pursue their vested interests at the expense of American society.

Before 1863, "state's rights" was the Civil War's defining issue. The North fought to preserve the Union on its terms, while the South fought to secede from the Union on its terms. After 1863, the continuation of slavery became the war's defining issue. For the North, emancipation became a moral imperative and was crucial to its ultimate victory.

For several decades, "volume" and "value" forces have battled for control of US healthcare. This "war" has centered on healthcare's escalating costs. As with emancipation, there is a moral imperative for the United States to establish universal healthcare coverage. The health, wellness, and productivity of the American people, their local communities, and the nation overall hang in the balance.

All Americans deserve the right to appropriate, accessible, and affordable healthcare services. Universal coverage, however, does not require a single-payer health insurance system. Indeed, freedom to choose appropriate health insurance coverage from multiple sources is as American as free markets. It is a natural manifestation of America's pluralistic and consumer-oriented society.

This is healthcare's "Emancipation Proclamation" moment. Now is the time to reinvent health and healthcare delivery. Revolutionary Healthcare empowers consumers to expect and receive appropriate and affordable care every day, every time, everywhere. To survive and thrive, health companies must make Revolutionary Healthcare the rule, not the exception.

EMANCIPATING HEALTHCARE

This book begins with President Dwight Eisenhower's 1961 description of America's military industrial complex and the dangers it posed to broader societal interests. Eisenhower warned Americans that their Congress, the defense industry, and the Department of Defense work in conjunction to promote mutual self-interests to the detriment of the country as a whole.

I have applied Eisenhower's "iron triangle" framework to healthcare to explain how an equivalent Healthcare Industrial Complex (the System) consumes vast and increasing amounts of societal resources without restraint. Even worse, the System's fragmented architecture fails to deliver the vital health and healthcare services Americans need.

Policy makers have long recognized the need to increase the value America receives for its considerable investment in healthcare services. Despite significant efforts to incrementally improve healthcare's outcomes, quality, and costs, the System has frustrated reform efforts and expanded its profligate and self-serving behaviors. Meanwhile, healthcare costs escalate at an unsustainable rate, life expectancy is actually declining, and Americans now fear the costs of treating a disease more than actually contracting a disease.

Lincoln began the Civil War intent on maintaining the union of states, then embraced emancipation as a second war objective. As the casualties mounted and the prospects for quick victory faded, Lincoln realized he was not only fighting to keep the country together, he was fighting to preserve its soul.

America has been waging a long-fought and frustrating war to increase the value of healthcare service provision. Yet, that war has not addressed the System's fundamental inequities. Just as Lincoln did in signing the Emancipation Proclamation, Revolutionary Healthcare must amplify its moral imperative. Beyond pursuit of value-based care delivery, Revolutionary Healthcare must fight for universal healthcare coverage. In that way, healthcare will recapture its soul and fulfill its true purpose.

Therefore, Revolutionary Healthcare has a two-pronged battle mission. It must blow up the Healthcare Industrial Complex and build a new system that delivers kinder, smarter, affordable care to all Americans. To achieve this vision, governments must establish balanced regulatory policies and police them vigorously. They also must eliminate the influence peddling that tilts healthcare's competitive landscape in favor of incumbents. The American people deserve nothing less.

IRONY THEN AND NOW

Lincoln's Gettysburg Address is the most celebrated statement of national purpose in American history. Generations of schoolchildren have recited it at speech contests. Its concise eloquence resonates through time. Here are its opening and closing lines:

> Four score and seven years ago our fathers brought forth on this continent a new nation, conceived in liberty, and dedicated to the proposition that all men are created equal.
>
> Now we are engaged in a great civil war, testing whether that nation, or any nation so conceived and so dedicated, can long endure . . .
>
> that this nation, under God, shall have a new birth of freedom— and that government of the people, by the people, for the people, shall not perish from the earth.

In his opening sentence, Lincoln references the "All men are created equal" proclamation from the Declaration of Independence. American society did not then and has not yet achieved this expansive democratic vision of a just society.

Lincoln kept the Union together at enormous cost, but with clear purpose and a deep understanding of America's unfulfilled potential. In December 1862, Lincoln described the United States as "the last best hope on earth." Before the Civil War, Americans said, *"The United States are . . . "* Afterward, it became *"The United States is . . . "* The many had become one.

It is ironic that a nation founded on equality had to fight a brutal civil war to guarantee it. It is equally ironic that the people living in a nation that spends far more per capita on healthcare than any other experience subpar health status. Healthcare cannot transform until it honestly addresses its internal contradictions and aligns payment with desired outcomes.

FRAGMENTED AT CREATION

President Lyndon Johnson spoke with Lincoln-like passion as he signed Medicare and Medicaid into law on July 30, 1965:

> But there is another tradition that we share today. It calls upon us never to be indifferent toward despair. It commands us never to turn away from helplessness. It directs us never to ignore or to spurn those untended in a land that is bursting with abundance.

Unfortunately, the reality of American healthcare has not measured up to President Johnson's lofty rhetoric. Fragmented at birth, the System dispenses high-cost care through an uncoordinated network of facilities and practitioners. Outcomes are suboptimal. The System ignores consumer needs and preferences. Unpaid medical expenses are the leading cause of personal bankruptcy.

US healthcare employs complex, centrally developed payment formularies that private-market participants exploit for their own economic benefit. The result is a payment system that at best invites manipulation and at worst stimulates massive fraud. Lax regulatory enforcement and capture of legislative process by industry insiders exacerbate the damage.

More troubling than the System's profligacy is the toll it takes on consumers and clinicians. Consumers navigate through byzantine treatment labyrinths that depersonalize care, generate suboptimal outcomes, and marginalize customer experience. For clinicians, doing the right thing for patients often requires heroic effort. An unbearable administrative burden limits their time with patients and leads to excessive burnout. On balance, American healthcare is cruel, unfair, unfeeling, and mistake prone.

Fifty-plus years of operating in this artificial economic environment has created major structural distortions. These include a massive asset bubble in acute care facilities, severe access limitations, an outdated academic medicine platform, and deplorable underinvestment in basic care services, health promotion, and social determinants of health.

The sins of forefathers (and mothers) have returned to haunt later generations. American healthcare is now engaged in a great revolution, testing whether its healthcare system can deliver on the promise of Revolutionary Healthcare—providing the right care at the right time in the right place at the right price within a personalized, holistic, and compassionate ecosystem.

On one side is an American society that wants better, more affordable, convenient, holistic, and compassionate healthcare. On the other side is an entrenched Healthcare Industrial Complex with powerful incumbents fighting to keep the System intact.

REVOLUTIONARY MIGHT

The heroes of this battle are visionary leaders, frontline care professionals, and revolutionary organizations (new and old, big and small) delivering better health and healthcare outcomes at lower costs in customer-friendly settings. This alliance is solving consumers' three healthcare "jobs-to-be-done."

- Fix me when I'm broken.

- Sustain my health.

- Enhance my health.

Revolutionaries are winning market share by delivering great health and healthcare services to consumers. Upstart organizations see opportunities to serve consumers with innovation and customer-centric business models. Enlightened incumbents are changing business models so they can compete more effectively in a transforming marketplace. Discerning employers demand insurance and wellness programs that deliver better health outcomes for their employees. Empowered and educated consumers push the marketplace forward with informed medical decision making.

Healthcare's revolutionaries go into battle with powerful forces on their side. These include:

- **Full-risk contracting vehicles that align payer, provider, and consumer interests** in pursuing Revolutionary Healthcare.

- **Empowered buyers** who use their purchasing power to demand and receive Revolutionary Healthcare.

- **Liberated data** that flows where it's needed most to optimize care delivery in real time, enhance medical decision making, educate consumers, reduce medical error, and ease the stresses of care delivery for both clinicians and consumers.

- **New management models supported by data systems** that enable teams of teams to work with a "shared consciousness," through which frontline professionals have the data, knowledge, tools, and authority to do the right thing for consumers in real time.

- **A greater public understanding of the System's dysfunction and more transparency tools to guide consumer decision making** on identifying higher-quality healthcare services, knowing how much they cost, and determining when and where to receive care.

- **Greater regulatory willingness to support market-based policies** that shift care risk to third parties, level the competitive playing field, and address areas of market failure in service pricing.

Consumer Revolutionaries are demanding information about costs and better care. Buyers are making their presence felt and shaping healthcare products and services through their purchases. Demand-driven change generates revolutionary results. Some markets have already achieved sufficient critical mass that payers and providers are vertically integrating to manage the episodic and long-term care needs of distinct populations. This is the path to Revolutionary Healthcare.

More and more health companies are accepting the risks of managing the health of targeted populations. As this happens, it becomes paramount for these companies to address the social and environmental factors that influence health and shape healthcare spending. Achieving desired care outcomes, broad-based improvement in health status, market relevance, and financial stability depend upon it.

The emergence of transformative and disruptive business models, most notably the rise in enhanced primary care services, testify to increasing effectiveness of the private companies to solve consumers jobs to be done in healthcare. As they do, Revolutionary Healthcare captures more hearts, minds, and wallets.

JUSTICE AND VALUE

What does "government of, by, and for the people" mean in postindustrial, multicultural America? There's never been a true pluralistic democracy in the history of the world, so the American Experiment continues. Healthcare is an embodiment of the larger American commitment to justice, fairness, progress, and equality. Balancing the needs of the many while protecting the rights of all is an ongoing challenge and responsibility for the nation's leaders.

American healthcare must work for all its people. It should increase national equality. It should reduce levels of chronic disease and increase healthy life years. It should elevate the health status of individuals and communities. The nation can achieve these broadly distributed benefits by providing universal health coverage that delivers affordable access to appropriate health and healthcare services as needed.

The best way of achieving affordable and universal healthcare is by turning more consumers into customers. Customers use their purchasing power to buy products and services that meet individual needs. Their purchasing decisions send powerful signals to the marketplace where companies reconfigure offerings to keep existing customers and find new ones.

Unleashing America's innovation engine on solving the nation's health and healthcare challenges is America's "last best hope" for transforming its inefficient, uneven, fragmented, and ridiculously expensive healthcare delivery system.

Paraphrasing Lincoln, market-based healthcare reform must appeal to the "better angels of our nature." Markets are the best mechanisms for allocating societal resources efficiently.

High-functioning marketplaces require level-field competition, consumer protections, and ongoing monitoring to guarantee buyers and sellers transact on equal terms. They also require constant adjustment to maintain their competitiveness and fairness. Revolutionary Healthcare is on the march, but it has a long battle ahead to break the System's stranglehold on healthcare payment and delivery.

The preamble to the US Constitution begins with the phrase, "We the People of the United States, in Order to form a more perfect union . . . " This language recognizes the imperfect state of the current union and the ongoing need to improve its form, function, and fairness.

What is true for the nation at large is poignantly true for American healthcare. The nation does not need to spend 18 percent of its economy to provide superior healthcare to everyone in the country.

Revolutionary Healthcare isn't mysterious, miraculous, or mythical. It combines the best of human spirit with science and technology to deliver the care people need when and where they need it. It elevates while healing. It's within reach and coming fast.

America has the capacity to build a "more perfect" healthcare system. Delivering better healthcare to all Americans for less money will free up enormous resources to fund other pressing needs and invest in more productive enterprise. Market-driven, value-driven healthcare reform will produce a stronger national economy with healthier individuals and communities.

Given its importance, cost, and reach, fixing American healthcare is this generation's major public policy challenge. At issue is whether we can give birth to a new American Healthcare that engages with the people to provide better health and healthcare services for the American people.

America fought a Civil War to emancipate the slaves and guarantee equality under the law. Today, the System forces Americans to receive healthcare services on its terms, not theirs. Healthcare revolutionaries are fighting to guarantee appropriate, accessible, and affordable health and healthcare services for all Americans. Are you ready to join the revolution?

ACKNOWLEDGMENTS

The creation process for *The Customer Revolution in Healthcare* consists of three concentric circles of effort working in unison. Inside the "bull's-eye," Keith Hollihan, Lindsay Morrison, and I produced the manuscript. The middle circle combined the collective efforts of 4sight Health and McGraw-Hill to review, edit, design, produce, market, and distribute *The Customer Revolution in Healthcare*. The final circle is a vast network of professional contacts with whom I share perspectives, debate policies, explore anomalies, and develop thought leadership. Great writing is a team effort.

INNER CIRCLE

Keith and I worked closely together on my 2016 book, *Market vs. Medicine*, and collaborate on thought leadership engagements. We have exceptional chemistry. Keith has a Svengali-like ability to understand my thinking, support it with research, and amplify it with creative metaphors. For Keith, great writing is both an elegant dance and a contact sport! He pushes me and the rest of our 4sight Health team to explore new topics, think more boldly, and be more provocative. He's passionate about making healthcare smarter, kinder, and more just. Keith believes now is the time for *The Customer Revolution in Healthcare*. Let's march!

Lindsay joined 4sight Health as our content and marketing director at the end of 2017. With a English degree from Northwestern and a distinguished career in media, Lindsay quickly became invaluable. She organized 4sH's digital footprint, upgraded our content platform, standardized our business practices, and managed our professional services. Then she turned her attention to the new book. Wow! Lindsay's unique blend of editorial savvy, content knowledge, and organizational wizardry put our production process into high gear and kept it there throughout. Lindsay is directing 4sH's marketing, sales, and outreach efforts to spread *The Customer Revolution in Healthcare* nationwide. When you join the revolution, look for Lindsay's raised fist going over the barricades.

MIDDLE CIRCLE

The 4sight Health family of contributors were Michelle Lange (graphic design); Nathan Bays, Karen Handmaker, Dave Burda, and Terri Brady (content review); Lalitha Ramachandran (research); Alina Bonn (social media connection); Shannon Morfin (professional outreach); and Amanda Butterworth (logistics). What a team!

My editor at McGraw-Hill, Casey Ebro, leads the charge, with support from a well-trained army of copy editors, designers, and proofreaders. They are a superb group that meets deadlines, thinks outside the box, and delivers a superior product. Casey runs the "business of healthcare" product line for McGraw-Hill. For that reason, Casey is the ideal partner and editor for *The Customer Revolution in Healthcare*. She knows the subject matter and is part coach, part cheerleader, and part drillmaster, as required, in getting the publishing job done. We are in great hands with Casey!

OUTER CIRCLE

In *Market vs. Medicine*, I identified a couple hundred individuals from my network who inform and inspire my work across the full spectrum of healthcare activity. That list has only gotten longer and deeper, so I won't repeat the exercise. What I can tell you is that there are remarkable people fighting every day to fix our broken healthcare system. They're natural revolutionaries who understand the stakes and are taking up the charge.

NOTES

INTRODUCTION

1. "Transcript of President Dwight D. Eisenhower's Farewell Address (1961)," https://www.ourdocuments.gov/doc.php?flash=false&doc=90&page=transcript.
2. "A Typical American Birth Costs as Much as Delivering a Royal Baby," *The Economist*, April 23, 2018, https://www.economist.com/graphic-detail/2018/04/23/a-typical-american-birth-costs-as-much-as-delivering-a-royal-baby.

CHAPTER 1

1. "How Have Healthcare Prices Grown in the U.S. over Time?," Peterson-Kaiser Health System Tracker, n.d., https://www.healthsystemtracker.org/chart-collection/how-have-healthcare-prices-grown-in-the-u-s-over-time/#item-the-average-price-of-knee-replacement-has-increased-faster-than-general-inflation.
2. "A Study of Cost Variations for Knee and Hip Replacement Surgeries in the U.S.," Blue Cross Blue Shield, January 21, 2015, https://www.bcbs.com/the-health-of-america/reports/study-of-cost-variations-knee-and-hip-replacement-surgeries-the-us.
3. Melanie Evans, "What Does Knee Surgery Cost? Few Know, and That's a Problem," *Wall Street Journal*, August 21, 2018, https://www.wsj.com/articles/what-does-knee-surgery-cost-few-know-and-thats-a-problem-1534865358.
4. Section 1886(d)(5)(A) of the [Medicare] [AC] Act, Outlier Payments.
5. Elizabeth Rosenthal, "Those Indecipherable Medical Bills? They're One Reason Health Care Costs So Much," *New York Times*, March 29, 2017, https://www.nytimes.com/2017/03/29/magazine/those-indecipherable-medical-bills-theyre-one-reason-health-care-costs-so-much.html.
6. "A Comparison of Hospital Administrative Costs in Eight Nations: US Costs Exceed All Others by Far," The Physician Payments Sunshine Act, accessed January 5, 2019, https://www.healthaffairs.org/doi/10.1377/hlthaff.2013.1327.

7. Gregg S. Meyer, Akinluwa A. Demehin, Xiu Liu, and Duncan Neuhauser, "Two Hundred Years of Hospital Costs and Mortality—MGH and Four Eras of Value in Medicine," *New England Journal of Medicine*, June 7, 2012, https://www.nejm.org/doi/full/10.1056/NEJMp1202628.

8. Christopher Howard, "Tax Expenditures: What They Are and Who Benefits," Scholars Strategy Network, January 1, 2012, https://scholars.org/brief/tax-expenditures-what-they-are-and-who-benefits.

9. M. I. Roemer, "Bed Supply and Hospital Utilization: A Natural Experiment," *Hospitals*, November 1, 1961, 36–42.

10. Donald M. Berwick, "Eliminating Waste in US Health Care," *JAMA*, April 11, 2012, https://jamanetwork.com/journals/jama/article-abstract/1148376.

11. Rabah Kamal and Cynthia Cox, "How Do Healthcare Prices and Use in the U.S. Compare to Other Countries?," Peterson-Kaiser Health System Tracker, May 8, 2018, https://www.healthsystemtracker.org/chart-collection/how-do-healthcare-prices-and-use-in-the-u-s-compare-to-other-countries/#item-start.

12. Bruce Steinwald, Paul Ginsburg, Caitlin Brandt, Sobin Lee, and Kavita Patel, "Medicare Graduate Medical Education Funding Is Not Addressing the Primary Care Shortage: We Need a Radically Different Approach," Brookings.edu, December 3, 2018, https://www.brookings.edu/research/medicare-graduate-medical-education-funding-is-not-addressing-the-primary-care-shortage-we-need-a-radically-different-approach/.

13. Alex Kacik, "Medicare Doctor Fees Need Changing to Promote Primary Care," *Modern Healthcare*, December 6, 2018, https://www.modernhealthcare.com/article/20181206/NEWS/181209949.

14. Katie Thomas and Charles Ornstein, "Top Sloan Kettering Cancer Doctor Resigns After Failing to Disclose Industry Ties," *New York Times*, September 13, 2018, https://www.nytimes.com/2018/09/13/health/jose-baselga-cancer-memorial-sloan-kettering.html.

15. Charles Ornstein and Katie Thomas, "What These Medical Journals Don't Reveal: Top Doctors' Ties to Industry," *New York Times*, December 8, 2018, https://www.nytimes.com/2018/12/08/health/medical-journals-conflicts-of-interest.html.

16. David Lazarus, "Direct-to-Consumer Drug Ads: A Bad Idea That's About to Get Worse," *Los Angeles Times*, February 15, 2017, http://www.latimes.com/business/la-fi-lazarus-drugadvertising-20170215-story.html.

17. Beth Snyder Bulik, "Doctor Payments Back on the Table at GlaxoSmith-Kline with Rollback of Its Total Ban," FiercePharma, October 3, 2018, https://www.fiercepharma.com/marketing/doctor-payments-back-table-at-gsk-a-rollback-its-total-ban-to-allow-some-exceptions.

18. Alia Paavola, "Reversing Course: GlaxoSmithKline Will Resume Paying Physicians Who Promote Its Drugs," *Becker's Hospital Review*, October 3, 2018, https://www.beckershospitalreview.com/pharmacy/reversing-course -glaxosmithkline-will-resume-paying-physicians-who-promote-its-drugs .html.

CHAPTER 2

1. Alison Kodjak, "Surprised by a Medical Bill? Join the Club. Most Americans Say They Have Been," NPR, September 2, 2018, https://www.npr.org /sections/health-shots/2018/09/02/643708098/surprised-by-a-medical -bill-join-the-club-most-americans-say-they-have-been.

2. Scott Hensley, "Share Your Medical Bill with Us," NPR, February 16, 2018, https://www.npr.org/sections/health-shots/2018/02/16/585549568 /share-your-medical-bill-with-us.

3. Jordan Rau, "Bill of the Month: $43,208 for Repeat Surgery to Replace Broken Medical Device," NPR, December 18, 2018, https://www.npr.org /sections/health-shots/2018/12/18/677330646/bill-of-the-month-43-208 -for-repeat-surgery-to-replace-broken-medical-device.

4. Barbara Feder Ostrov, "Bill of the Month: A $48,329 Allergy Test Is a Lot of Scratch," NPR, October 29, 2018, https://www.npr.org/sections/health -shots/2018/10/29/660330047/bill-of-the-month-a-48-329-allergy-test-is -a-lot-of-scratch.

5. Fred Schulte, "How a Urine Test After Back Surgery Triggered a $17,850 Bill," NPR, February 16, 2018, https://www.npr.org/sections/health-shots /2018/02/16/584296663/how-a-urine-test-after-back-surgery-triggered -a-17-800-bill.

6. "NHE Fact Sheet 2017," CMS.gov Centers for Medicare and Medicaid Services, December 6, 2018, https://www.cms.gov/research-statistics-data -and-systems/statistics-trends-and-reports/nationalhealthexpenddata/nhe -fact-sheet.html.

7. "CMS Office of the Actuary Releases 2017–2026 Projections of National Health Expenditures," CMS.gov Centers for Medicare and Medicaid Services, February 14, 2018.

8. Donald M. Berwick, "Eliminating Waste in US Health Care," *JAMA*, April 11, 2012, https://www.icsi.org/_asset/y74drr/eliminating-waste-in -the-us-healthcare-2012.pdf.

9. David W. Johnson, "Good Intentions Aren't Enough: Choosing Wisely Misses the Target," 4sight Health, November 15, 2017, http://www .4sighthealth.com/good-intentions-arent-enough-choosing-wisely-misses -the-target/.

10. David W. Johnson, *Market vs Medicine: America's Epic Fight for Better, Affordable Healthcare* (Chicago: David W. Johnson, 2016), 313–14.

11. "Columbus | Ohio | 2018 | Market Overview (Event Driven) | Research & Reports," August 16, 2018, https://decisionresourcesgroup.com/report /1006483-marketaccess-columbus-ohio-2018-market-overview-event/.

12. John Hargraves, "HMI Price Index Tool," 2016 Health Care Cost and Utilization Report—HCCI, https://www.healthcostinstitute.org/research /hmi/interactive.

13. Ross Margulies, "Baker Administration Submits 1115 Waiver Request to CMS, Including Major Change to Drug Coverage," Medicaid and the Law, April 13, 2017, http://www.medicaidandthelaw.com/2017/09/13 /baker-administration-submits-1115-waiver-request-to-cms-including -major-change-to-drug-coverage/.

14. Katie Thomas, "Insurers Battle Families Over Costly Drug for Fatal Disease," *New York Times*, June 22, 2017, https://www.nytimes.com/2017/06 /22/health/duchenne-muscular-dystrophy-drug-exondys-51.html.

15. Katie Thomas, "Costly Drug for Fatal Muscular Disease Wins F.D.A. Approval," *New York Times*, December 30, 2016, https://www.nytimes .com/2016/12/30/business/spinraza-price.html?_r=1.

16. Dustin L. Richter and David R. Diduch, "Cost Comparison of Outpatient Versus Inpatient Unicompartmental Knee Arthroplasty," *Orthopaedic Journal of Sports Medicine* 5, no. 3 (March 2017), doi:10.1177 /2325967117694352.

17. "Construction Put in Place Estimated for the United States: 3rd Quarter 2018 Forecast (based on 2nd Quarter 2018 Actuals)," Fails Management Institute (FMI) 2018, www.fminet.com/wp-content/uploads/2018/09 /PIP_Tables_Q3_Outlook_2018.pdf.

18. "Health Care Construction," *FMI*, July 26, 2017, www.fminet.com /outlook-nonresidential/health-care/.

19. Alia Paavola, "12 Hospital Construction Projects Worth $1B or More in 2018," *Becker's Hospital Review*, December 20, 2018, www .beckershospitalreview.com/facilities-management/12-hospital -construction-projects-worth-1b-or-more-in-2018.html; David W. Johnson and David Morlock, "Brand-Heavy and Asset-Light: Moving Beyond the Acute-Care Mindset," 4sight Health, November 14, 2018, www .4sighthealth.com/brand-heavy-and-asset-light-moving-beyond-the -acute-care-mindset/.

20. "Rush Plans Major New Outpatient Care Center at Ashland Avenue and Harrison Street," Rush University Medical Center, August 8, 2018, www .rush.edu/news/press-releases/rush-plans-major-new-outpatient-care-center.

21. Eve Kerr, "Choosing Wisely. A Special Report on the First Five Years," *Choosing Wisely*, @ABIMFoundation, 2017, www.choosingwisely.org/wp -content/uploads/2017/10/Choosing-Wisely-at-Five.pdf.

22. "Choosing Wisely: How to Fulfill the Promise in the Next 5 Years," *Health Affairs*, October 24, 2017, www.healthaffairs.org/doi/10.1377/hlthaff.2017 .0953.

23. Maria Castellucci, "Low-Value Care Persists Five Years into Choosing Wisely Campaign," *Modern Healthcare*, October 24, 2017, www .modernhealthcare.com/article/20171024/NEWS/171029941.

24. Upton Sinclair, *I, Candidate for Governor, and How I Got Licked*, (University of California Press, 1994).

CHAPTER 3

1. Joyce Frieden, "A Doctor's Life at the Nation's Oldest Hospital, Now on TV," Medpage Today, September 25, 2018, https://www.medpagetoday .com/hospitalbasedmedicine/generalhospitalpractice/75311.

2. Sarah Kliff, "The Problem Is the Prices," Vox.com, October 16, 2017, https://www.vox.com/policy-and-politics/2017/10/16/16357790/health -care-prices-problem.

3. Barbara Feder Ostrov, "Bill of the Month: A $48,329 Allergy Test Is a Lot of Scratch," NPR, October 29, 2018, https://www.npr.org/sections /health-shots/2018/10/29/660330047/bill-of-the-month-a-48-329 -allergy-test-is-a-lot-of-scratch?utm_source=npr_newsletter&utm _medium=email&utm_content=20181104&utm_campaign=health& utm_term=nprnews.

4. Elisabeth Rosenthal, "After Surgery, Surprise $117,000 Medical Bill from Doctor He Didn't Know," *New York Times*, September 20, 2014, https:// www.nytimes.com/2014/09/21/us/drive-by-doctoring-surprise-medical -bills.html.

5. Gallup, Inc., "Healthcare System," Gallup.com, November 2018, http:// www.gallup.com/poll/4708/healthcare-system.aspx.

6. "2018 Employer Health Benefits Survey—Summary of Findings," The Henry J. Kaiser Family Foundation, October 9, 2018, https://www.kff .org/report-section/2018-employer-health-benefits-survey-summary-of -findings/.

7. chrome-extension://oemmndcbldboiebfnladdacbdfmadadm/http:// sentierresearch.com/reports/Sentier_Household_Income_Trends_Report _June_2018_07_24_18.pdf.

8. Sara R. Collins and David C Radley, "The Cost of Employer Insurance Is a Growing Burden for Middle-Income Families," Commonwealth

Fund, December 2, 2018, www.commonwealthfund.org/publications /issue-briefs/2018/dec/cost-employer-insurance-growing-burden-middle -income-families.

9. Scott Crichlow, "Race for the Senate 2018: Key Issues in West Virginia," Brookings.edu, November 2, 2018, https://www.brookings.edu/blog /fixgov/2018/10/23/race-for-the-senate-2018-key-issues-in-west-virginia/.

10. Howard Berkes et al., "An Epidemic Is Killing Thousands of Coal Miners. Regulators Could Have Stopped It," *Portside*, NPR, December 30, 2018, portside.org/2018-12-30/epidemic-killing-thousands-coal-miners -regulators-could-have-stopped-it.

11. Steven Wine, "VoteCast: Health Care, Gun Issues Helped Manchin," AP News, November 7, 2018, https://www.apnews.com/5ec995814f8b48cd90 c7dcce89c5120a.

12. "America's Health Rankings Annual Report," America's Health Ratings, United Health Foundation, 2017, 6, https://www.americashealthrankings .org/learn/reports/2016-annual-report/comparison-with-other-nations.

13. "Life Expectancy at Birth (in years)," The Henry J. Kaiser Family Foundation, May 2, 2017, https://www.kff.org/other/state-indicator /life-expectancy/?currentTimeframe=0&selectedDistributions=life -expectancy-at-birth-years&sortModel=%7B%22colId%22:%22Location %22,%22sort%22:%22asc%22%7D.

14. Alan S. Blinder, *After the Music Stopped: The Financial Crisis, the Response, and the Work Ahead* (Penguin Books, 2016), Chapter 15.

15. "NHE Fact Sheet 2017," CMS.gov Centers for Medicare & Medicaid Services, December 6, 2018, www.cms.gov/research-statistics-data-and -systems/statistics-trends-and-reports/nationalhealthexpenddata/nhe-fact -sheet.html.

16. Luke Mintz, "Photo of Dead Syrian Boy Boosts Fundraising 100-fold—Study," Reuters, January 11, 2017, https://af.reuters.com/article /worldNews/idAFKBN14V2GE.

CHAPTER 4

1. "Heroin in Cincinnati: This Is What an Epidemic Looks Like," *Cincinnati Enquirer*, September 10, 2017, www.cincinnati.com/pages/interactives /seven-days-of-heroin-epidemic-cincinnati/.

2. David W. Johnson, "Crony Capitalism Has Consequences: Opioid Distribution, Destruction and Death," 4sight Health, November 3, 2017, http://www.4sighthealth.com/crony-capitalism-has-consequences-opioid -distribution-destruction-and-death/.

3. Sara Sidner, "Fentanyl: The Opioid That Killed Prince," CNN, October 25, 2017, http://www.cnn.com/2016/05/10/health/fentanyl-new-heroin -deadlier/.

4. "Surgeon General's Report on Alcohol, Drugs, and Health," Executive Summary, accessed December 15, 2018, https://addiction.surgeongeneral .gov/.

5. Elizabeth Chuck and Erika Edwards, "Surgeon General Calls on America to Face Addiction Crisis," NBCNews.com, November 17, 2016, http:// www.nbcnews.com/health/health-news/78-people-die-day-opioid -overdose-surgeon-general-says-landmark-n685366.

6. Holly Hedegaard, Li-Hui Chen, and Margaret Warner, "Drug-Poisoning Deaths Involving Heroin: United States, 2000–2013," Centers for Disease Control and Prevention, March 4, 2015, https://www.cdc.gov/nchs/data /databriefs/db190.htm.

7. "Opioid Overdose," Centers for Disease Control and Prevention, December 19, 2018, https://www.cdc.gov/drugoverdose/data/statedeaths.html.

8. International Narcotics Control Board, *Narcotic Drugs 2017: Estimated World Requirements for 2018—Statistics for 2016* (United Nations, 2018), https://www.incb.org/incb/en/narcotic-drugs/Technical_Reports /narcotic_drugs_reports.html.

9. Brian F. Mandell, Daniel G. Tobin, Rebecca Andrews, William C. Becker, and Marissa Galicia-Castillo, "The Fifth Vital Sign: A Complex Story of Politics and Patient Care," MDedge Psychiatry, August 16, 2017, https://www.mdedge.com/ccjm/article/109138/drug-therapy/fifth-vital -sign-complex-story-politics-and-patient-care.

10. Sonya Collins, "Opioids: A Crisis Decades in the Making," WebMD, March 14, 2018, https://www.webmd.com/special-reports/opioids-pain /20180314/opioids-pain.

11. Caitlin Esch, "How One Sentence Helped Set off the Opioid Crisis," Marketplace, December 13, 2017, https://www.marketplace.org/2017/12 /13/health-care/uncertain-hour/opioid.

12. Harriet Ryan, Lisa Girion, and Scott Glover, "'You Want a Description of Hell?' OxyContin's 12-hour Problem #InvestigatingOxy," *Los Angeles Times*, May 5, 2016, http://www.latimes.com/projects/oxycontin-part1/.

13. Barry Meier, "In Guilty Plea, OxyContin Maker to Pay $600 Million," *New York Times*, May 10, 2007, http://www.nytimes.com/2007/05/10 /business/11drug-web.html.

14. "Pharmaceutical Executives Charged in Racketeering Scheme," The United States Department of Justice, December 9, 2016, https://www.justice.gov /usao-ma/pr/pharmaceutical-executives-charged-racketeering-scheme.

15. German Lopez, "Elizabeth Warren Wants the CDC to Consider Fighting the Opioid Epidemic . . . with Marijuana," Vox.com, February 12, 2016, http://www.vox.com/2016/2/12/10979326/elizabeth-warren-marijuana -opioids.

16. Eric Eyre, "Drug Firms Poured 780M Painkillers into WV amid Rise of Overdoses," *Charleston Gazette-Mail*, December 17, 2016, https:// www.wvgazettemail.com/news/health/drug-firms-poured-m-painkillers -into-wv-amid-rise-of/article_78963590-b050-11e7-8186-f7e8c8a1b804 .html.

17. "Surgeon General's Report on Alcohol, Drugs, and Health," Executive Summary, accessed December 15, 2018, https://addiction.surgeongeneral .gov/.

18. "How Congress Allied with Drug Company Lobbyists to Derail the DEA's War on Opioids," *Washington Post*, October 15, 2017, https://www .washingtonpost.com/graphics/2017/investigations/dea-drug-industry -congress/?utm_term=.4af249e98016.

19. Graphics, "How Congress Allied with Drug Company Lobbyists to Derail the DEA's War on Opioids," *Washington Post*, October 15, 2017, https://www.washingtonpost.com/graphics/2017/investigations/dea-drug -industry-congress/?utm_term=.4af249e98016.

20. "This Day in Quotes," February 7, 2015, http://www.thisdayinquotes.com /2010/02/it-became-necessary-to-destroy-town-to.html.

21. "S.483 - 114th Congress (2015-2016): Ensuring Patient Access and Effec- tive Drug Enforcement Act of 2016," Congress.gov, April 19, 2016, https://www.congress.gov/bill/114th-congress/senate-bill/483.

22. Eric Lipton and Katie Thomas, "Drug Lobbyists' Battle Cry Over Prices: Blame the Others," *New York Times*, May 29, 2017, https://www.nytimes .com/2017/05/29/health/drug-lobbyists-battle-cry-over-prices-blame-the -others.html?smprod=nytcore-ipad&smid=nytcore-ipad-share&_r=1.

23. "Top Lobbying Industries in the U.S. 2017," Statista, 2018, https://www .statista.com/statistics/257364/top-lobbying-industries-in-the-us/.

24. David Greene, "Senate Democrat Calls on Trump to Withdraw Tom Marino's Nomination," NPR, October 17, 2017, https://www.npr.org /2017/10/17/558267052/senate-democrat-calls-on-trump-to-withdraw -tom-marinos-nomination.

25. Ravi Gupta, Nilah D. Shaw, and Joseph S. Ross, "The Rising Price of Nal- oxone—Risks to Efforts to Stem Overdose Deaths," *New England Journal of Medicine*, December 8, 2016, https://www.nejm.org/doi/full/10.1056 /NEJMp1609578.

26. Office of the Commissioner, "Press Announcements—Statement from FDA Commissioner Scott Gottlieb, M.D., on Agency's Approval of

Dsuvia and the FDA's Future Consideration of New Opioids," US Food and Drug Administration, November 2, 2018, https://www.fda.gov /NewsEvents/Newsroom/PressAnnouncements/ucm624968.htm.

27. Ed Silverman, "FDA Approves Controversial New Opioid 10 Times More Powerful Than Fentanyl," *Scientific American*, November 2, 2018, https://www.scientificamerican.com/article/fda-approves-controversial -new-opioid-10-times-more-powerful-than-fentanyl/.

PART I CONCLUSION

1. "The Declaration of Independence: Full Text," UShistory.org, http://www .ushistory.org/declaration/document/.

CHAPTER 5

1. Sara R. Collins and David C. Radley, "The Cost of Employer Insurance Is a Growing Burden for Middle-Income Families," Commonwealth Fund, December 7, 2018, https://www.commonwealthfund.org/publications /issue-briefs/2018/dec/cost-employer-insurance-growing-burden-middle -income-families.

2. Angelica LaVito, "Walmart Makes Reducing Health-Care Costs a Top Priority—for Customers, Too," CNBC, October 12, 2018, https://www .cnbc.com/2018/10/12/walmart-makes-cutting-health-care-costs-top -priority.html.

3. Ayla Ellison, "Walmart Wants to Cut Healthcare Costs for Cus- tomers," *Becker's Hospital Review*, October 12, 2018, https://www .beckershospitalreview.com/finance/walmart-wants-to-cut-customers -healthcare-costs.html.

4. Mackenzie Garrity, "Walmart to Implement Mandatory Travel Policy for Employees' Spine Surgeries," *Becker's Spine Review*, November 4, 2018, https://www.beckersspine.com/spine/item/43523-walmart-to-implement -mandatory-travel-policy-for-employees-spine-surgeries.html.

5. Tami Luhby, "Walmart Wants to Bring Its 'Everyday Low Prices' to Health Care," CNNMoney, September 19, 2018, https://money.cnn.com /2018/09/19/news/companies/walmart-health-care/index.html.

6. David W. Johnson, "Geeking-Up Healthcare: Consumer Giant Best Buy Makes a Big Move," 4sight Health, September 19, 2018, http://www .4sighthealth.com/geeking-up-healthcare-consumer-giant-best-buy -makes-a-big-move/.

7. Clayton M. Christensen, Taddy Hall, Karen Dillon, and David S. Dun- can, "Know Your Customers' 'Jobs to Be Done,'" *Harvard Business Review*, August 24, 2016, https://hbr.org/2016/09/know-your-customers-jobs-to -be-done.

8. "Health Insurance Coverage of the Total Population," Timeframe: 2017, The Henry J. Kaiser Family Foundation, November 29, 2018, https://www .kff.org/other/state-indicator/total-population.

9. Rabah Kamal and Cynthia Cox, "How Has US Spending on Healthcare Changed over Time?," Peterson-Kaiser Health System Tracker, December 10, 2018, https://www.healthsystemtracker.org/chart-collection /u-s-spending-healthcare-changed-time/#item-per-capita-out-of-pocket -expenditures-have-grown-since-1970_2017.

10. https://www.hcinnovationgroup.com/policy-value-based-care/news /13030872/hhs-secretary-azar-hhs-is-planning-new-mandatory-bundled -payment-models.

11. Jay Greene, "In a First for Michigan, Henry Ford Health Has Signed a Direct Contract to Provide a Wide Range of Healthcare Services for GM Employees," *Modern Healthcare*, August 6, 2018, https://www .modernhealthcare.com/article/20180806/NEWS/180809937.

12. "MassHealth Partners with 17 Health Care Organizations to Improve Health Care Outcomes for Members," Mass.gov, August 17, 2017, https://www.mass.gov/news/masshealth-partners-with-17-health-care -organizations-to-improve-health-care-outcomes-for.

13. https://www.fiercehealthcare.com/payer/cmmi-s-adam-boehler-wants-to -blow-up-fee-for-service.

14. "Medicare Advantage Achieves Cost-Effective Care and Better Outcomes for Beneficiaries with Chronic Conditions Relative to Fee-for-Service Medicare," Avalere Study, July 2018, July 11, 2018.

15. Vijay Pande, "Devoted," Andreessen Horowitz, October 18, 2018, https:// a16z.com/2018/10/16/devoted/.

16. https://www.modernhealthcare.com/article/20180901/NEWS /180839977/insurers-profit-from-medicare-advantage-s-incentive-to-add -coding-that-boosts-reimbursement

17. Richard Kronick, "Projected Coding Intensity in Medicare Advantage Could Increase Medicare Spending by $200 Billion Over Ten Years," *Health Affairs*, February 2017, https://www.healthaffairs.org/doi/10.1377 /hlthaff.2016.0768.

18. "CMS Geographic Payment Variation Dashboard," Timeframe: 2016, CMS.gov, Center for Medicare and Medicaid, n.d., https://portal.cms .gov/wps/portal/unauthportal/unauthmicrostrategyreportslink?evt= 2048001&src=mstrWeb.2048001&documentID=881776D811E8577F0 0000080EF85EDD0&visMode=0¤tViewMedia=1&Server=E48V126P &Project=OIPDA-BI_Prod&Port=0&connmode=8&ru=1&share=1& hiddensections=header,path,dockTop,dockLeft,footer.

19. "Cost of Living," Numbeo.com, n.d., accessed December 15, 2018, https://www.numbeo.com/cost-of-living/.

20. Daniel R. Levinson, "Medicare Advantage Appeal Outcomes and Audit Findings Raise Concerns About Service and Payment Denials," OIG .HHS.gov, Office of the Inspector General, US Department of Health and Human Services, September 16, 2018, https://oig.hhs.gov/oei/reports /oei-09-16-00410.pdf.

21. https://www.newyorker.com/magazine/2019/02/04/the-personal-toll-of -whistle-blowing.

22. "Geographic Variation in Standardized Medicare Spending: County Level," CMS Enterprise Portal—Reports Link, accessed December 2018, https://portal.cms.gov/wps/portal.

23. William Gibson, quoted in Scott Rosenberg, "Virtual Reality Check Digital Daydreams, Cyberspace Nightmares," *San Francisco Examiner*, Section: Styles, Page C1, April 19, 1992.

24. "Apple TV Commercial, 'Someday at Christmas' Featuring Stevie Wonder, Andra Day," ISpot.tv, accessed December 2018, https://www.ispot.tv /ad/AI1A/apple-someday-at-christmas-featuring-stevie-wonder-andra -day.

25. Davide Scialpi, "Jeff Bezos's Quotes About Success and Leadership— Founder of Amazon," Medium.com, May 8, 2018, https://medium .com/@davidescialpi/jeff-bezoss-quotes-about-success-and-leadership -4fd245202795.

CHAPTER 6

1. Sarah Zhang, "How a Genealogy Website Led to the Alleged Golden State Killer," *The Atlantic*, April 28, 2018, https://www.theatlantic .com/science/archive/2018/04/golden-state-killer-east-area-rapist-dna -genealogy/559070/.

2. Bernard Marr, "How Much Data Do We Create Every Day? The Mind-Blowing Stats Everyone Should Read," *Forbes*, July 9, 2018, https://www .forbes.com/sites/bernardmarr/2018/05/21/how-much-data-do-we-create -every-day-the-mind-blowing-stats-everyone-should-read/.

3. Katharine Grayson, "Fairview CEO Says Epic an 'Impediment' to Innovation, Calls for 'March on Madison,'" *Biz Journals*, January 16, 2018, https://www.bizjournals.com/twincities/news/2018/01/16/fairview-ceo -says-epic-an-impediment-to.html.

4. Atul Gawande, "Why Doctors Hate Their Computers," *New Yorker*, November 12, 2018, https://www.newyorker.com/magazine/2018/11/12 /why-doctors-hate-their-computers.

5. John T. James, "A New, Evidence-Based Estimate of Patient Harms Associated with Hospital Care," *Journal of Patient Safety* 9, no. 3 (September 2013): 122–28, doi:10.1097/pts.0b013e3182948a69,

6. https://khn.org/news/death-by-a-thousand-clicks/?utm_campaign=KHN %3A%20First%(20Edition&utm_source=hs_email&utm_medium=email &utm_content=70864706&_hsenc=p2ANqtz-9GysDIrJ0jbRqhuNjv-IC1 Xbs0PyywGshHrPzQD-waZ4Mz0-ZT0VE1LbF3OP5kEewCnSy6Uh Llm58wjmvAmdO0AKp26Q&_hsmi=70864706

7. Martin Makary and Michael Daniel, "Study Suggests Medical Errors Now Third Leading Cause of Death in the U.S.," May 3, 2016, https:// www.hopkinsmedicine.org/news/media/releases/study_suggests_medical _errors_now_third_leading_cause_of_death_in_the_us.

8. Ken Ong and Regina Cregin, "Electronic Health Record and Patient Safety," *Patient Safety*, 2013, 69–86, doi:10.1007/978-1-4614-7419-7_5.

9. Medscape Annual Survey 2017.

10. https://www.forbes.com/sites/zinamoukheiber/2012/04/18/epic-systems -tough-billionaire/#4f85eafd58d9

11. https://www.beckershospitalreview.com/healthcare-information -technology/epic-founder-judy-faulkner-comes-in-3rd-on-forbes-richest -women-list.html

12. Peter Densen, "Challenges and Opportunities Facing Medical Education," *Transactions of the American Clinical and Climatological Association*, 2011, 48–58, https://www.ncbi.nlm.nih.gov/pmc/articles/PMC3116346/.

13. John Hagel III, John Seely Brown, and Lang Davison, "Abandon Stocks, Embrace Flows," *Harvard Business Review*, January 27, 2009, https://hbr .org/2009/01/abandon-stocks-embrace-flows.html.

14. Accenture, "2018 Consumer Survey on Digital Health," 2018, https:// www.accenture.com/t20180306T103559Z__w__/us-en/_acnmedia/PDF -71/accenture-health-2018-consumer-survey-digital-health.pdf.

15. https://apervita.com/the-joint-commission-selects-apervita-to-enable -easier-electronic-quality-measure-submission-for-hospitals/.

16. https://www.jointcommission.org/us_hospitals_transitioning_to_the_joint _commission%E2%80%99s_new_direct_data_submission_platform/.

17. Will Kenton, "Moore's Law," Investopedia, December 13, 2018, https:// www.investopedia.com/terms/m/mooreslaw.asp.

18. Jakob Nielsen, "Nielsen's Law of Internet Bandwidth," Nielsen Norman Group, April 5, 1998, https://www.nngroup.com/articles/law-of -bandwidth/.

19. Gordon Bell, "Bell's Law for the Birth and Death of Computer Classes: A Theory of the Computer's Evolution," Software Asset Management— Microsoft SAM, November 1, 2007, https://www.microsoft.com/en-us

/research/publication/bells-law-for-the-birth-and-death-of-computer
-classes-a-theory-of-the-computers-evolution/.

20. "Cryptocurrency Market Capitalizations," CoinMarketCap, accessed
December 12, 2018, https://coinmarketcap.com/.

21. "Big Pharma Turns to Blockchain to Track Meds," *Fortune*, September 21,
2017, http://fortune.com/2017/09/21/pharma-blockchain.

22. Michael Larkin, "Blockchain May Finally Go Mainstream in Industry This Year: Microsoft Azure," *Investor's Business Daily*, June 18, 2018,
https://www.investors.com/news/blockchain-mainstream-industry
-applications-microsoft-azure-cto/.

23. Andrew Rossow, "Why Walmart's Move to the Blockchain Could Do
More Than Prevent E. Coli Outbreaks," *Forbes*, September 26, 2018,
https://www.forbes.com/sites/andrewrossow/2018/09/25/why-walmarts
-move-to-the-blockchain-could-do-more-than-cure-e-coli-outbreaks
/#d553bdc1100a.

24. "Humana, Optum, Others Team Up for Blockchain-Enabled
Data-Sharing," *Modern Healthcare*, April 2, 2018, https://www
.modernhealthcare.com/article/20180402/NEWS/180409999.

25. "Let's Cut Through the Noise: A Reality Check on Blockchain," *Modern
Healthcare*, 2018, https://www.modernhealthcare.com/article/20180926
/SPONSORED/180929921.

26. Jill Frew, "How Blockchain Will Transform Healthcare," Cain Brothers,
December 18, 2017, https://www.cainbrothers.com/wp-content/uploads
/Industry-Insights_121817.pdf.

27. General Stanley McChrystal, *Team of Teams* (New York: Penguin, 2015),
https://www.mcchrystalgroup.com/insights/teamofteams/; and David
W. Johnson and Mudit Garg, "Frontline Decisions in Real Time: What
Health Systems Can Learn from the U.S. Military's Defeat of Al Qaeda
in Iraq," 4sight Health, December 12, 2018, http://www.4sighthealth.com
/frontline-decisions-in-real-time-what-health-systems-can-learn-from
-the-u-s-militarys-defeat-of-al-qaeda-in-iraq/.

CHAPTER 7

1. Sinclair on *The Jungle* in *Cosmopolitan*, October 1906.

2. "J&J Knew for Decades That Asbestos Lurked in Its Baby Powder," Reuters, December 14, 2018, https://www.reuters.com/investigates/special
-report/johnsonandjohnson-cancer/.

3. *Letter from Theodore Roosevelt to Ray Stannard Baker*. Theodore Roosevelt
Papers. Library of Congress Manuscript Division. https://www.theodore
rooseveltcenter.org/Research/Digital-Library/Record?libID=o266348.
Theodore Roosevelt Digital Library. Dickinson State University.

4. "When Business and Government Are Bedfellows," *The Economist*, August 23, 2012, https://www.economist.com/prospero/2012/08/23/when -business-and-government-are-bedfellows.

5. Hannah Fingerhut, "1. Trust in Government: 1958–2015," Pew Research Center for the People and the Press, September 18, 2018, http://www .people-press.org/2015/11/23/1-trust-in-government-1958-2015/.

6. Rebecca Lerner, "The 10 Richest Counties in America 2017," *Forbes*, December 7, 2017, https://www.forbes.com/sites/rebeccalerner/2017/07 /13/top-10-richest-counties-in-america-2017/#413cc2112ef3.

7. Louis Brandeis, *Other People's Money and How the Bankers Use It* (New York: Frederick A. Stokes, 1914).

8. "Opioid Crisis: The Lawsuits That Could Bankrupt Manufacturers and Distributors," CBS News, December 16, 2018, https://www.cbsnews.com /news/opioid-crisis-attorney-mike-moore-takes-on-manufacturers-and -distributors-at-the-center-of-the-epidemic-60-minutes/.

9. https://www.washingtonpost.com/national/health-science/purdue -pharma-state-of-oklahoma-reach-settlement-in-landmark-opioid -lawsuit/2019/03/26/69aa5cda-4f11-11e9-a3f7-78b7525a8d5f_story.html ?noredirect=on&utm_term=.4a60dad3f4f8.

10. National Institute on Drug Abuse, "Overdose Death Rates," NIDA, August 9, 2018, https://www.drugabuse.gov/related-topics/trends -statistics/overdose-death-rates.

11. https://www.ourdocuments.gov/doc.php?flash=false&doc=90&page= transcript.

12. Alex M. Azar II, "Value-Based Transformation of America's Healthcare System," HHS.gov, May 5, 2018, https://www.hhs.gov/about/leadership /secretary/speeches/2018-speeches/value-based-transformation-of -americas-healthcare-system.html.

13. Ibid.

14. David Burda, "HHS Goes All In on Competition as the Way to Fix Healthcare Woes," 4sight Health, December 17, 2018, http://www .4sighthealth.com/hhs-goes-all-in-on-competition-as-the-way-to-fix -healthcare-woes/.

15. http://www.4sighthealth.com/interoperability-battle-lines-data-freedom -fighters-vs-entrenched-data-blockers/

16. François De Brantes, Suzanne Delbanco, Erin Butto, Karina Patino-Maxmanian, and Lea Tessitore, "Price Transparency & Physician Quality Report Card 2017," Altarum, November 8, 2017, https://altarum.org/sites /default/files/uploaded-publication-files/Price Transparency and Physician Quality Report Card 2017_0.pdf.

17. "Statement on Proposed CY 2019 Outpatient OPPS Rule," American Hospital Association, July 25, 2018, https://www.aha.org/press-releases /2018-07-25-statement-proposed-cy-2019-outpatient-opps-rule.

18. Kashmira Gander, 2018, "From January 1, All U.S. Hospitals Must Publish Price Lists for All Services," *Newsweek*, December 27, 2018, https:// www.newsweek.com/end-hidden-costs-january-1st-all-us-hospitals-must -publish-price-lists-all-1272328.

19. William Shakespeare, *Julius Caesar*, Act I, Scene ii.

20. "U.S. News & World Report Announces the 2016–17 Best Hospitals," *U.S. News & World Report*, August 2, 2016, https://www.usnews.com/info /blogs/press-room/articles/2016-08-02/us-news-announces-the-201617 -best-hospitals.

21. Steve Findlay, "Consumers' Interest in Provider Ratings Grows, and Improved Report Cards and Other Steps Could Accelerate Their Use," *Health Affairs*, April 2016, https://www.healthaffairs.org/doi/abs/10.1377 /hlthaff.2015.1654.

22. John Commins, "CMS Releases 5-STAR Hospital Quality Rankings," *Health Leaders*, July 27, 2016, https://www.healthleadersmedia.com /strategy/cms-releases-5-star-hospital-quality-rankings.

23. Amitabh Chandra, Amy Finkelstein, Adam Sacarny, and Chad Syverson, "Healthcare Exceptionalism? Performance and Allocation in the U.S. Healthcare Sector," NBER Working Paper No. 21603, October 2015, doi:10.3386/w21603.

24. Austin, J. Matthew, Ashish K. Jha, Patrick S. Romano, Sara J. Singer, Timothy J. Vogus, Robert M. Wachter, and Peter J. Pronovost, "National Hospital Ratings Systems Share Few Common Scores and May Generate Confusion Instead of Clarity," *Health Affairs* 34, no. 3 (March 2015): 423– 30, doi:10.1377/hlthaff.2014.0201.

25. Medicare.gov, Hospital Compare, Quality of Care Profile Page, accessed December 2018, https://www.medicare.gov/hospitalcompare/profile .html#profTab=0&ID=240010&loc=ROCHESTER%2C%20MN &lat=44.0216306&lng=-92.4698992&name=MAYO%20CLINIC %20HOSPITAL%20ROCHESTER&Distn=0.8

26. Darrell Kirch, "Commentary: AAMC Says CMS' Flawed Methodology Skews Hospital Star Ratings @AAMCtoday," *Modern Healthcare*, August 6, 2018, https://www.modernhealthcare.com/article/20160806 /MAGAZINE/308069979.

27. Benjamin L. Ranard, Rachel M. Werner, Tadas Antanavicius, H. Andrew Schwartz, Robert J. Smith, Zachary F. Meisel, David A. Asch, Lyle H. Ungar, and Raina M. Merchant, "Yelp Reviews of Hospital Care Can

Supplement and Inform Traditional Surveys of the Patient Experience of Care," *Health Affairs*, April 2016, https://www.healthaffairs.org/doi/abs/10.1377/hlthaff.2015.1030.

PART III

1. Ron Chernow, *Washington, A Life* (Penguin Books Ltd., 2011), 448–51.

CHAPTER 8

1. Rob Davies, "Apple Becomes World's First Trillion-Dollar Company," *The Guardian*, August 2, 2018, https://www.theguardian.com/technology/2018/aug/02/apple-becomes-worlds-first-trillion-dollar-company.
2. Walter Isaacson, *Steve Jobs: A Biography* (Simon & Schuster, 2011), Chapter 15.
3. "1984" Apple ad, January 22, 1984, CBS.
4. Clayton M. Christensen, Michael E. Raynor, and Rory McDonald, "What Is Disruptive Innovation?," *Harvard Business Review*, December 19, 2016, https://hbr.org/2015/12/what-is-disruptive-innovation.
5. Clayton M. Christensen, *Innovators Dilemma: When New Technologies Cause Great Firms to Fail*, Management of Innovation and Change Series (Harvard Business Review Press, 1997).
6. https://hbr.org/2015/12/what-is-disruptive-innovation.
7. Theodore Levitt, "Marketing Myopia," *Harvard Business Review*, March 20, 2017, https://hbr.org/2004/07/marketing-myopia.
8. Clayton M. Christensen, Taddy Hall, Karen Dillon, and David S Duncan, "Know Your Customers' 'Jobs to Be Done,'" *Harvard Business Review*, August 24, 2016, https://hbr.org/2016/09/know-your-customers-jobs-to-be-done.
9. Carmen Nobel, "Clay Christensen's Milkshake Marketing," HBS Working Knowledge, February 14, 2011, https://hbswk.hbs.edu/item/clay-christensens-milkshake-marketing; and "Clay Christensen: The 'Job' of a McDonald's Milkshake," YouTube video, 7:09, posted by HubSpot Academy, October 5, 2017.
10. David W. Johnson and Andrew Waldeck, "Gawande's Gift: Re-Imagining Corporate Wellness and Healthcare," 4sight Health, July 7, 2018, http://www.4sighthealth.com/gawandes-gift-re-imagining-corporate-wellness-and-healthcare/.
11. Lydia Ramsey, "Investors Are Betting $660 Million That Companies That Ship Viagra and Hair Loss Pills to Your Door Is the Future of Medicine—but Some Doctors Are Worried," *Business Insider*, October 22, 2018, https://www.businessinsider.com/booming-direct-consumer-healthcare-business-2018-10.

12. Nona Tepper, "DuPage Medical Group Snags $1.45 Billion to Expand Outside Metro Chicago," *Crain's Chicago Business*, August 16, 2017, http://www.chicagobusiness.com/article/20170816/NEWS03/170819899/dupage-medical-group-snags-1-45-billion-from-ares-management.
13. "Jitterbug: The Anti-MVNO," FierceWireless, June 15, 2007, https://www.fiercewireless.com/wireless/jitterbug-anti-mvno.
14. Mike Dano, "Best Buy's Biggest Acquisition Ever Is GreatCall, an MVNO Targeting Seniors," FierceWireless, August 16, 2018, https://www.fiercewireless.com/wireless/best-buy-s-biggest-acquisition-ever-greatcall-mvno-targeting-seniors.
15. "Best Buy Acquires GreatCall, a Leading Connected Health Services Provider," Best Buy Co., Inc., April 15, 2018, http://investors.bestbuy.com/investor-relations/news-and-events/financial-releases/news-details/2018/Best-Buy-Acquires-GreatCall-a-Leading-Connected-Health-Services-Provider/default.aspx.
16. https://www.businessinsider.com/bright-health-insurance-startup-financial-results-aca-medicare-advantage-2019-3.
17. https://www.healthleadersmedia.com/finance/demand-health-insurance-shows-promise-can-it-deliver.
18. David Galloppa, "Think Different," http://www.thecrazyones.it/spot-en.html.

CHAPTER 9

1. Caroline Hallemann, "How Lord Altrincham Changed the Monarchy Forever," *Town & Country*, September 19, 2018, https://www.townandcountrymag.com/society/tradition/a14273687/lord-altrincham-john-grigg-role-british-history/.
2. Katie Frost, "The Heartbreaking Royal Romance of Princess Margaret and Peter Townsend," *Town & Country*, June 6, 2018, https://www.townandcountrymag.com/society/tradition/news/a8139/princess-margaret-peter-townsend-love-affair/.
3. "Humana Announces Agreement to Acquire a 40 Percent Minority Interest in Kindred's Homecare Business for Approximately $800 Million Through a Joint Venture with an Entity Owned by TPG Capital and Welsh, Carson, Anderson & Stowe," Humana, December 19, 2017, https://press.humana.com/press-release/current-releases/humana-announces-agreement-acquire-40-percent-minority-interest-kindr.
4. Nick Wingfield, Katie Thomas, and Reed Abelson, "Amazon, Berkshire Hathaway and JPMorgan Team Up to Try to Disrupt Health Care," *New York Times*, January 30, 2018, https://www.nytimes.com/2018/01/30/technology/amazon-berkshire-hathaway-jpmorgan-health-care.html.

5. David W. Johnson, "Value Quest: Capital Formation Challenges for Non-Profit Health Systems," 4sight Health, October 26, 2016, http://www .4sighthealth.com/value-quest-capital-formation-challenges-non-profit -health-systems/.

6. Scott D. Anthony, Clark G. Gilbert, and Mark W. Johnson, *Dual Transformation: How to Reposition Today's Business While Creating the Future* (Cambridge, MA: Harvard Business Review, 2017).

7. Clayton Christensen, Andrew Waldeck, and Rebecca Fogg, "How Disruptive Innovation Can Finally Revolutionize Healthcare," Christensen Institute, Spring 2017.

8. David W. Johnson and Amy Compton-Phillips, "Platforming Healthcare: Owning Hospitals Is so 2015," 4sight Health, February 21, 2018, http:// www.4sighthealth.com/platforming-healthcare-owning-hospitals-is-so -2015.

9. Trefis Team, "CVS to Buy All of Target's Pharmacy Stores—a Win-Win for Both," June 30, 2015, https://www.forbes.com/sites/greatspeculations /2015/06/30/cvs-to-buy-all-of-targets-pharmacy-stores-a-win-win-for -both/#7b25d682508c; and Nathan Bomey, "5 Reasons Why Target Sold Pharmacy Biz to CVS," *USA Today*, June 15, 2015, https://www.usatoday .com/story/money/2015/06/15/target-cvs-pharmacy-sale/71248932/.

10. Kate Vitasek, "Vested Outsourcing: Five Rules That Will Transform Outsourcing," *Vested*, September 25, 2013, http://www.vestedway.com/vested -outsourcing/.

11. Robert Fraiman and David W. Johnson, "Letting Go: Steward Sells Its Hospitals and Embraces Patient-Centric Care," 4sight Health, January 23, 2017, http://www.4sighthealth.com/letting-go-steward-sells-hospitals -embraces-patient-centric-care/.

12. Maria Castellucci, "Steward Says $1.25 Billion Real Estate Deal Will Fund National Expansion," *Modern Healthcare*, September 27, 2016, https://www.modernhealthcare.com/article/20160927/NEWS /160929891.

13. David W. Johnson, "The Why, The How and The What: Consumerism, Trust and Brand Love," 4sight Health, November 17, 2015, http://www .4sighthealth.com/the-why-the-how-and-the-what-consumerism-trust -and-brand-love/.

14. "Intermountain Healthcare Announces a New Mission Vision and Values Statement," Intermountainhealthcare.org, November 14, 2014, https:// intermountainhealthcare.org/blogs/topics/transforming-healthcare/2014 /11/intermountain-healthcare-announces-a-new-mission-vision-and -values-statement/.

15. David W. Johnson, "Mission First: Mission Health's Surprising Sale to HCA," 4sight Health, April 17, 2018, http://www.4sighthealth.com /mission-first-mission-healths-surprising-sale-to-hca/.

CHAPTER 10
1. "2018 Healthcare in Canada Survey Results," April 22, 2018, https:// mcgill.ca/hcic-sssc/files/hcic-sssc/hcic_2018_press_release_en.pdf.
2. "Unnecessary Care in Canada," July 11, 2017, https://www.cihi.ca/en /unnecessary-care-in-canada.
3. Stuart Laidlaw, "Public Health Care Scores Big in Poll as MDs Study Privatization," August 12, 2009, https://www.thestar.com/life/health _wellness/2009/08/12/public_health_care_scores_big_in_poll_as_mds _study_privatization.html.
4. "Americans Still Hold Dim View of U.S. Healthcare System," December 11, 2017, https://news.gallup.com/poll/223403/americans-hold-dim-view -healthcare-system.aspx.
5. Jeffrey M. Jones, "U.S. Concerns About Healthcare High; Energy, Unemployment Low," March 26, 2018, https://news.gallup.com/poll/231533 /concerns-healthcare-high-energy-unemployment-low.aspx.
6. Lewis Thomas, ed., *The Making of a Socialist: The Recollections of T. C. Douglas* (Edmonton: The University of Alberta Press, 1982), 6–7.
7. Jean Larmour, "Saskatchewan Doctors' Strike," The Canadian Encyclopedia, February 7, 2006, https://www.thecanadianencyclopedia.ca/en/article /saskatchewan-doctors-strike.
8. "Milestones: Universal Policies," Canadian Public Health Association, accessed December 15, 2018, https://www.cpha.ca/milestones-universal -policies.
9. "Spending on Health: Latest Trends," Oecd.org, June 2018, http://www .oecd.org/health/health-systems/Health-Spending-Latest-Trends-Brief.pdf.
10. June E. O'Neill and Dave M. O'Neill, "Health Status, Health Care and Inequality: Canada vs. the U.S.," NBER, September 21, 2007, https:// www.nber.org/papers/w13429.
11. Jeffrey M. Jones and RJ Reinhart, "Americans Remain Dissatisfied with Healthcare Costs," Gallup.com, November 28, 2018, https://news.gallup .com/poll/245054/americans-remain-dissatisfied-healthcare-costs.aspx.
12. Lydia Saad, "Computer, Restaurant Sectors Still Top-Rated U.S. Industries," Gallup.com, September 5, 2018, https://news.gallup.com/poll /241892/computer-restaurant-sectors-top-rated-industries.aspx.
13. Liz Hamel, Mira Norton, Karen Pollitz, Larry Levitt, Gary Claxton, and Mollyann Brodie, "The Burden of Medical Debt: Results from the

Kaiser Family Foundation/New York Times Medical Bills Survey—
Section 3: Consequences of Medical Bill Problems," January 5, 2016,
https://www.kff.org/report-section/the-burden-of-medical-debt-section
-3-consequences-of-medical-bill-problems/.

14. "Americans' Views of Healthcare Costs, Coverage, and Policy," National
Opinion Research Center, March 2018, http://www.norc.org/PDFs
/WHI Healthcare Costs Coverage and Policy/WHI Healthcare Costs
Coverage and Policy Issue Brief.pdf.

15. Margot Sanger-Katz, "Advice from Health Care's Power Users," October 20, 2018, https://www.nytimes.com/2018/10/20/upshot/advice-from
-health-cares-power-users.html.

16. "Click Here to Support Hedda's Heart Transplant Organized by Hedda
Elizabeth Britt," Gofundme.com, November 24, 2018, https://www
.gofundme.com/hedda-needs-a-heart-transplant; and JC Reindl,
"Grand Rapids Woman Meets Gofundme Goal, Now Hopes for Heart
Transplant," *Detroit Free Press*, November 26, 2018, https://www.freep
.com/story/money/2018/11/26/grand-rapids-woman-heart-transplant
-gofundme-goal-met/2116805002/.

17. "Almost Half of the Money Raised Through GoFundMe Campaigns
Was for Healthcare," June 15, 2017, https://index.qz.com/1006412
/crowdfunding-health-services-almost-half-of-the-money-raised-through
-gofundme-went-to-medical-campaigns/.

18. Lauren S. Berliner and Nora J. Kenworthy, "Producing a Worthy Ill-
ness: Personal Crowdfunding Amidst Financial Crisis," NeuroImage,
February 8, 2017, https://www.sciencedirect.com/science/article/abs/pii
/S0277953617300886.

19. Steven Lott, "Chronic Diseases Claim at Least 75% of Health Care
Spending in Most Developed Countries; Pose a Growing Economic Burden on Low-and Middle-Income Countries," April 28, 2011, http://www
.wardhealth.com/articles/chronic-diseases-claim-least-75-health-care
-spending-most-developed-countries-pose-growing-.

20. Lily Rothman, "Martin Luther King Jr's Letter from a Birmingham
Jail—Why He Was There," April 16, 2015, http://time.com/3773914/mlk
-birmingham-jail/.

21. Martin Luther King Jr., "Letter from a Birmingham Jail," April 16, 1963,
text at African Studies Center, University of Pennsylvania, https://www
.africa.upenn.edu/Articles_Gen/Letter_Birmingham.html.

22. Amanda Moore, "Tracking Down Martin Luther King, Jr.'s Words
on Health Care," *The Huffington Post*, March 20, 2013, https://www

.huffingtonpost.com/amanda-moore/martin-luther-king-health-care
_b_2506393.html.

23. David W. Johnson and Casey Quinn, "Destination Medicare Advantage:
A Quest for Great Health Insurance," 4sight Health, June 14, 2018, http://
www.4sighthealth.com.

24. Malcolm Gladwell, *The Tipping Point: How Little Things Can Make a Big
Difference* (Little, Brown, 2000).

25. Regina E. Herzlinger, Barak D. Richman, and Richard J. Boxer, "Opinion: How Health Care Hurts Your Paycheck," November 2, 2016, https://
www.nytimes.com/2016/11/02/opinion/how-health-care-hurts-your
-paycheck.html.

26. Chad Terhune and Heidi De Marco, "Why One California County Went
Surgery Shopping," September 1, 2017, https://khn.org/news/why-one
-california-county-went-surgery-shopping/.

27. "Canada's Health Care System," Canada.ca, February 26, 2018, https://
www.canada.ca/en/health-canada/services/health-care-system/reports
-publications/health-care-system/canada.html.

28. David W. Johnson, "Medicare at Fifty: More Yesterdays than Tomor-
rows?," 4sight Health, August 5, 2015, http://www.4sighthealth.com
/medicare-at-fifty-more-yesterdays-than-tomorrows/.

29. Michael E. Eidenmuller, "Ronald Reagan, Radio Address on Social-
ized Medicine," Top 100 Speeches of the 20th Century—American
Rhetoric, August 3, 2017, https://www.americanrhetoric.com/speeches
/ronaldreagansocializedmedicine.htm.

30. "CMS Program Data—Populations," CMS.gov Centers for Medicare and
Medicaid Services, August 1, 2018, https://www.cms.gov/fastfacts/.

31. Milton I. Roemer, "Hospital Bed Utilization: Increasing Throughout,"
JAMA, 1961, 36–42, doi:10.21236/ada432032, https://jamanetwork.com
/journals/jama/article-abstract/332264.

PART III CONCLUSION

1. Ron Chernow, *Washington: A Life* (Penguin Books Ltd., 2011), 448.

CONCLUSION

1. Louis P. Masur, "How the Emancipation Proclamation Came to Be
Signed," Smithsonian.com, January 2013, https://www.smithsonianmag
.com/history/how-the-emancipation-proclamation-came-to-be-signed
-165533991/.

INDEX

ABOUT THE AUTHOR

David W. Johnson is the founder and CEO of 4sight Health, a healthcare advisory firm at the intersection of strategy, innovation, economics, and capital formation. As long-tenured investment banker, he managed over $30 billion in healthcare revenue bonds and led significant strategic advisory engagements for his health system clients.

Johnson is the author of the widely acclaimed book *Market vs. Medicine: America's Epic Fight for Better, Affordable Healthcare* and the respected biweekly blog *Market Corner Commentaries*. He is the author-in-residence at MATTER, a Chicago-based healthcare incubator, and serves on the board or as an advisor to several early-stage companies.

His civic and professional affiliations have included the Harvard School of Public Health, Harvard Medical School, Harvard Kennedy School, the Chicago Council on Global Affairs, the University of Chicago, the British-American Project, The Community Builders, the Health Management Academy, CHRISTUS Health, and the Terence Cardinal Cooke Health Center.

Johnson holds a master's degree in public policy from Harvard University. A former Peace Corps volunteer, he maintains his own health and well-being, in part, by running, reading, and cooking.

Visit 4sighthealth.com.